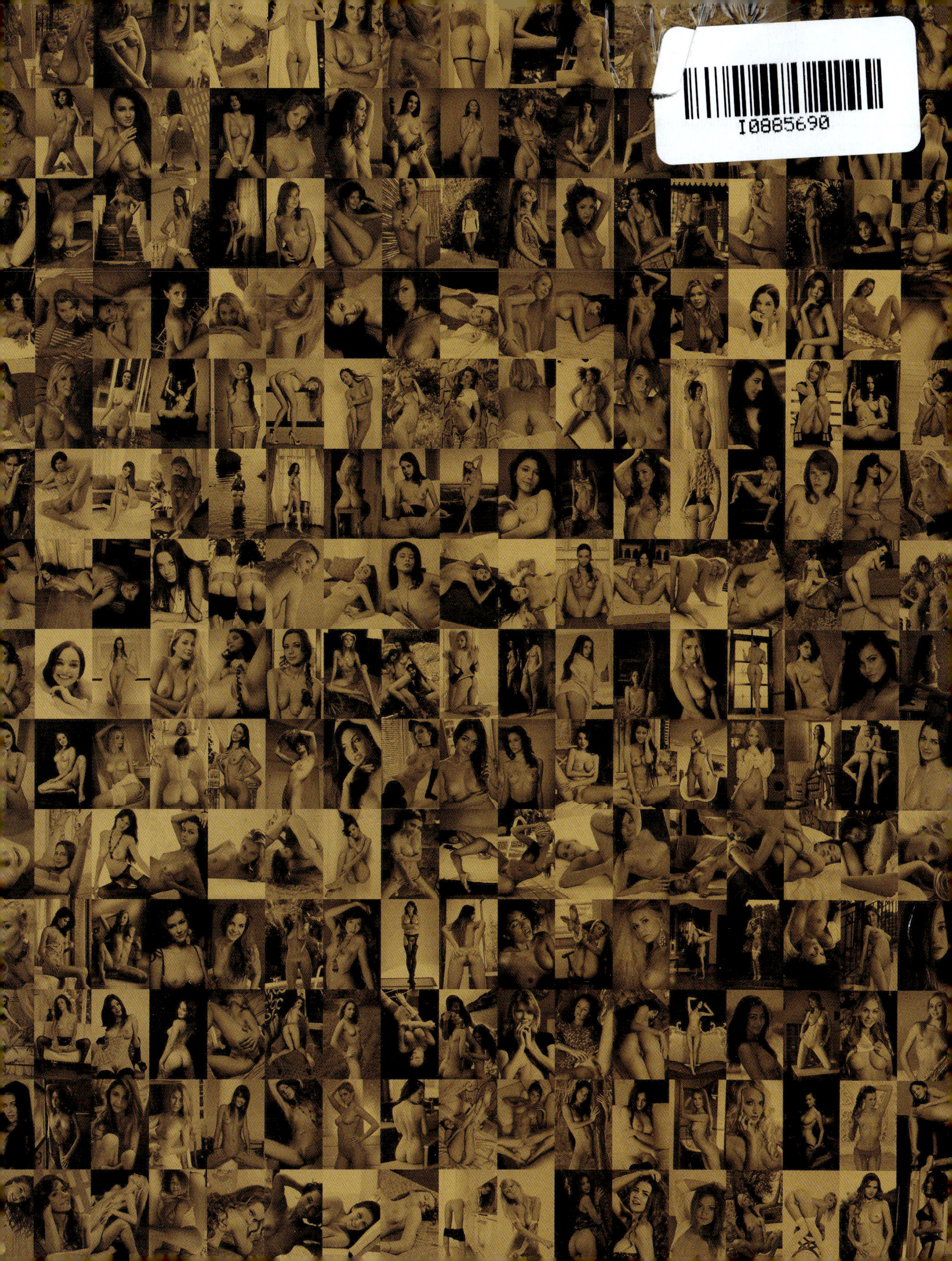

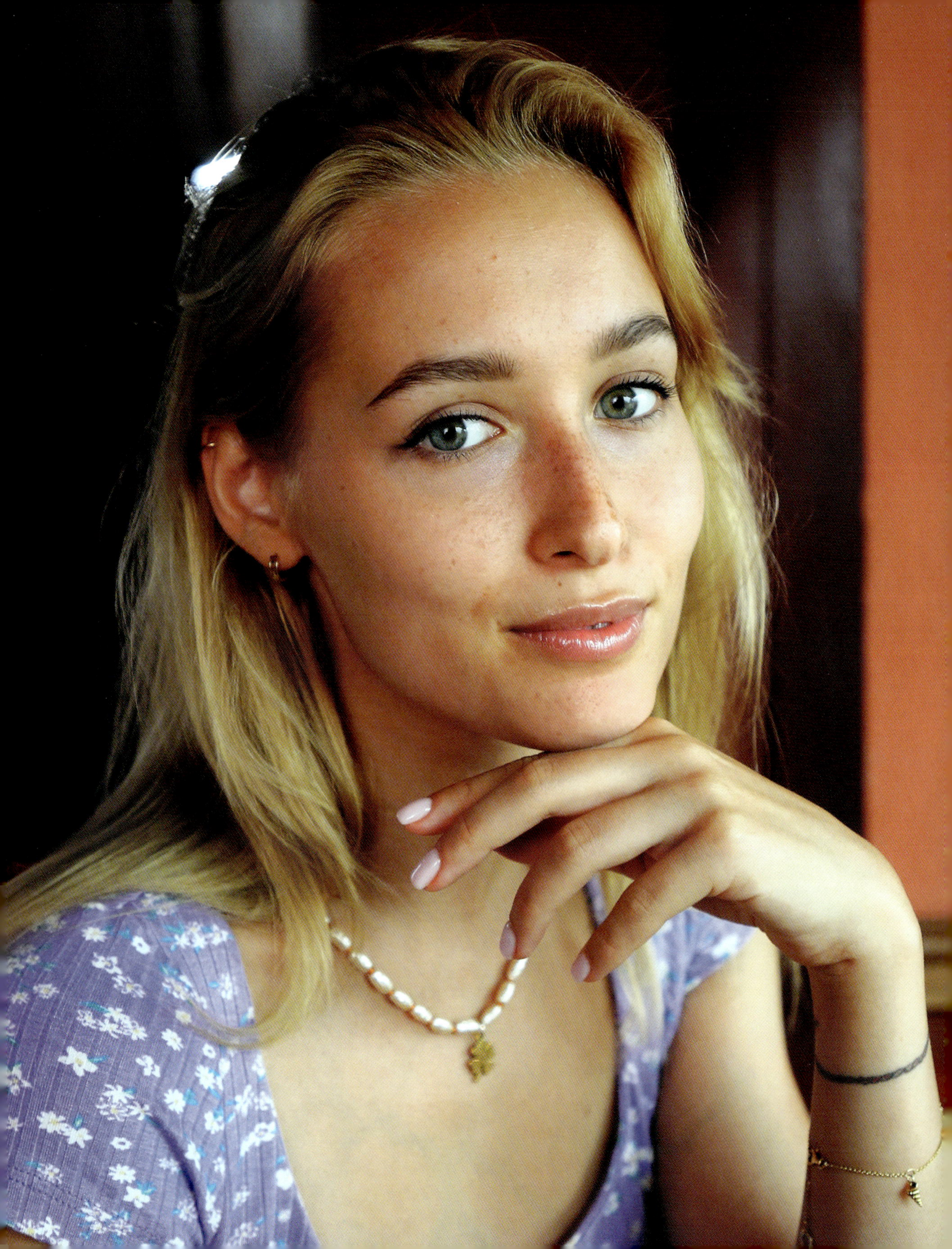

TOP MODELS OF

METART.COM™

WHERE FLAWLESS BEAUTY MEETS ART

KELLY COLLINS

COLLECTED AND EDITED BY ISABELLA CATALINA

EDITION Skylight

First edition 2026

EDITION SKYLIGHT
Rosengartenstrasse 13B
CH-8608 Bubikon / Zürich
Switzerland
info@edition-skylight.com
www.edition-skylight.com

ISBN 978-3-03766-717-0

Bibliographic information published by Die Deutsche Bibliothek
Die Deutsche Bibliothek lists this publication in the Deutsche Nationalbibliografie; detailed bibliographic data are available in the Internet at http://dnb.ddb.de.

Printed in Bosnia and Herzegovina

“WHEN IT COMES TO SEX, I HAVE SOME UNUSUAL PREFERENCES” – KELLY COLLINS

Stunning blonde Kelly Collins is one of the hottest new erotic models to emerge in recent years. Since her debut in May 2022, this Russian beauty has been captivating MetArt members with her charming smile, gorgeous body and vivacious manner. She especially likes her breasts, and keeps in shape playing tennis and doing gymnastics. She is a romantic person and she likes to have her hair played with. She has revealed that her nipples are very sensitive and even used to be pierced. Kelly has also made a considerable impression on our other sites, including MetArt X, SexArt, and VivThomas.com. With her boobs and sexy pussy lips, who can resist Kelly Collins?! And just to show you how bold she is, here is a selection of quotations taken from various interviews:
What do you like sexually? What gets Kelly wet? When it comes to sex, I have some unusual predilections. I get wet when I notice my partner sees things the way I do. (laughs) But physically, I am up to any fetish you'd care to mention because trying out new stuff and being dirty turn me on. The more the better! Anything that can take me to the limit! (laughs) **Are you submissive or dominant?** I like being dominated and being dominant; I like to switch between roles. I'm a foot fetishist, I guess, and I enjoy foreplay and dirty talk. **How often do you masturbate?** I think about three to four times a day, mostly because I'm bored. (laughs) I have a favourite toy... so I take it with me everywhere. Hands also work if I happen to leave my toy at home. **You've just won XBiz Europa Best New Starlet, how did that feel?** Agreeable, pleasant. (laughs) Of course, I feel very blessed because although I really wanted to win, I never thought it would actually happen. Now I'm bursting with energy and highly motivated to win best female performer in the next few years.

„WENN ES UM SEX GEHT, HABE ICH EINIGE UNGEWÖHNLICHE VORLIEBEN!“ – KELLY COLLINS

Die atemberaubende Blondine Kelly Collins zählt zu den heißesten neuen Erotikmodels der letzten Jahre. Die russische Schönheit begeistert die MetArt-Mitglieder seit ihrem Debüt im Mai 2022 mit ihrem charmanten Lächeln, ihrem umwerfenden Körper und ihrer lebhaften Art. Sie mag ihre Brüste und hält sich mit Tennis und Gymnastik fit. Sie ist romantisch veranlagt, liebt es, wenn man ihr durch die Haare streicht, und verrät, dass ihre Brustwarzen sehr empfindlich sind – sie hatte sie früher gepierct! Auch auf unseren anderen Seiten, darunter MetArt X, SexArt und Viv Thomas, hat Kelly einen bleibenden Eindruck hinterlassen. Wer kann Kelly Collins mit diesen Brüsten und ihren sexy Schamlippen schon widerstehen?! Und um Ihnen zu zeigen, wie mutig sie ist, hier eine Auswahl von Zitaten aus verschiedenen Interviews:
Was magst du sexuell? Was macht dich feucht? Ich habe ungewöhnliche Vorlieben beim Sex. Ich werde feucht, sobald ich merke, dass mein Partner die Dinge so sieht wie ich. (lacht) Aber körperlich bin ich normalerweise für jeden Fetisch zu haben, der mir vorgeschlagen wird, weil ich auf Neues und Schmutziges stehe. Je mehr, desto besser! Alles, was mich an meine Grenzen bringt! (lacht) **Bist du eher unterwürfig oder dominant?** Ich mag es, im selben Spiel sowohl dominant als auch dominiert zu sein. Meine Lieblingsfetische sind wohl Dirty Talk, Vorspiel und Fußfetisch. **Wie oft masturbierst du?** Ich glaube, so 3-4 Mal am Tag, meistens aus Langeweile. (lacht) Ich habe ein Lieblingsspielzeug... das nehme ich immer mit. Hände tun es auch, wenn ich mein Spielzeug mal vergessen habe. **Du hast gerade den XBiz Europa Award als beste Nachwuchsschauspielerin gewonnen, wie hat sich das angefühlt?** Angenehm. (lacht) Natürlich fühle ich mich unglaublich geehrt, diesen Preis zu gewinnen, weil ich ihn mir so sehr gewünscht habe, aber nie damit gerechnet hätte. Jetzt bin ich voller Energie für die Arbeit und hochmotiviert, in den nächsten Jahren als beste Darstellerin ausgezeichnet zu werden.

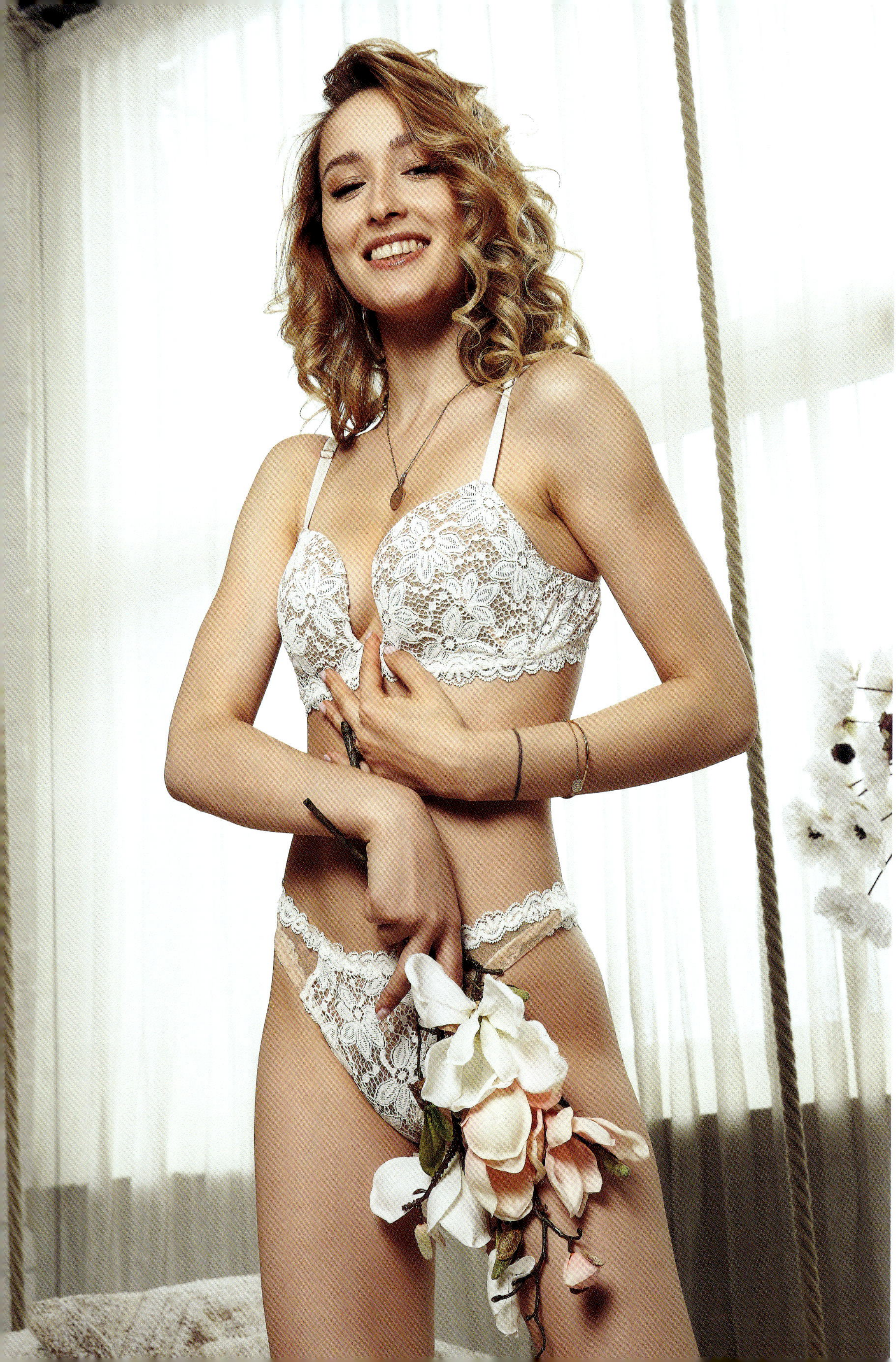

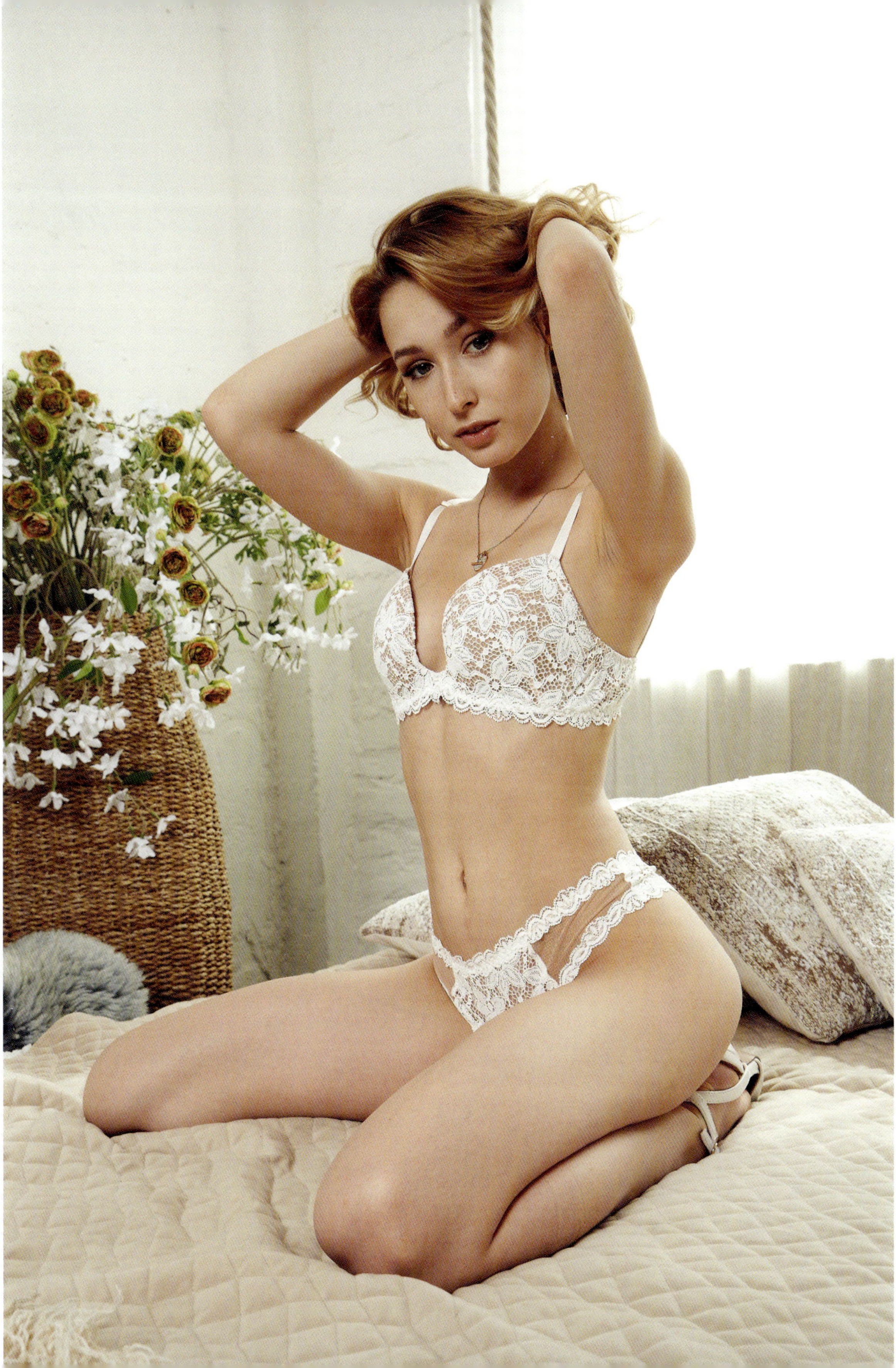

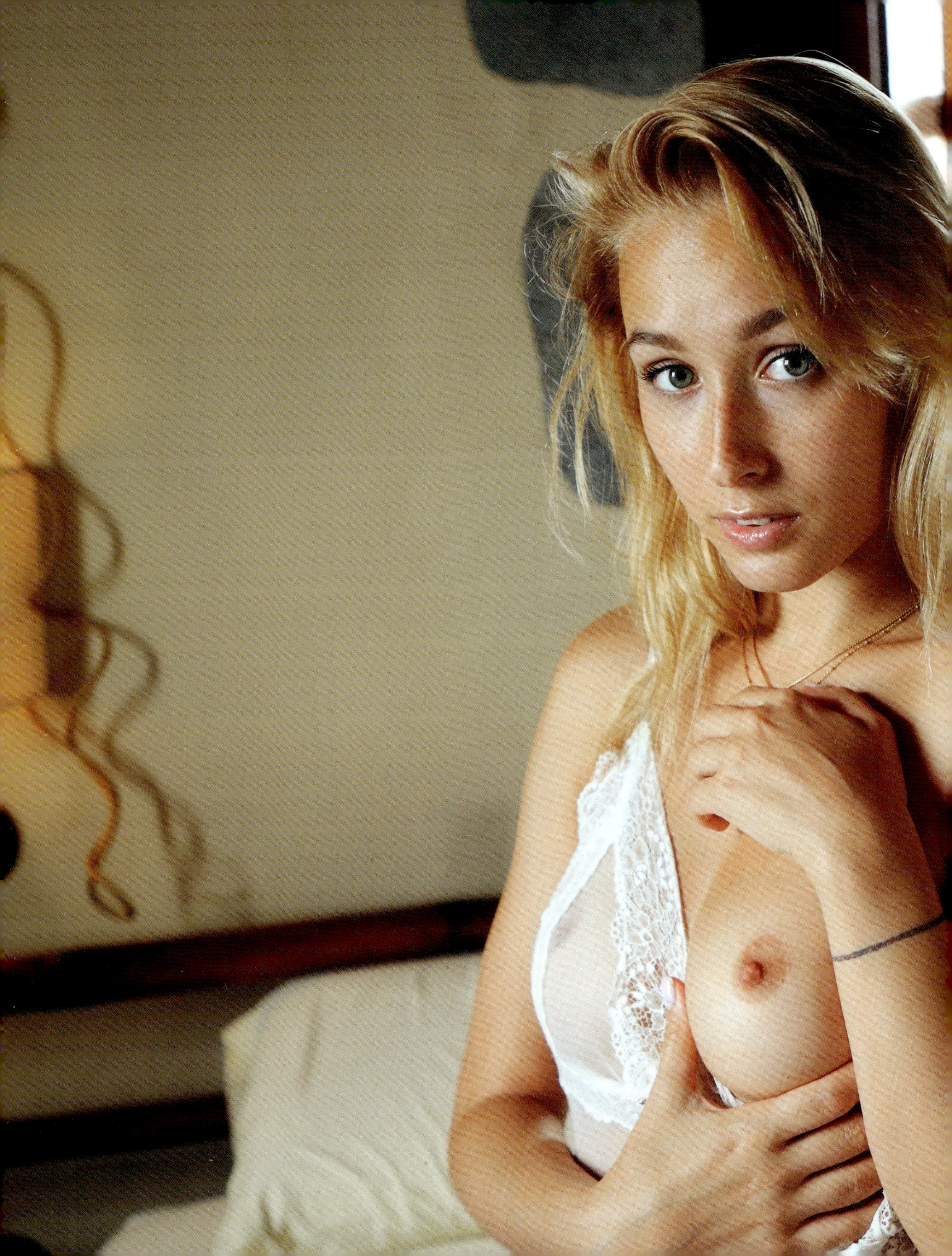

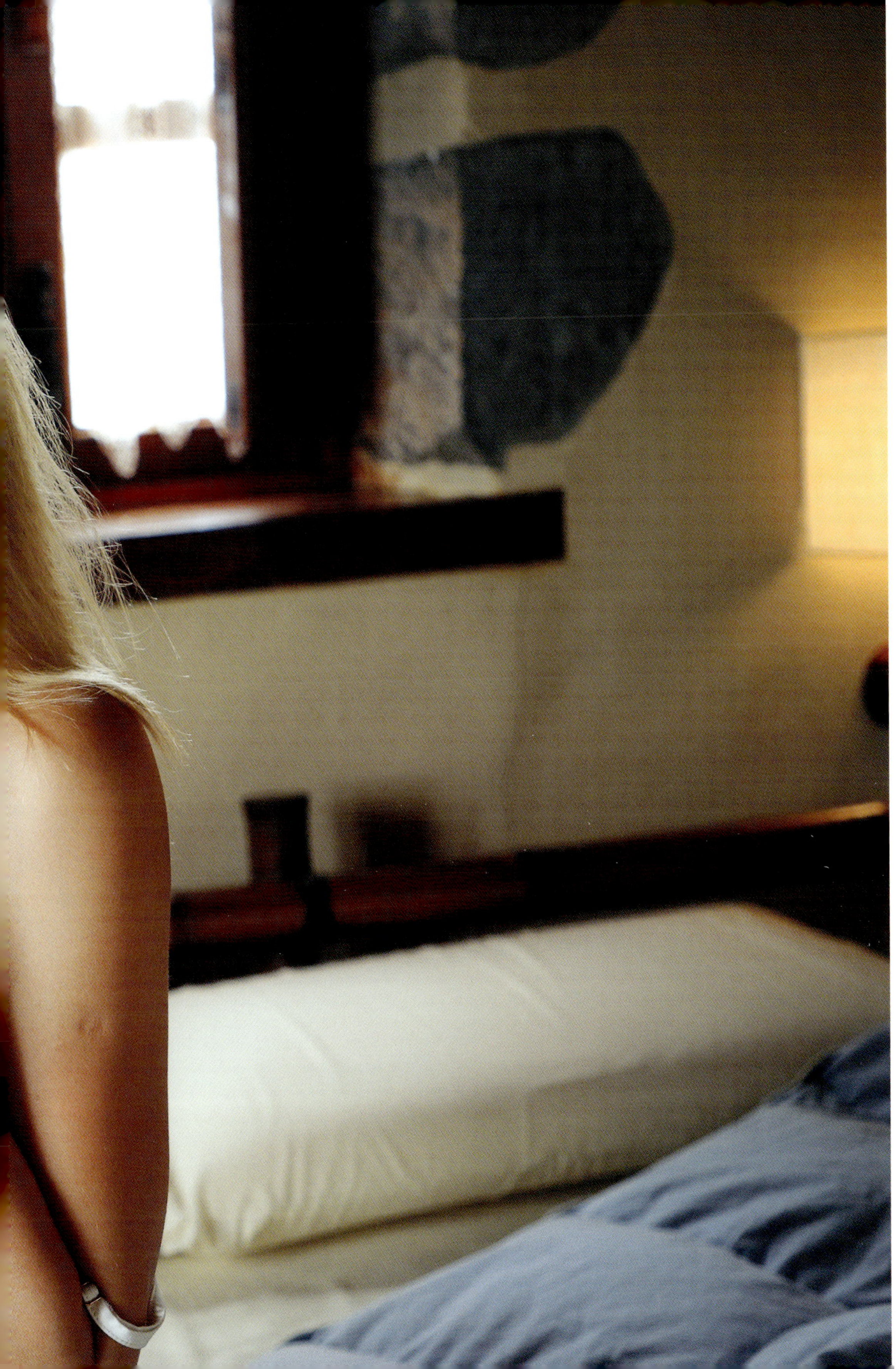

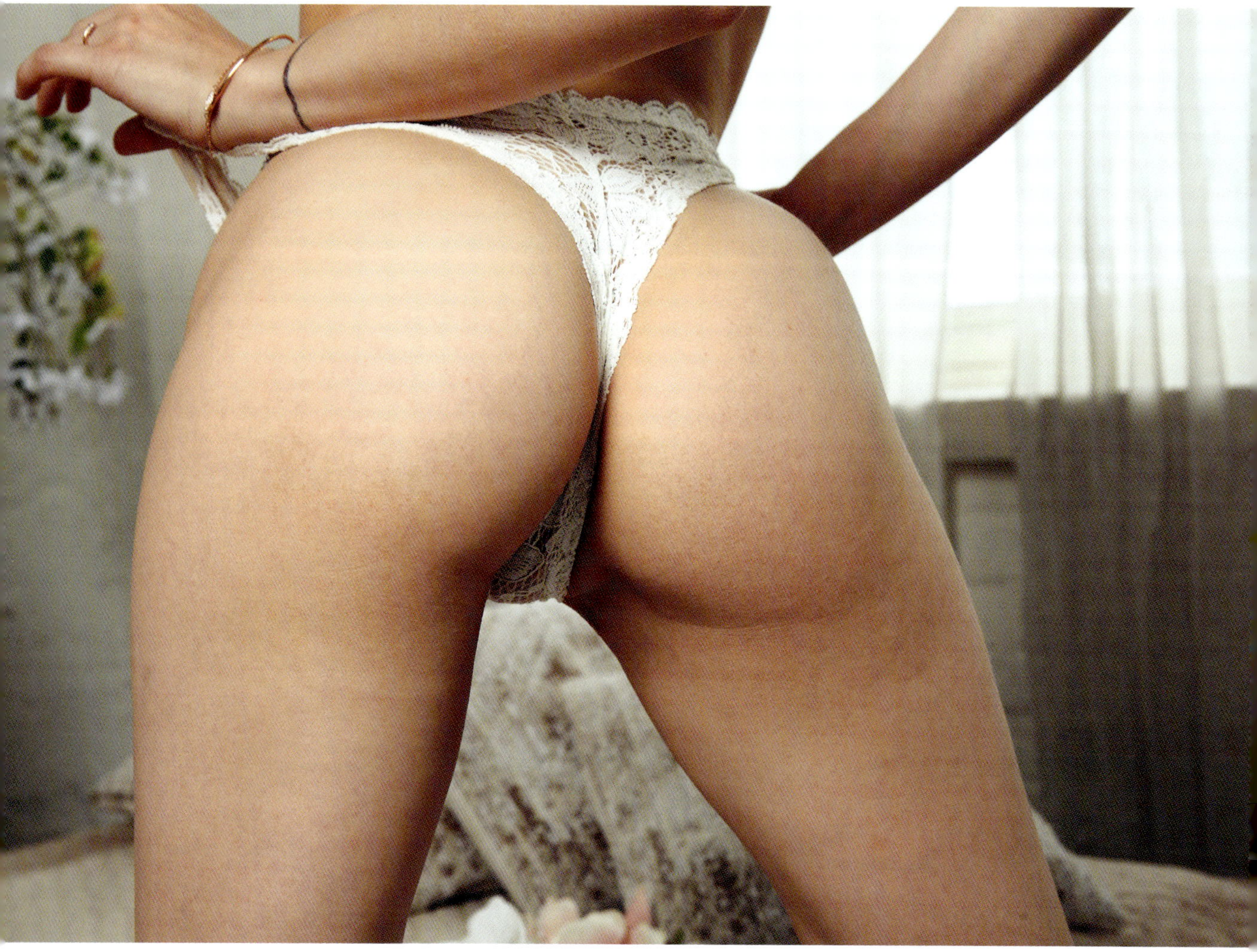

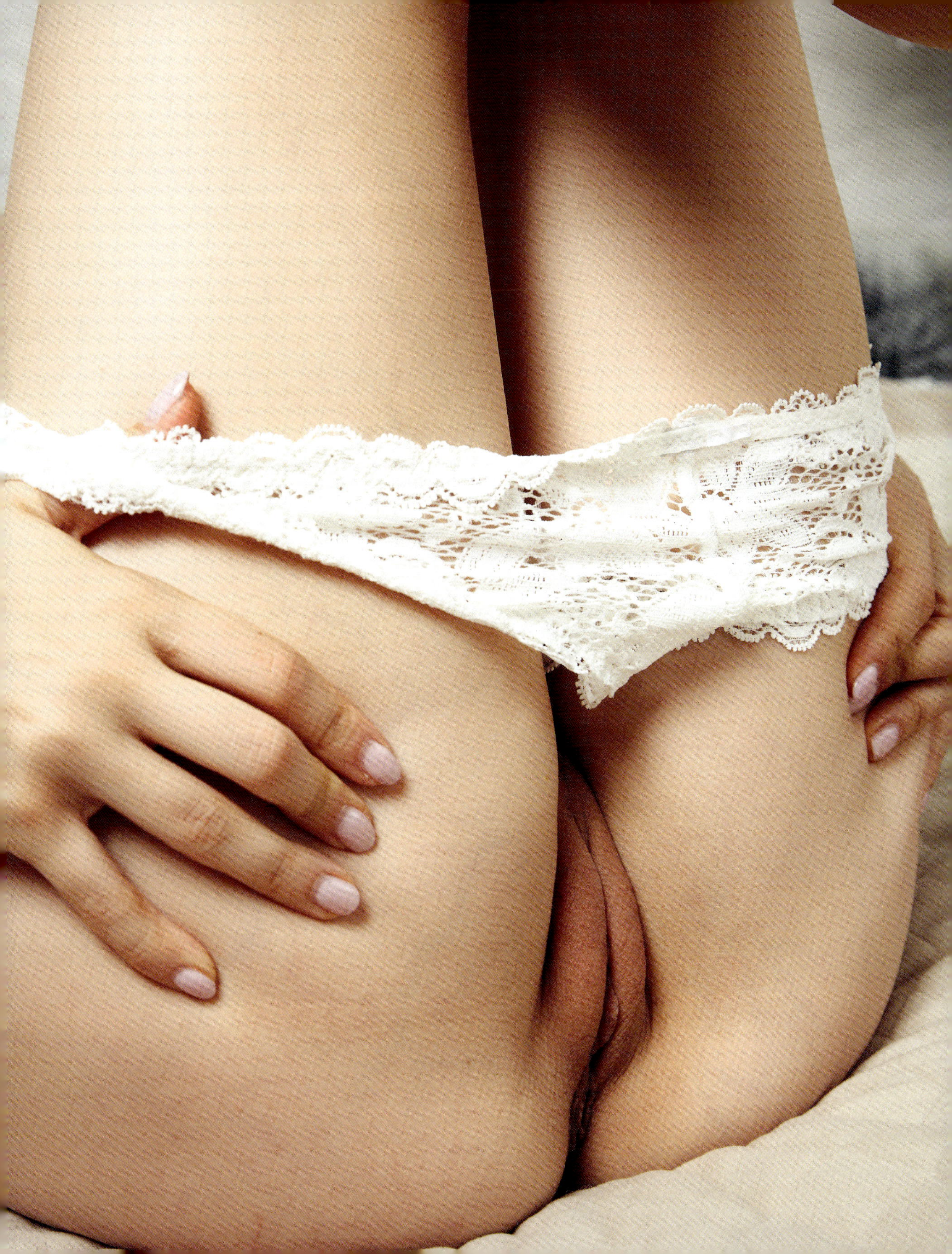

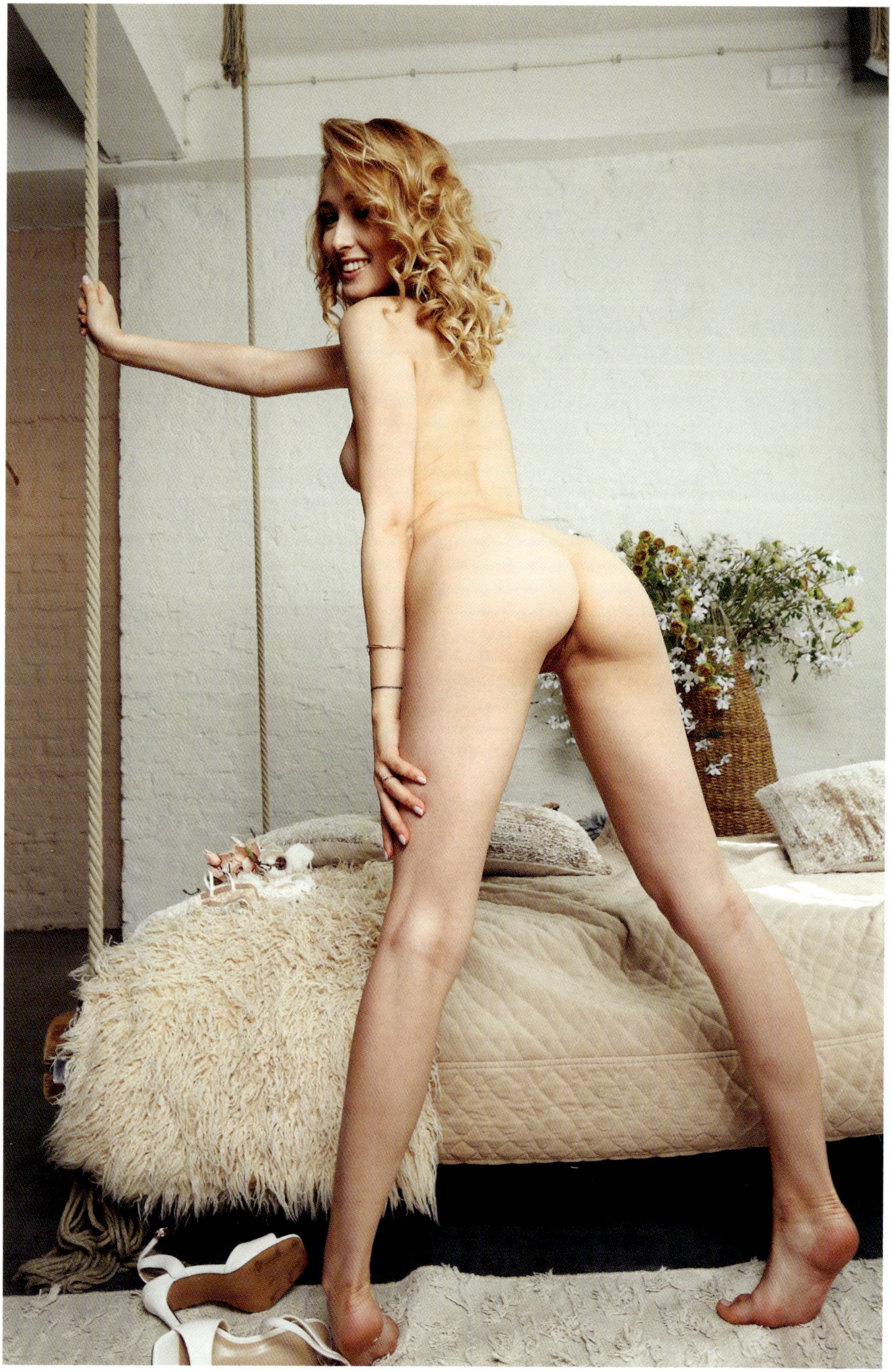

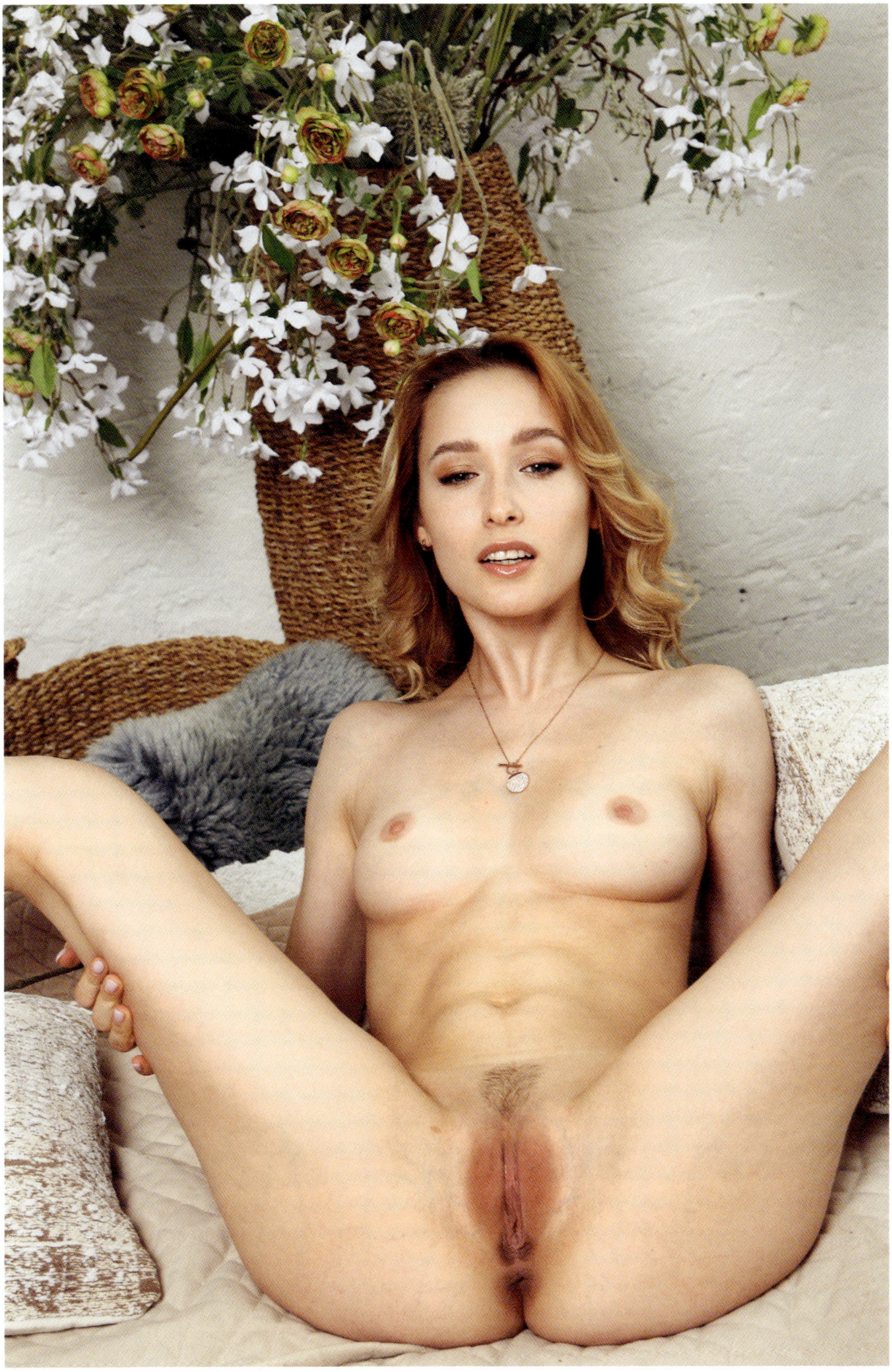

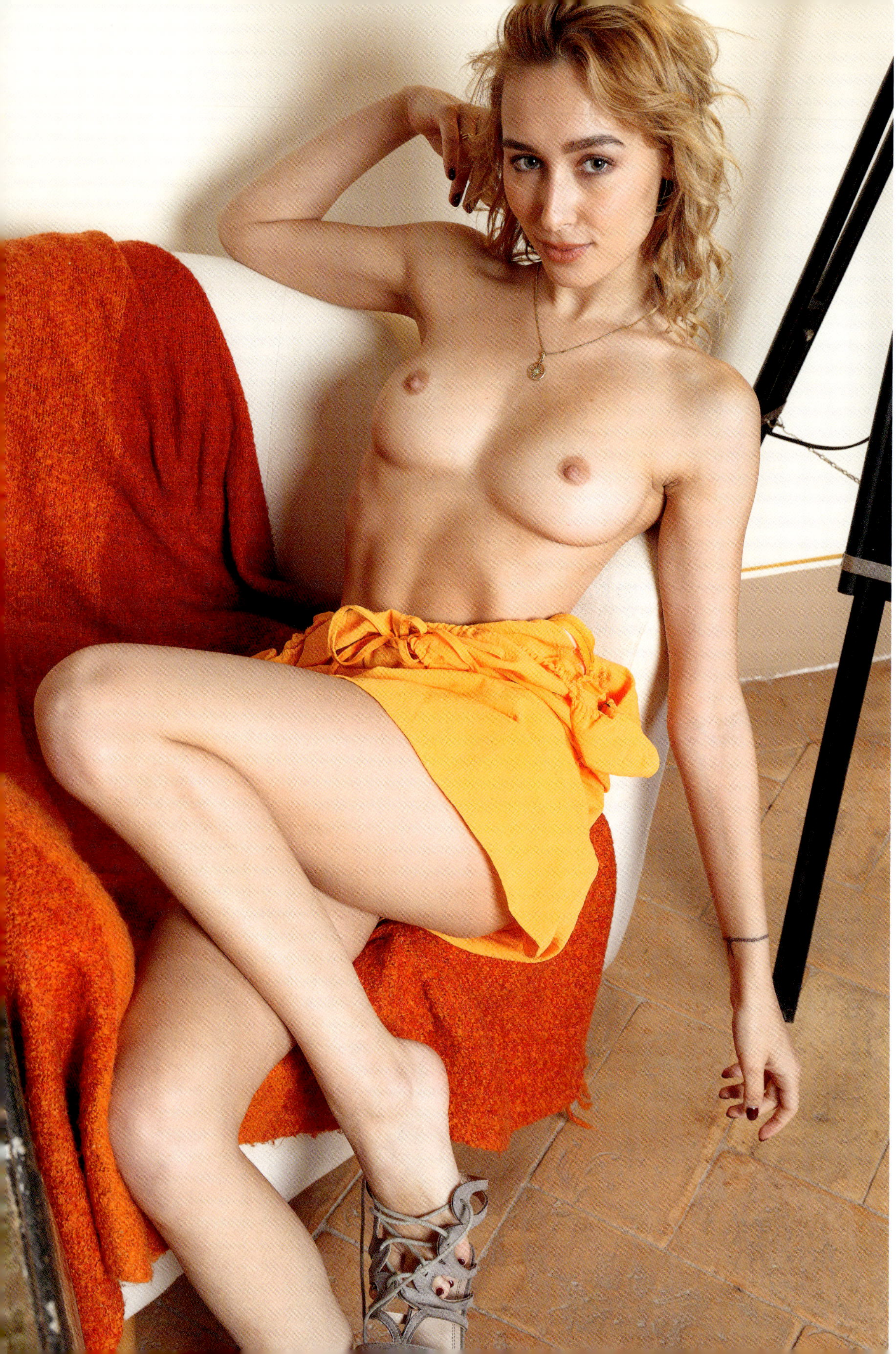

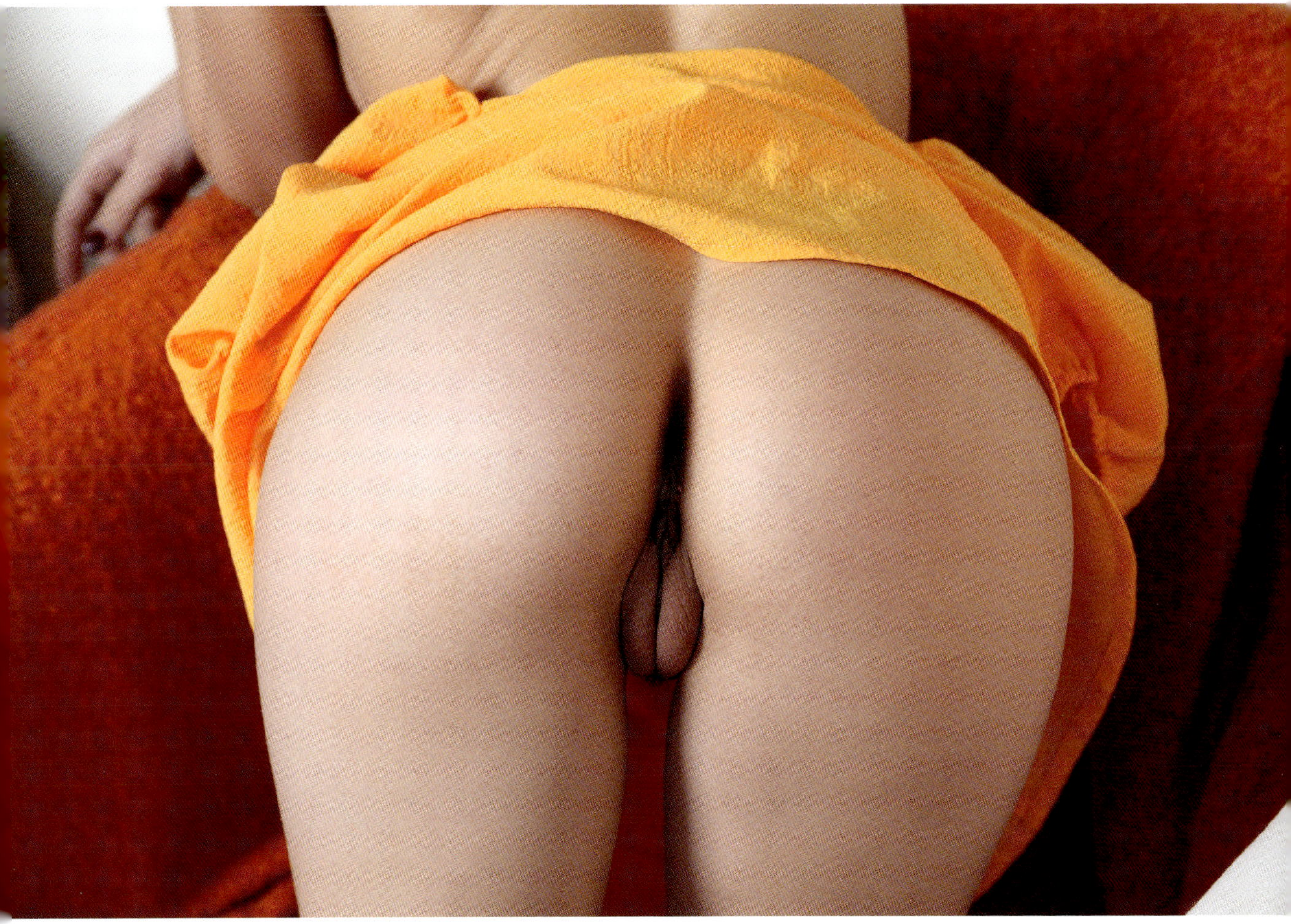

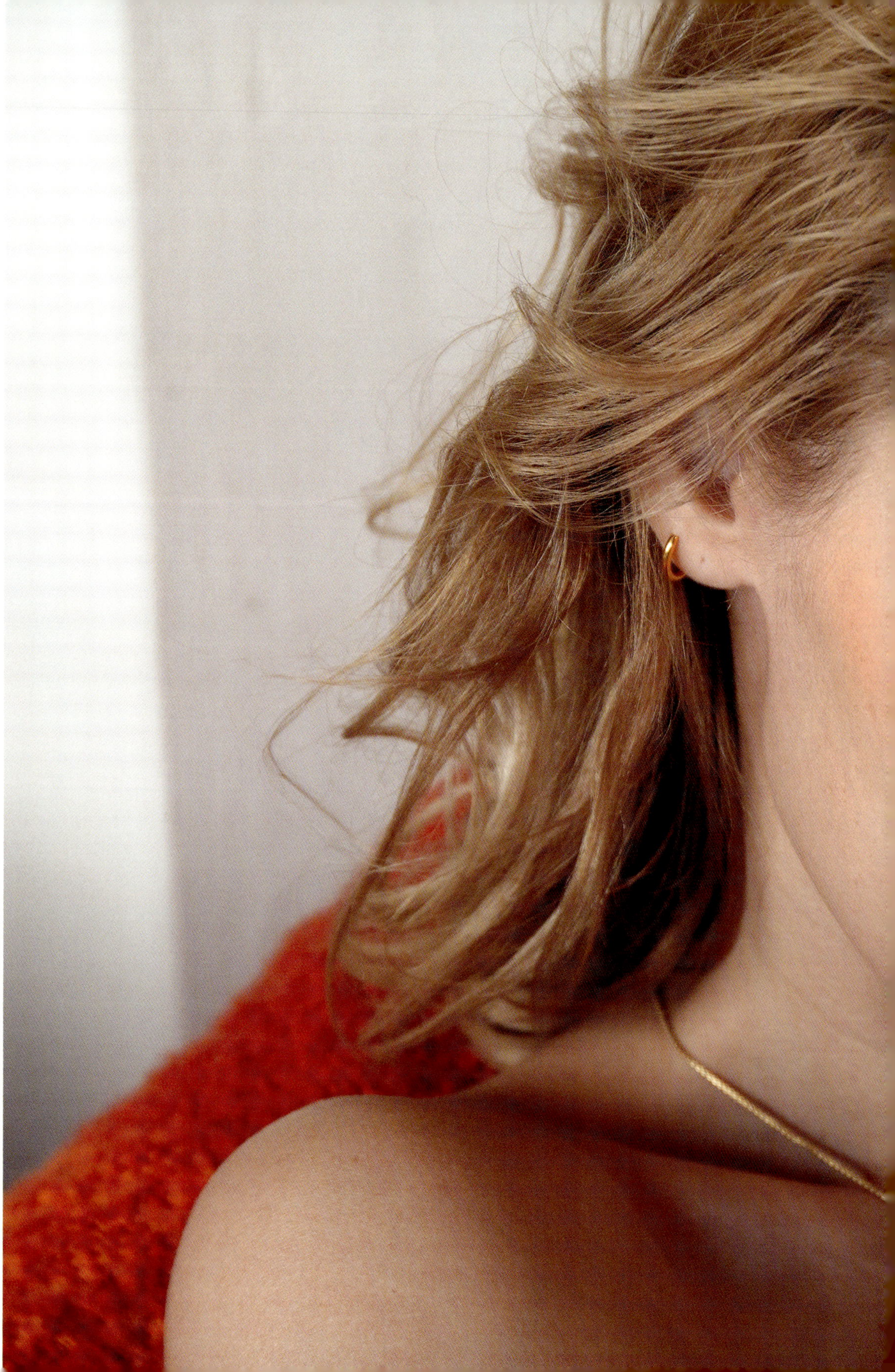

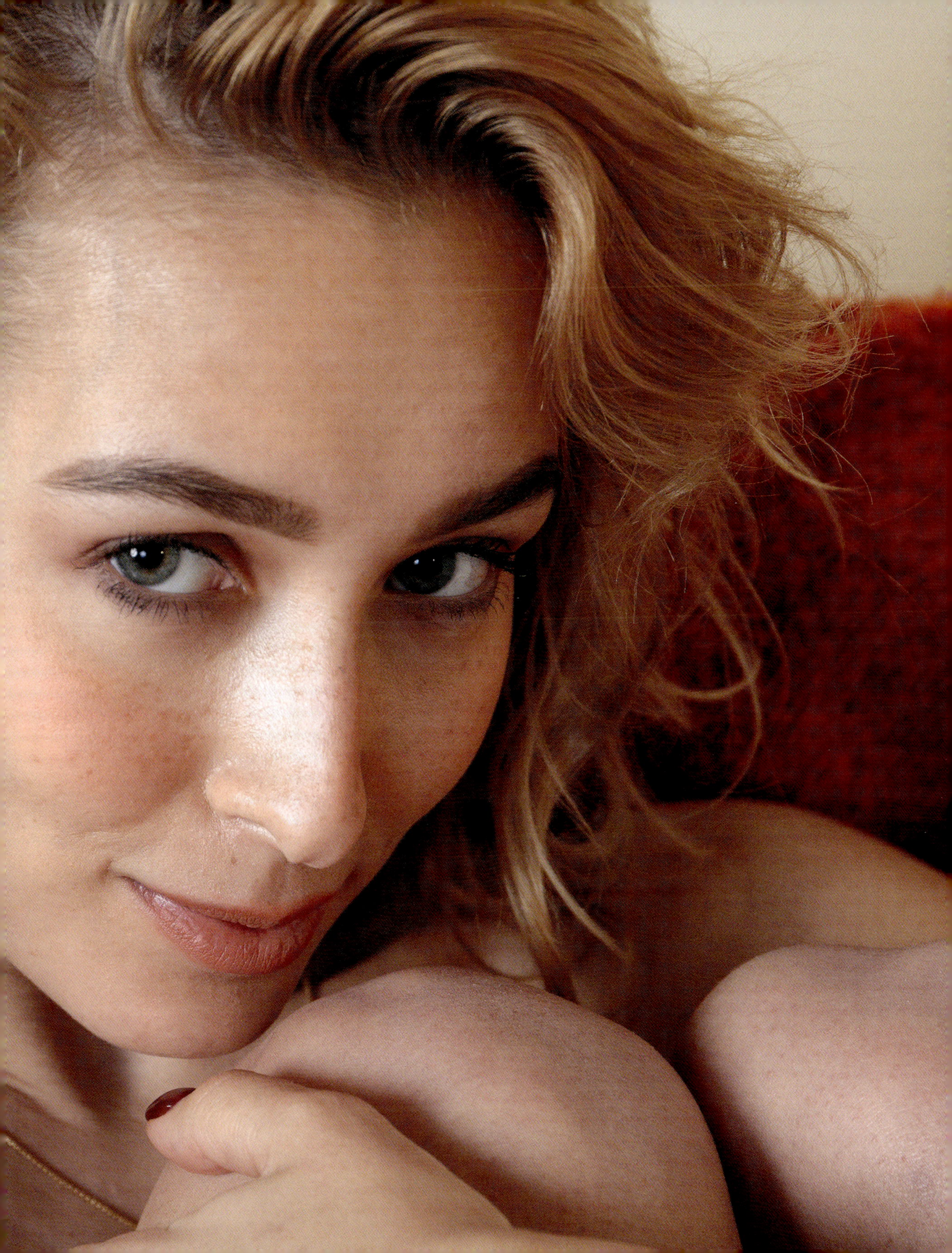

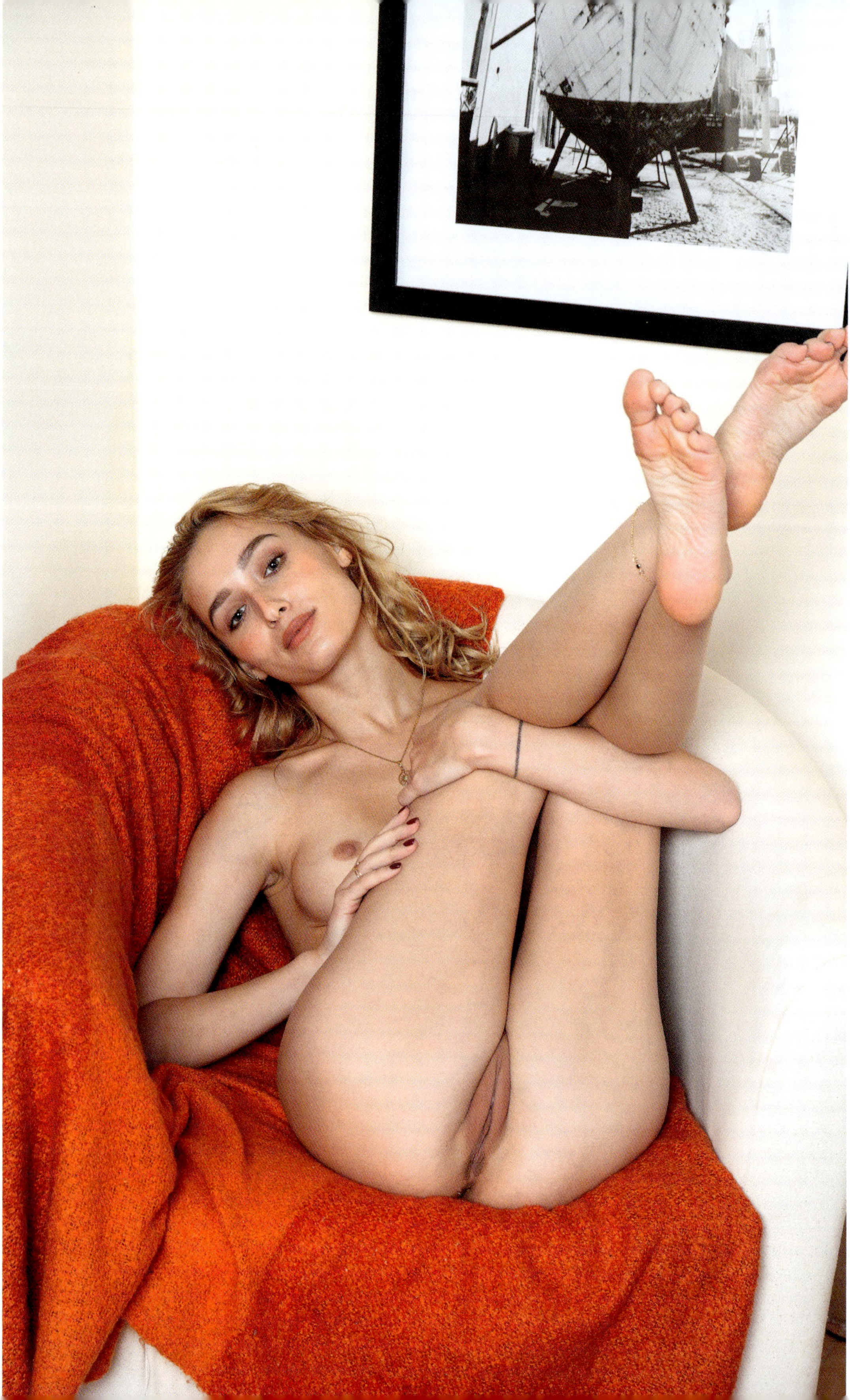

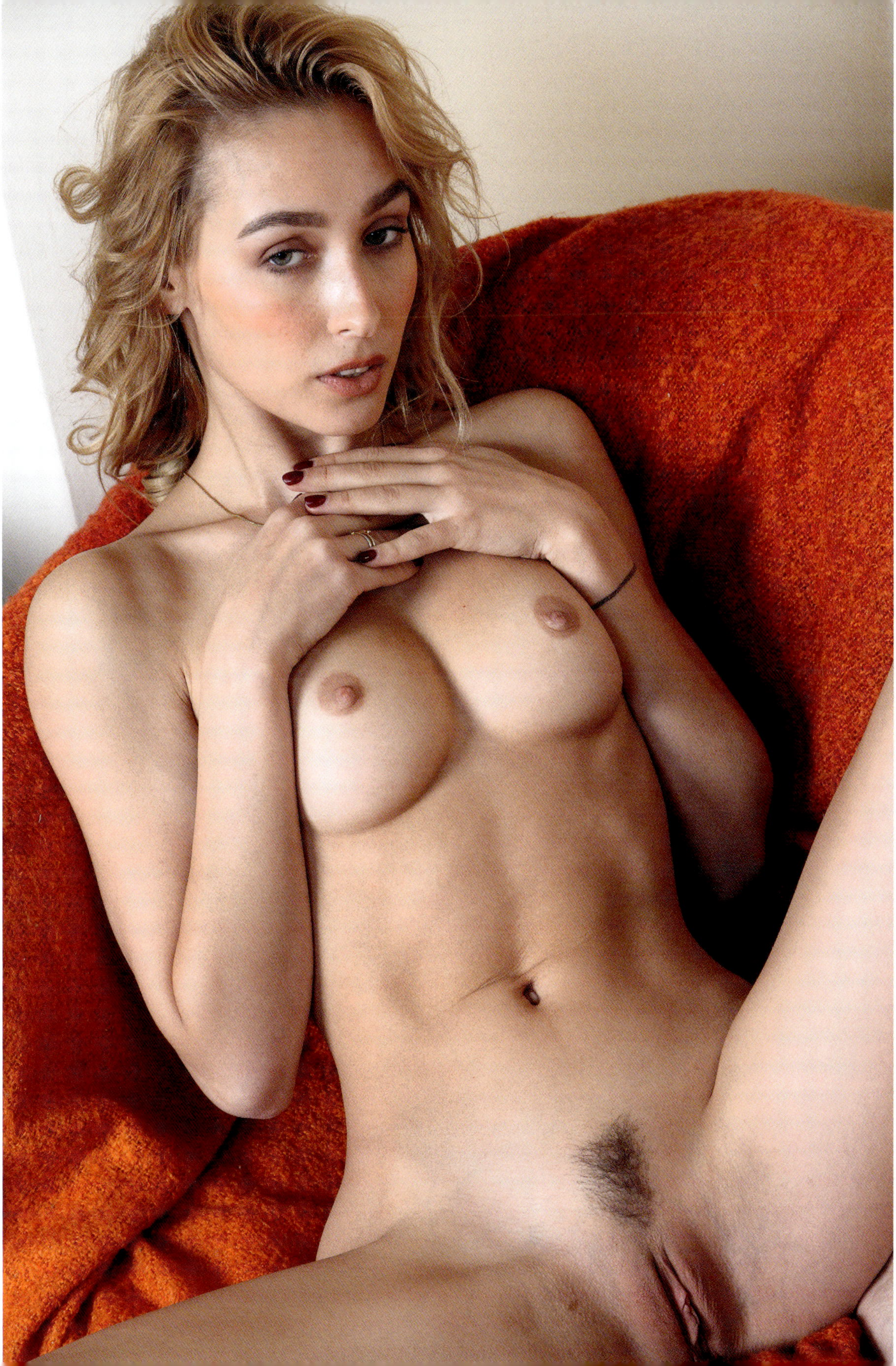

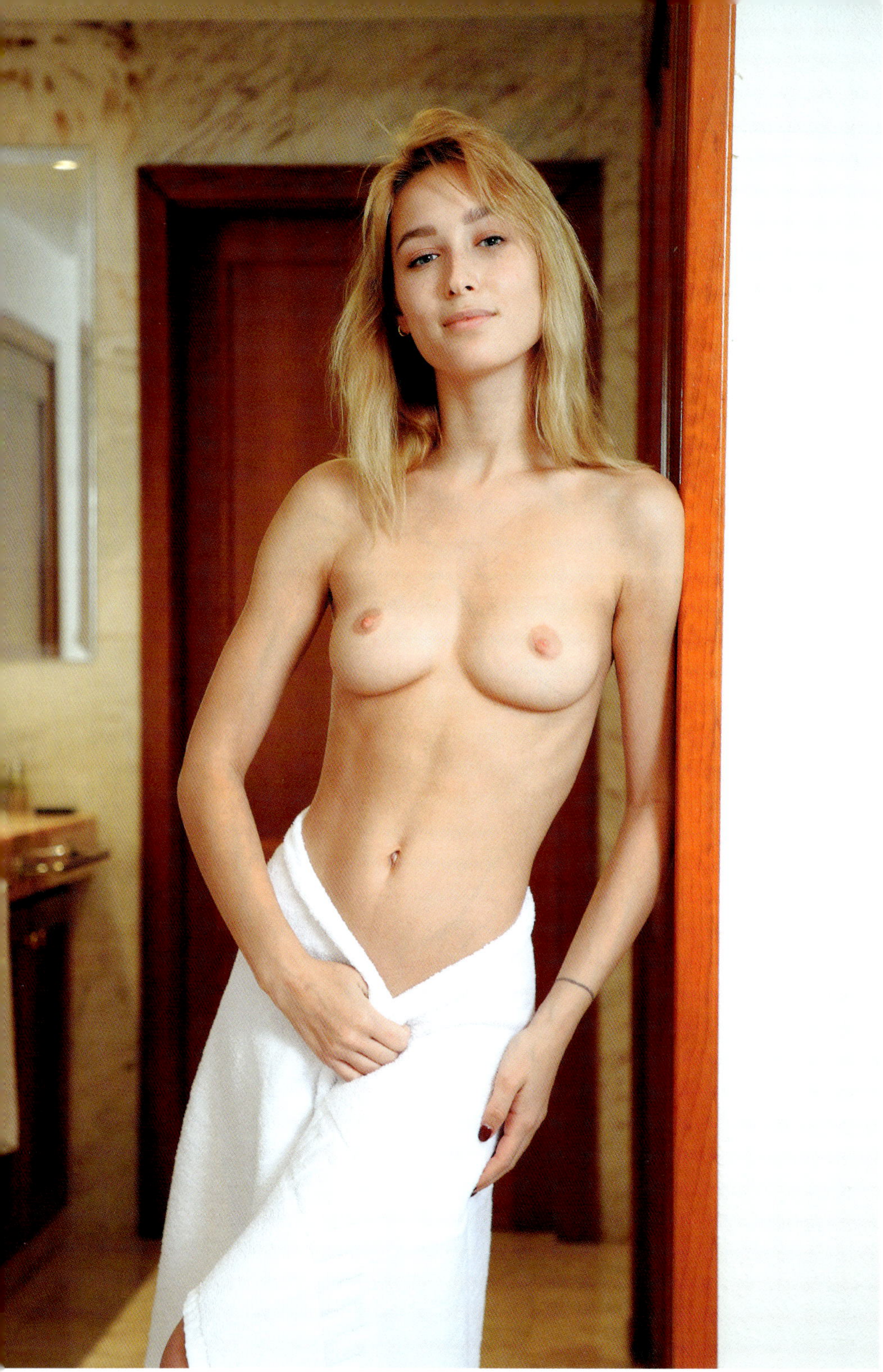

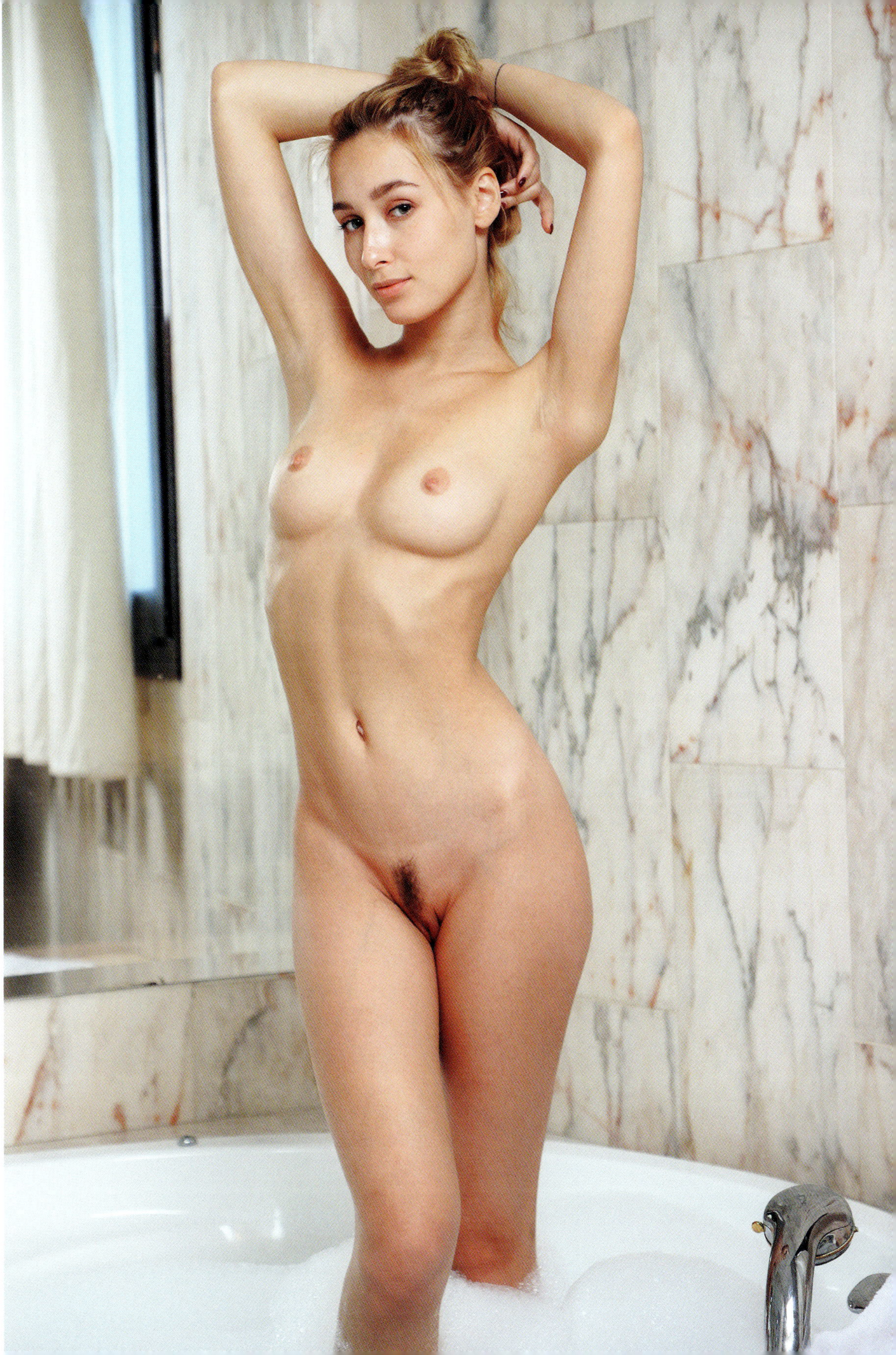

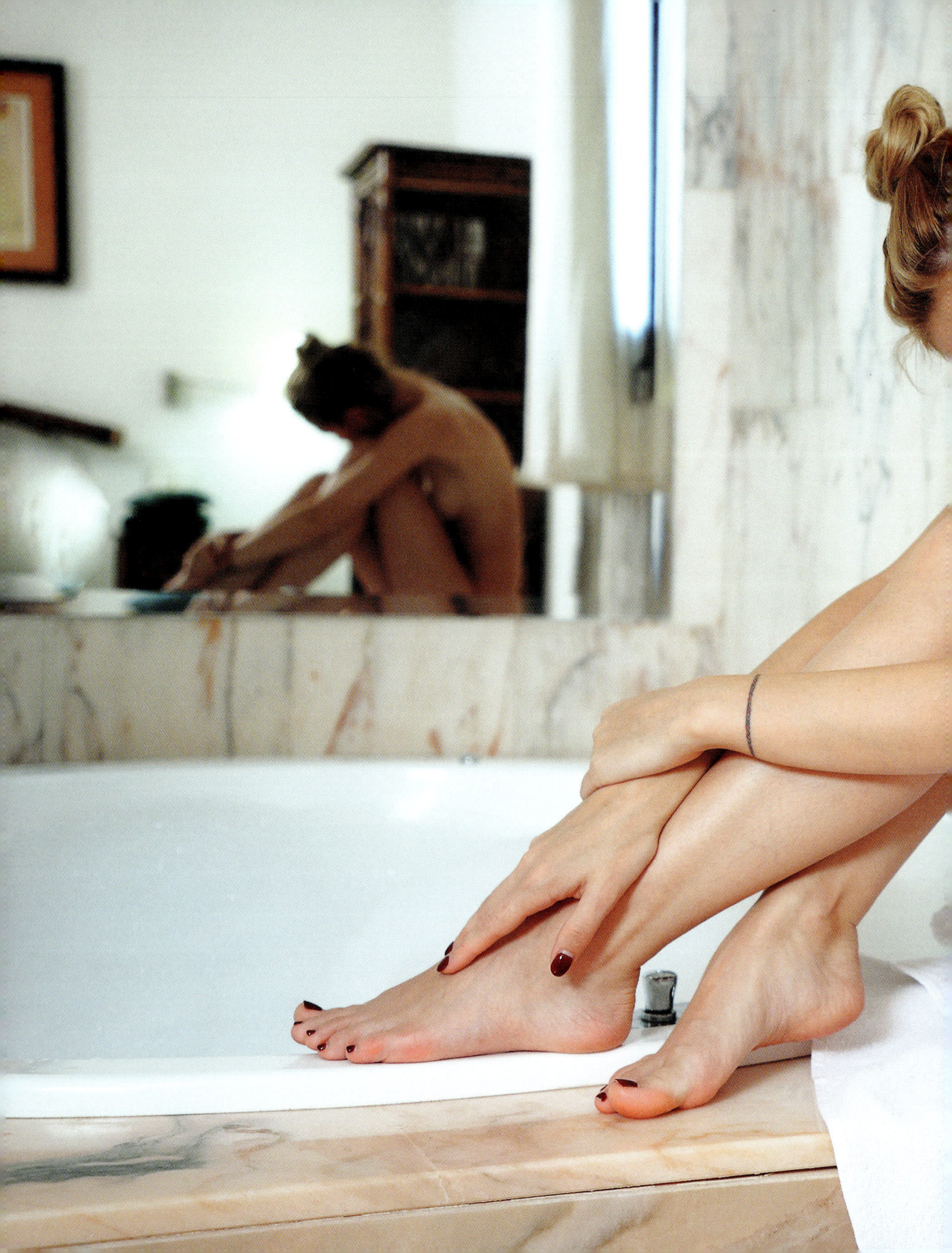

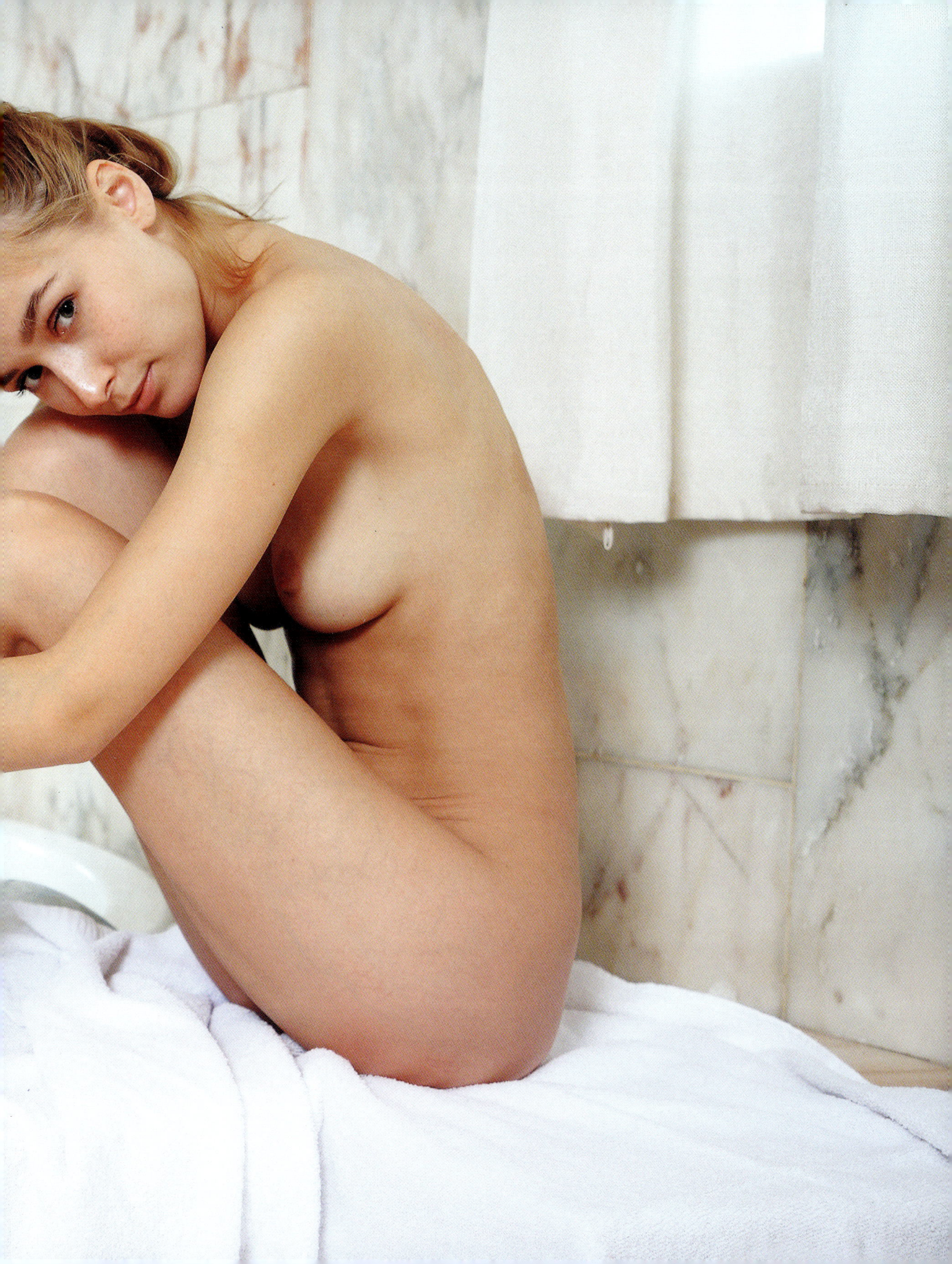

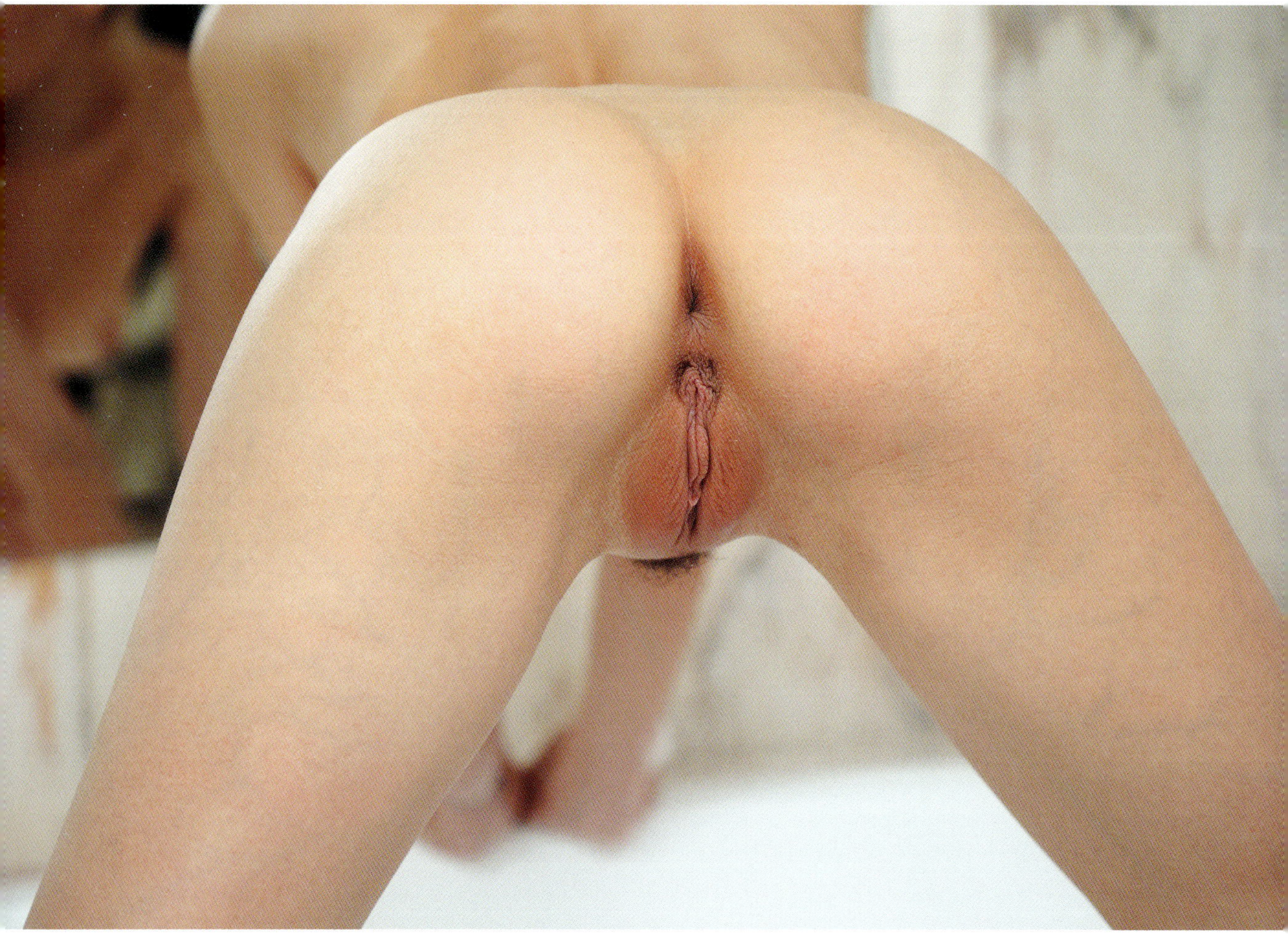

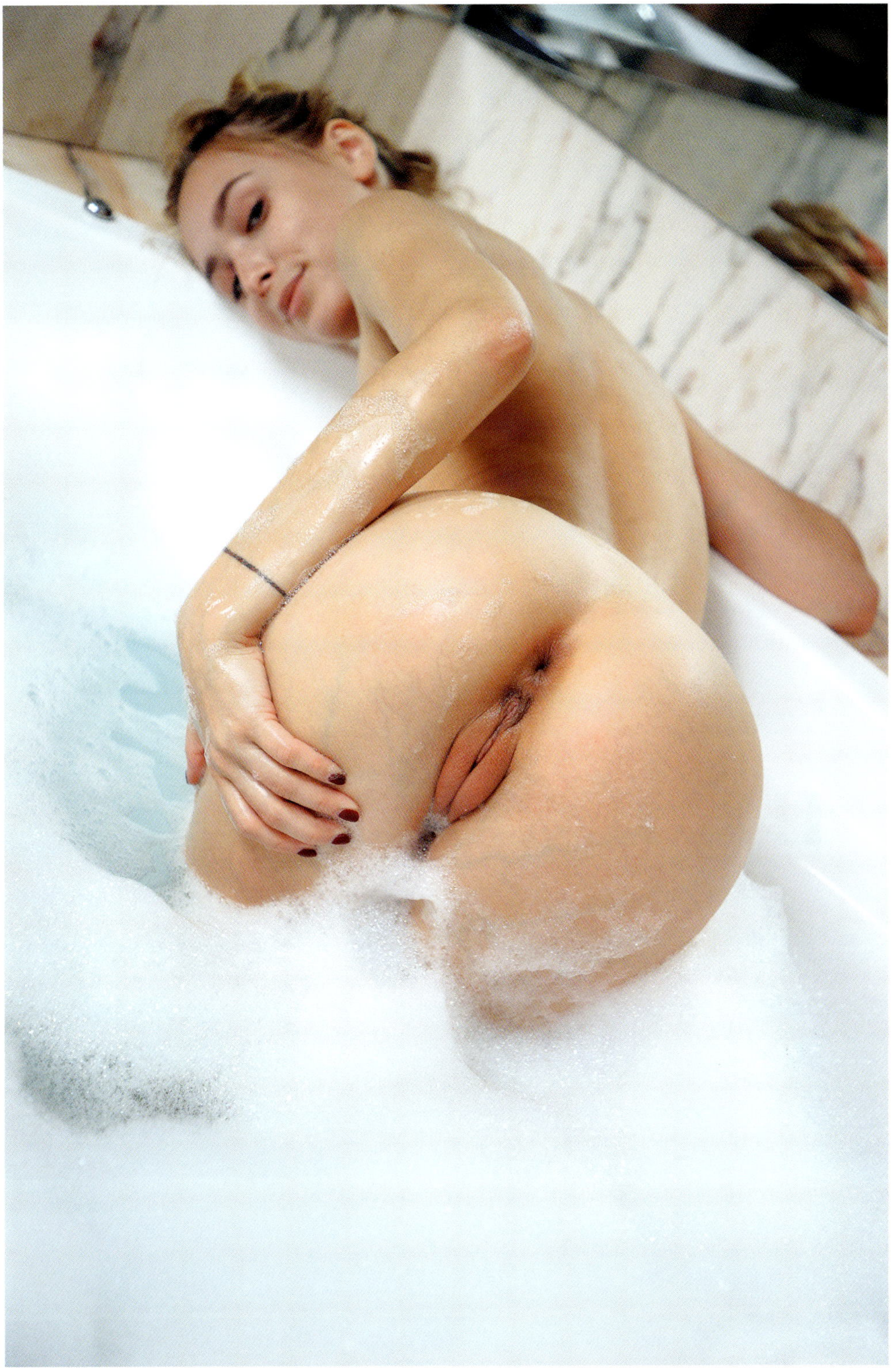

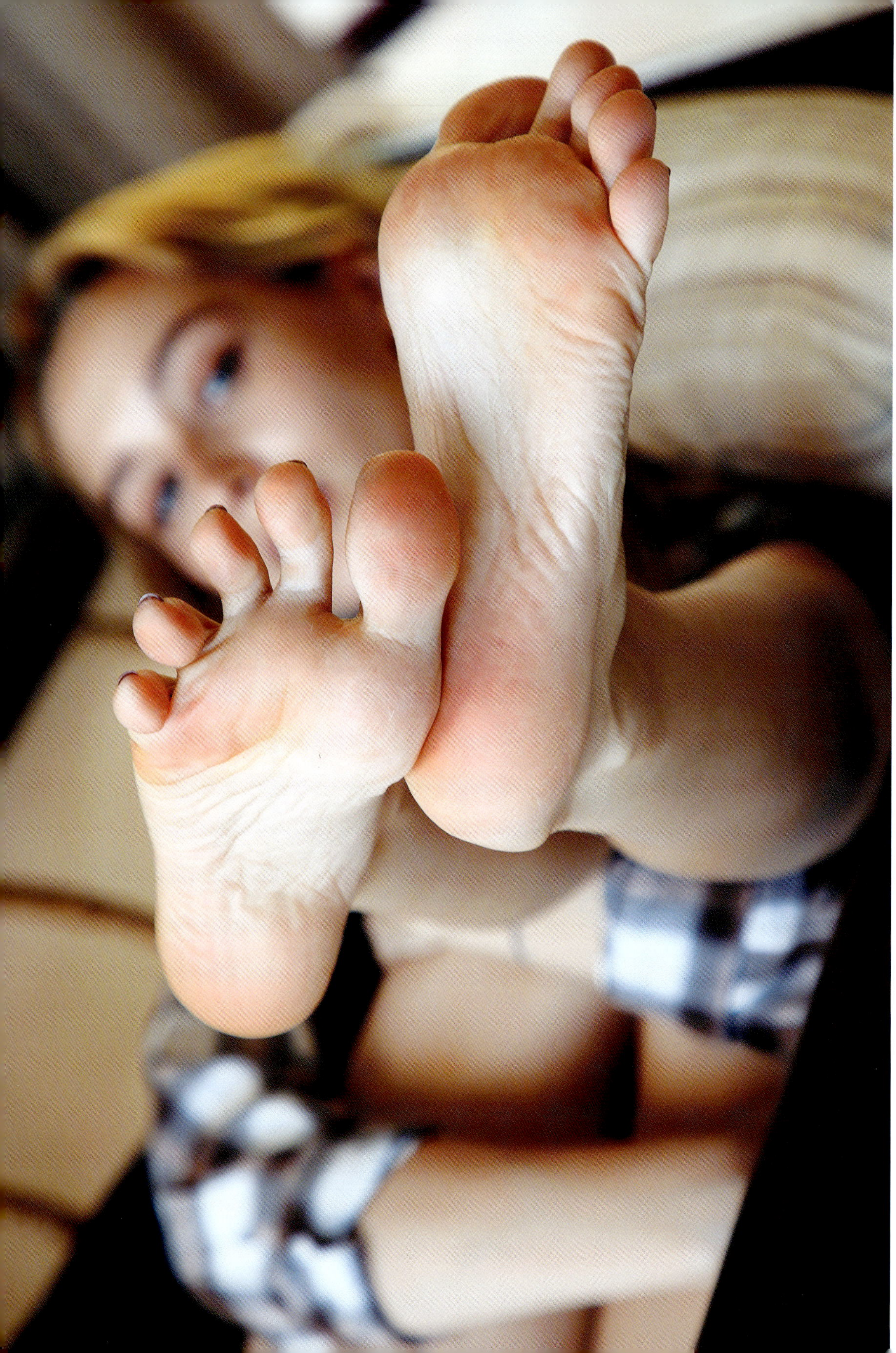

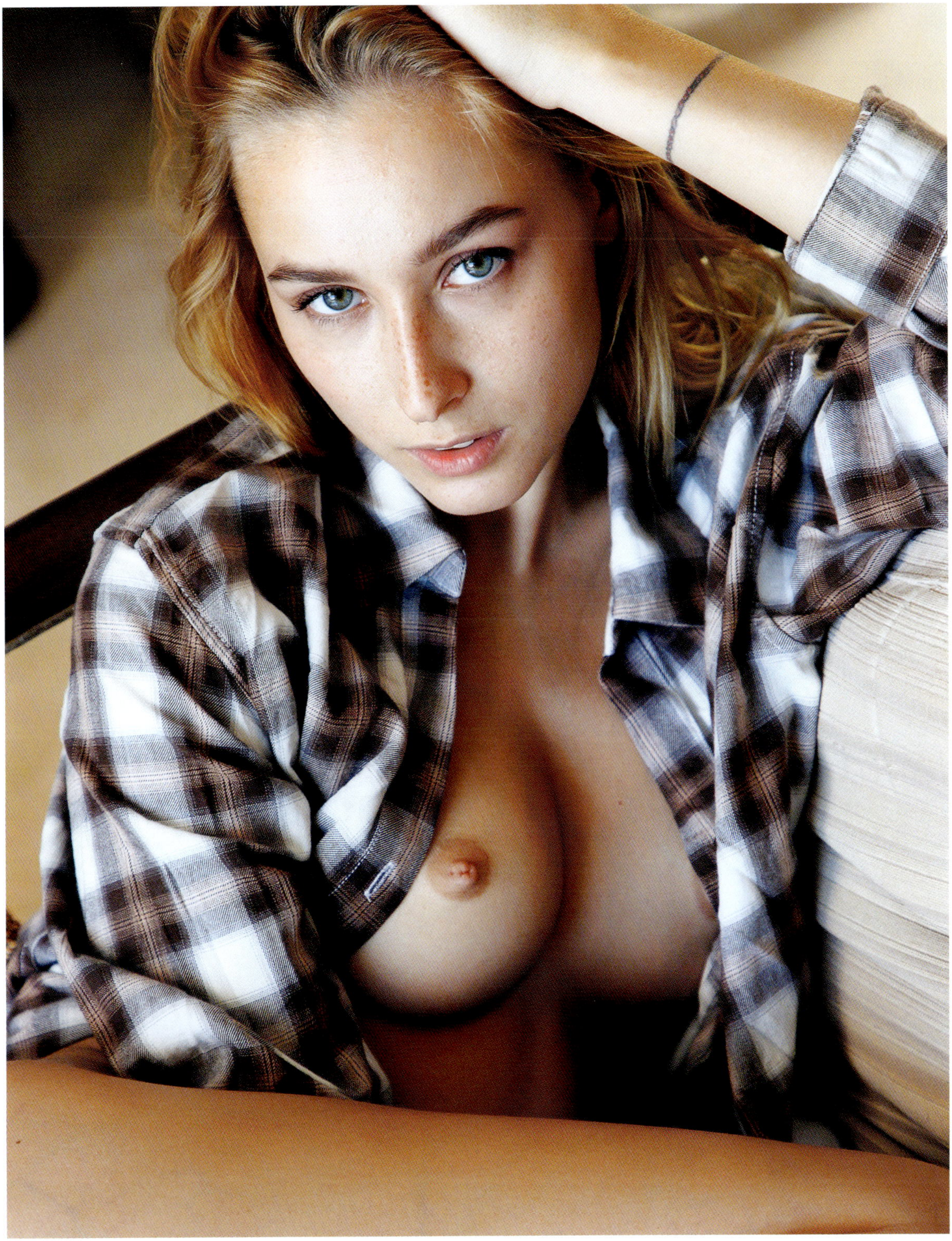

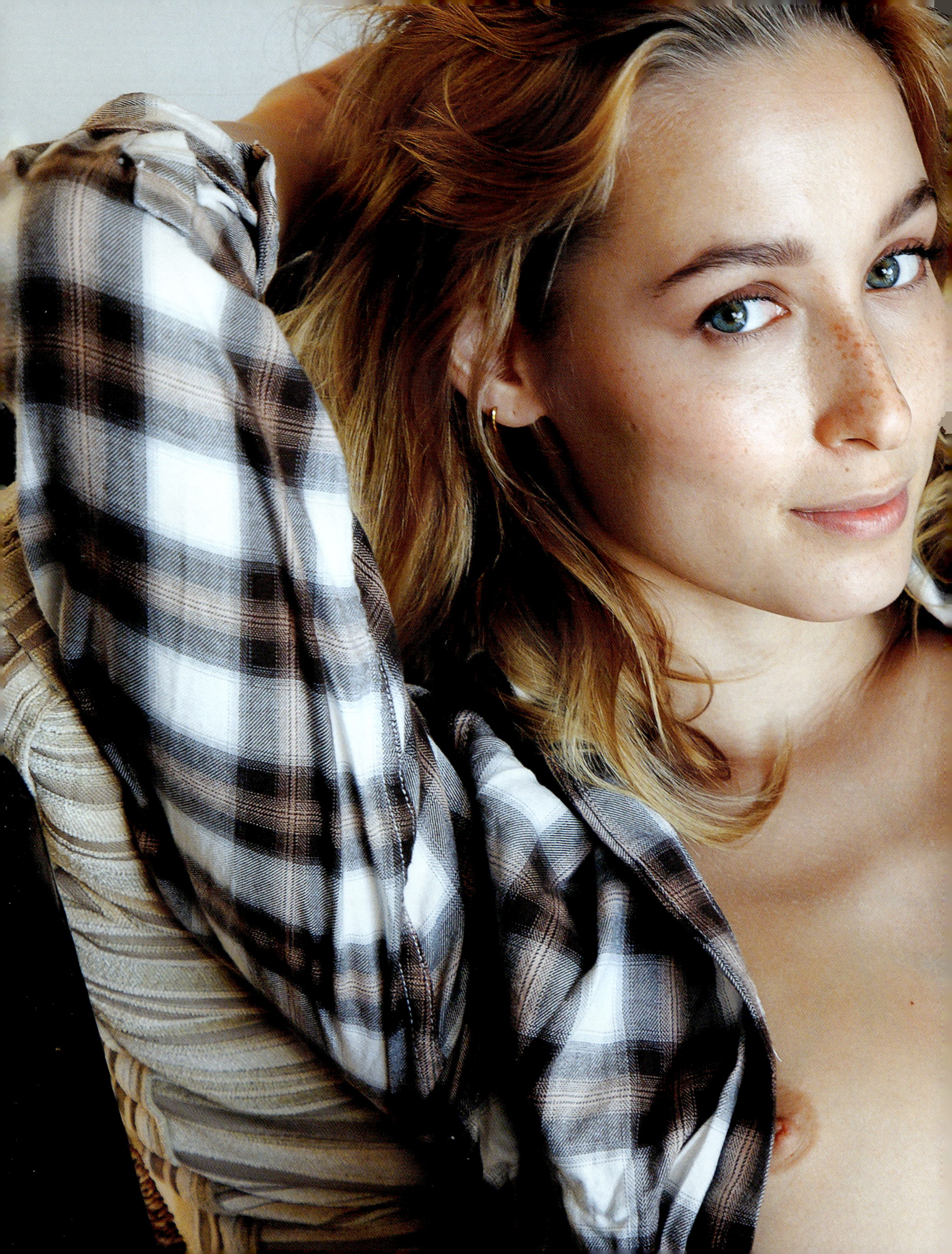

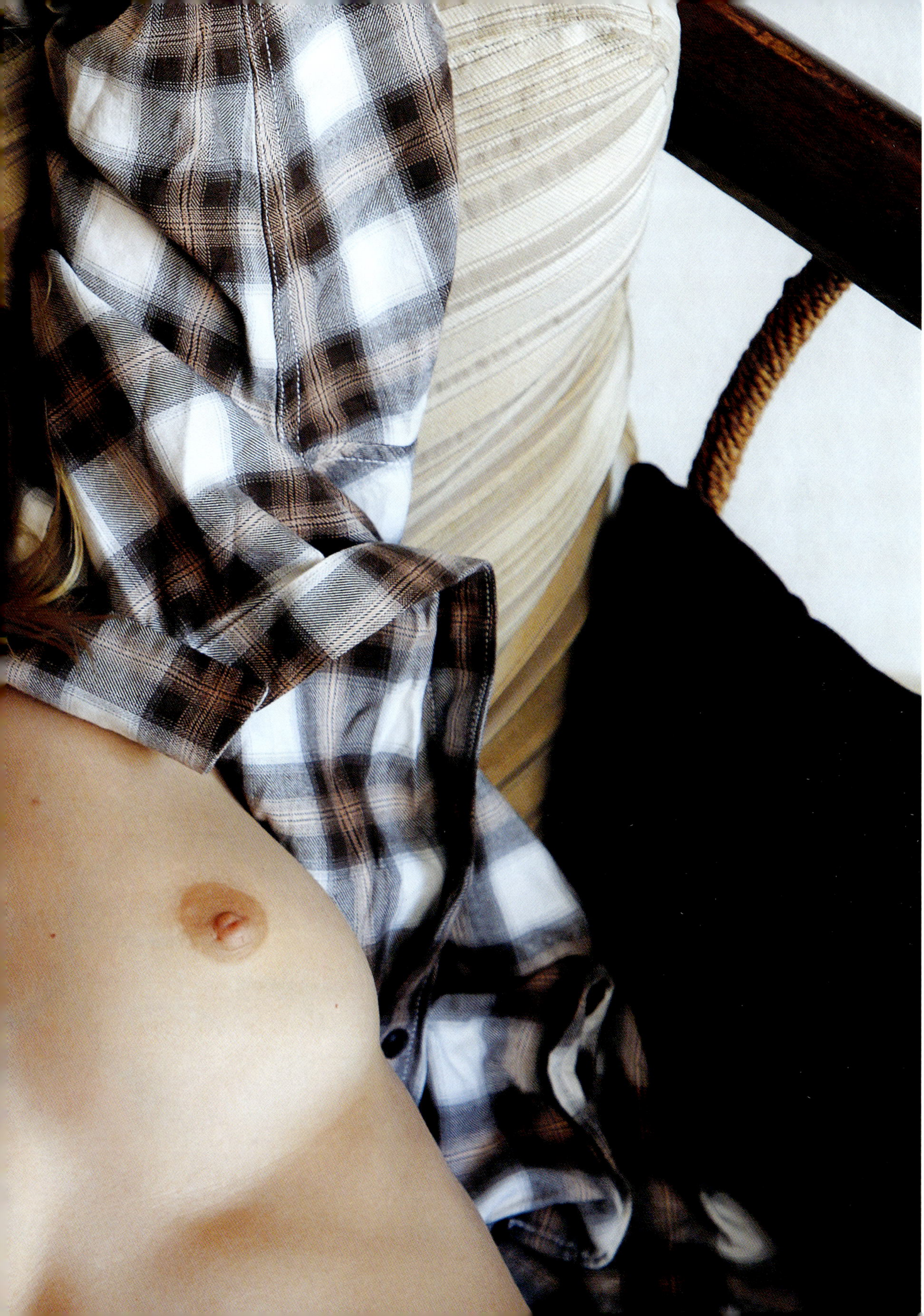

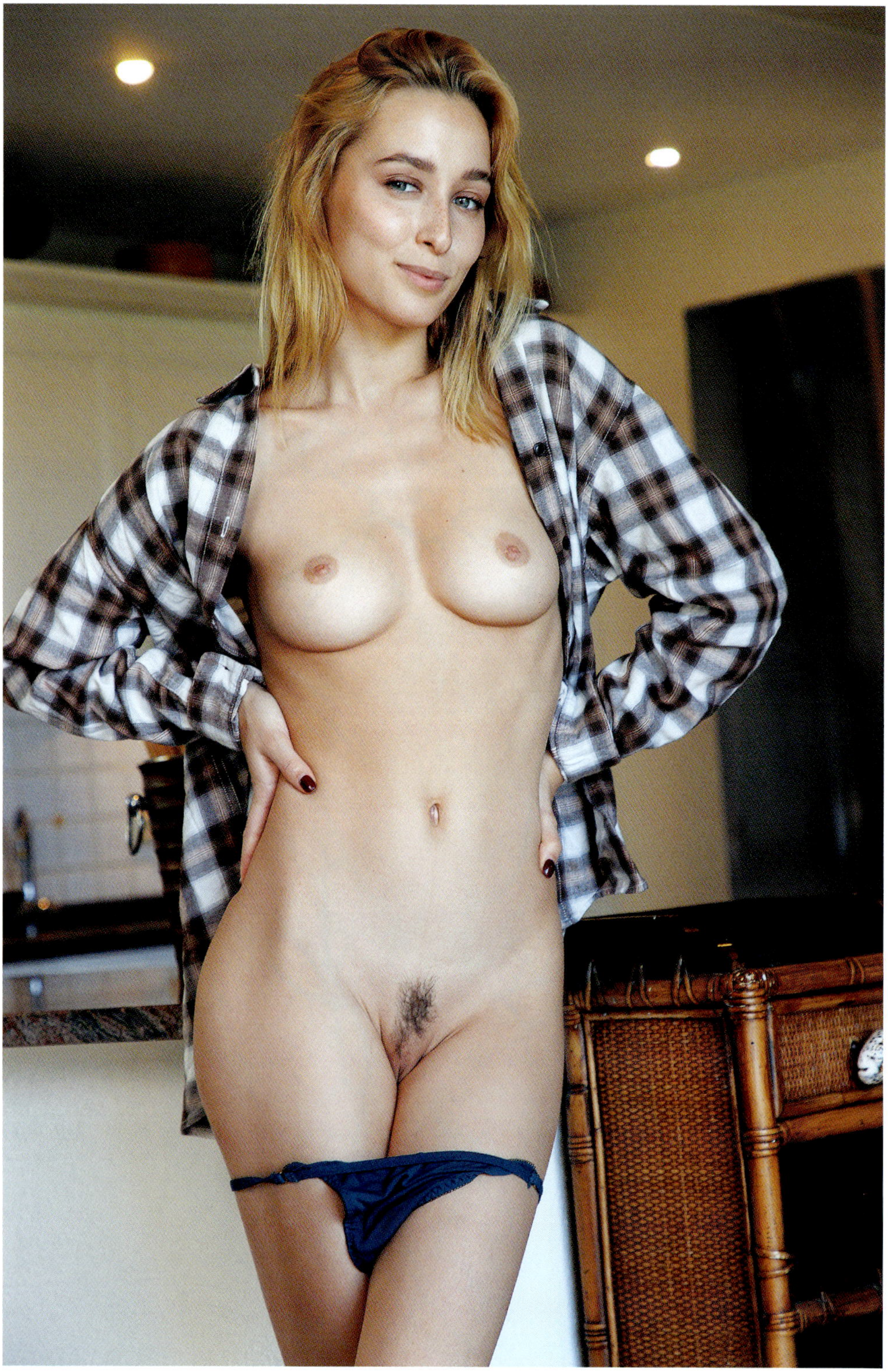

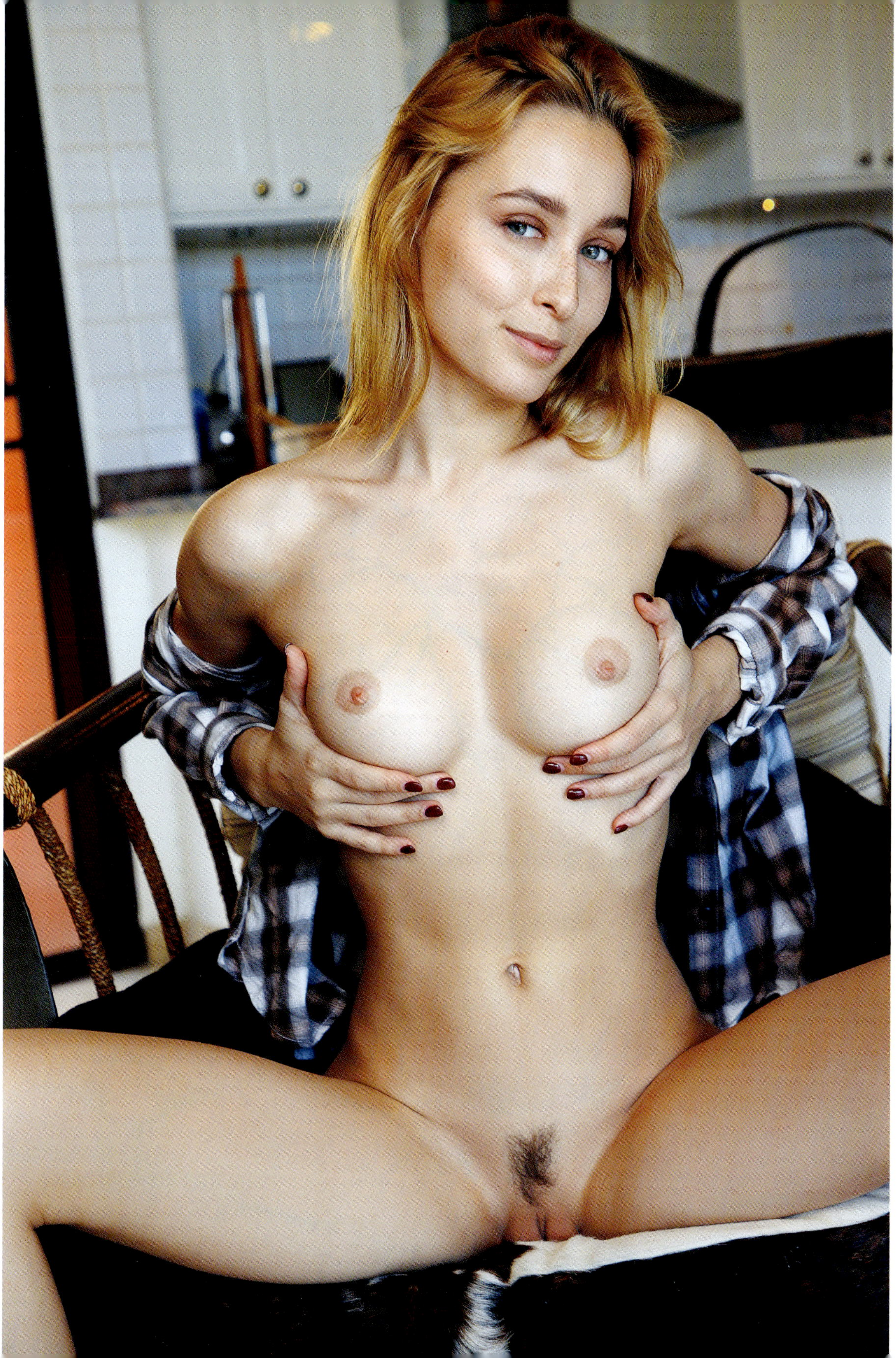

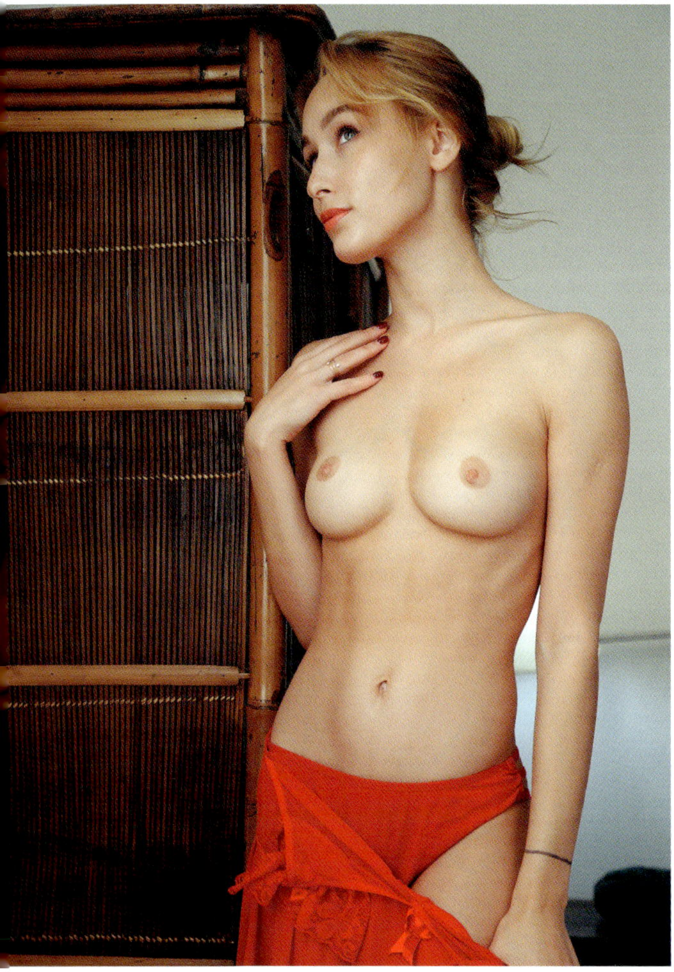

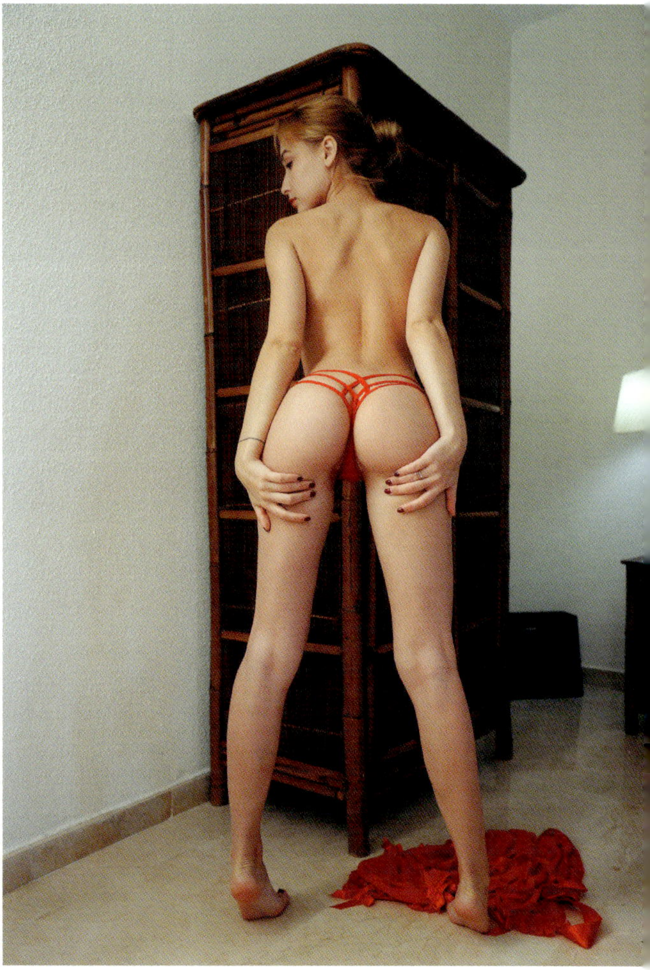

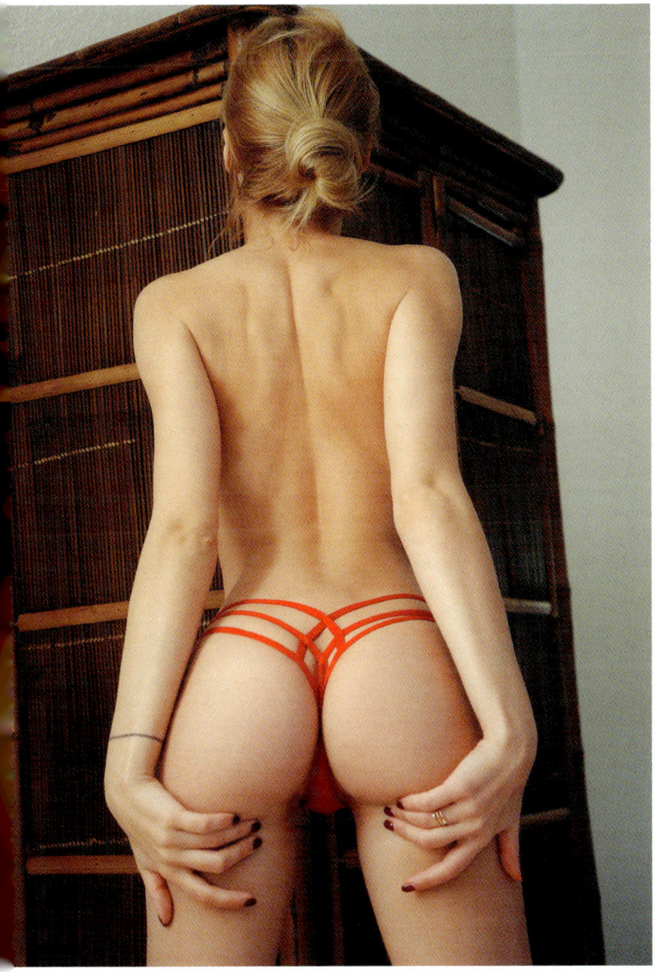

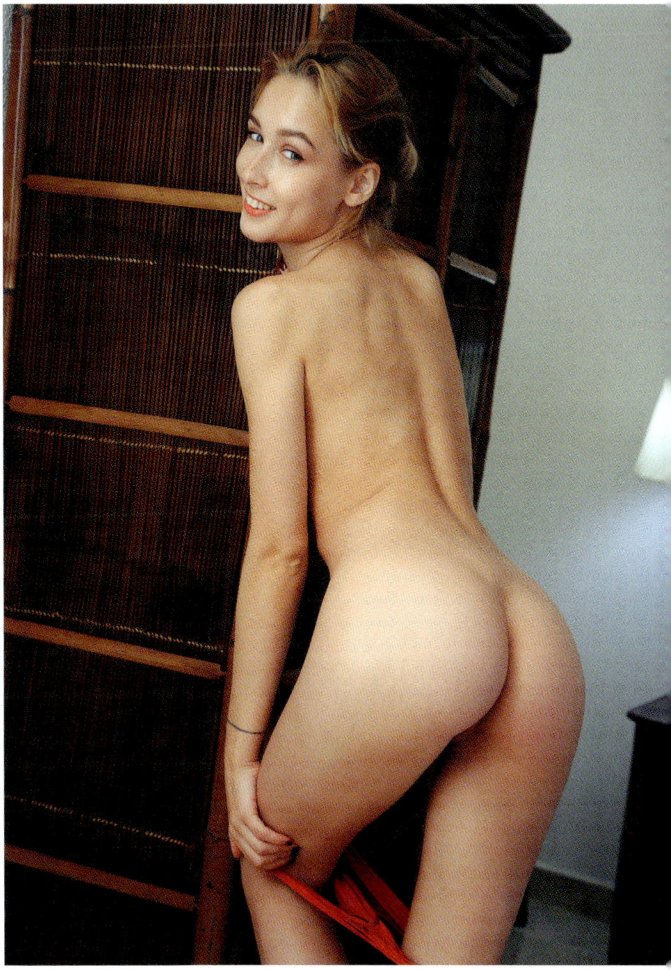

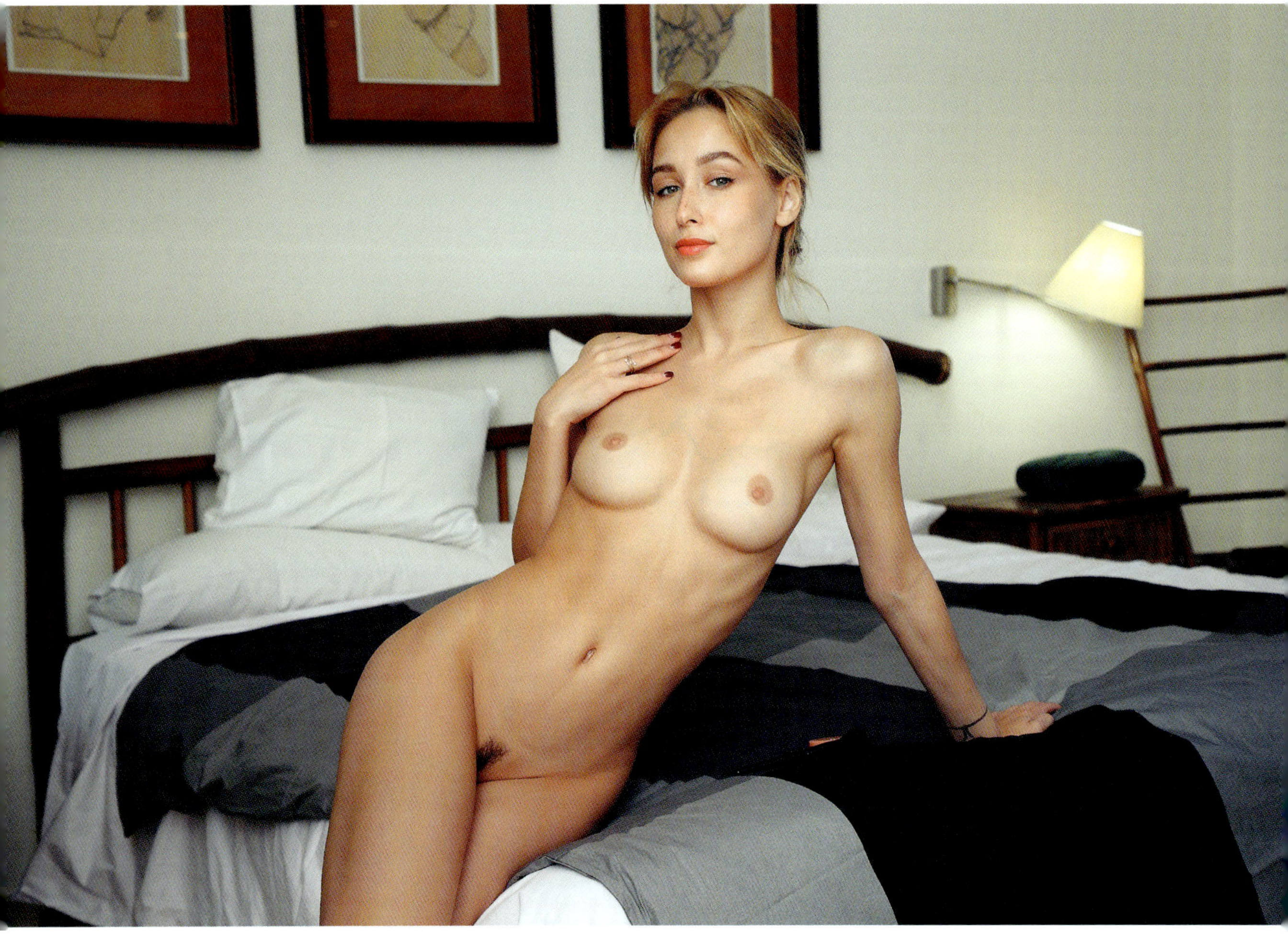

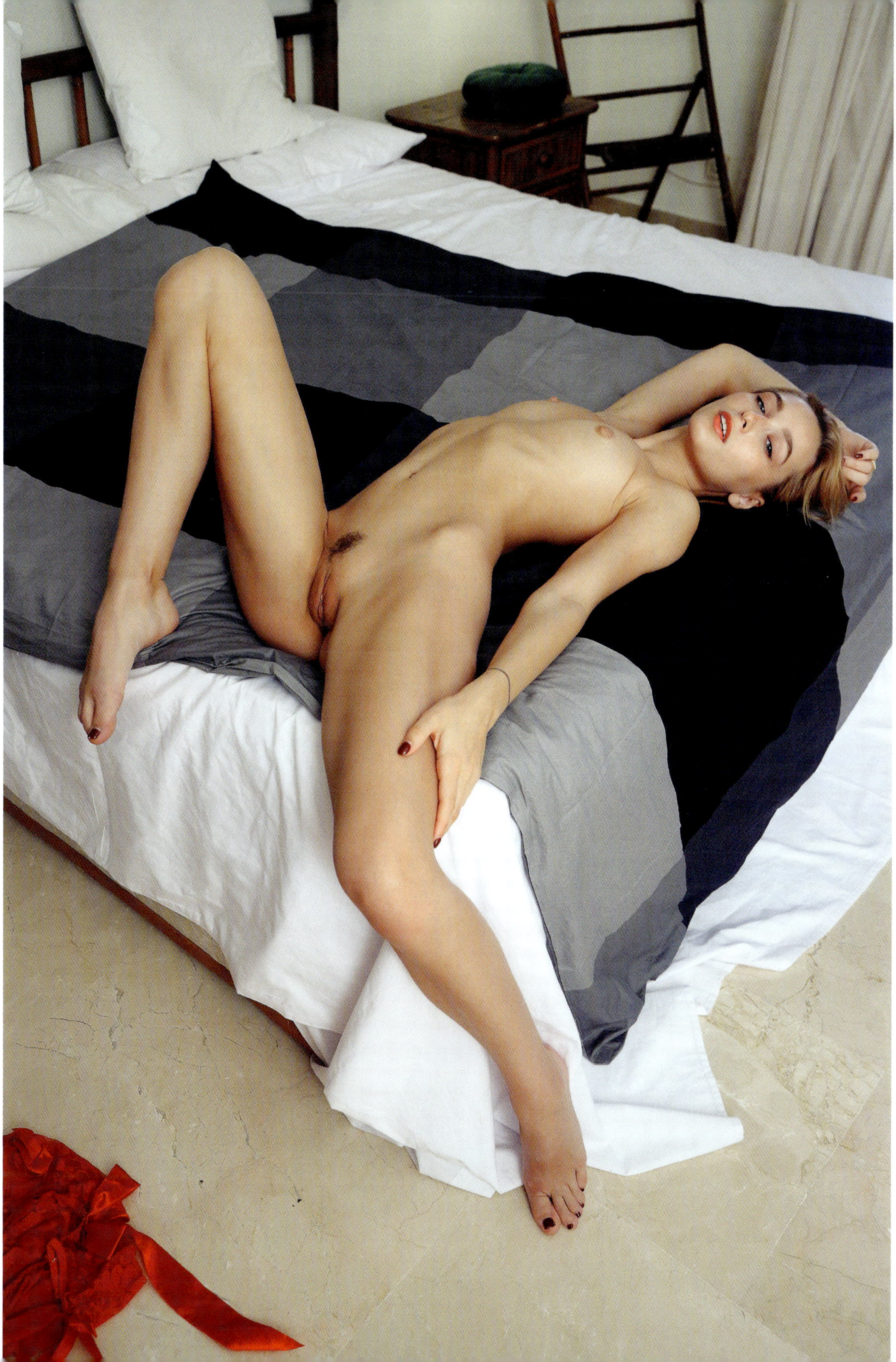

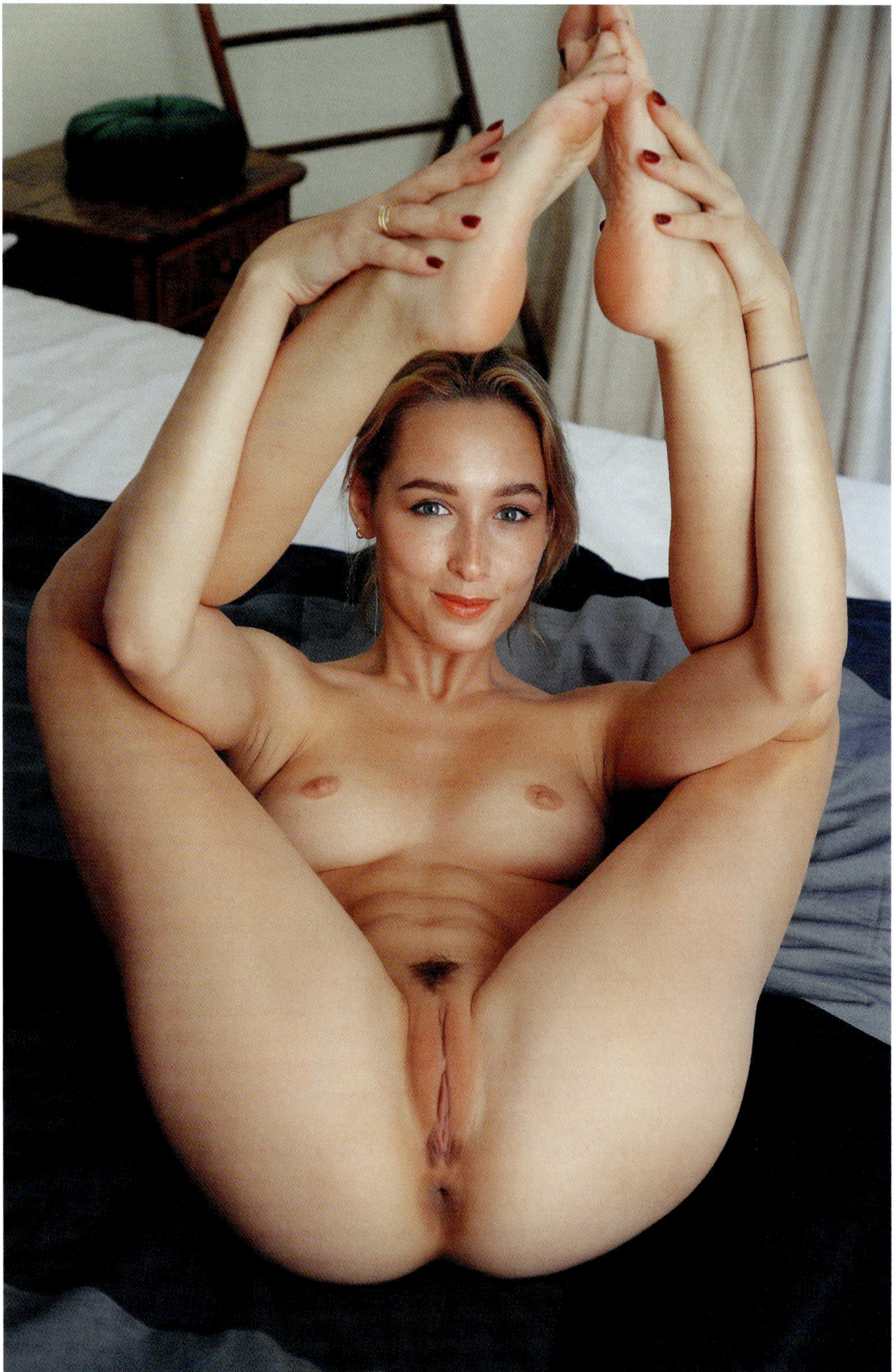

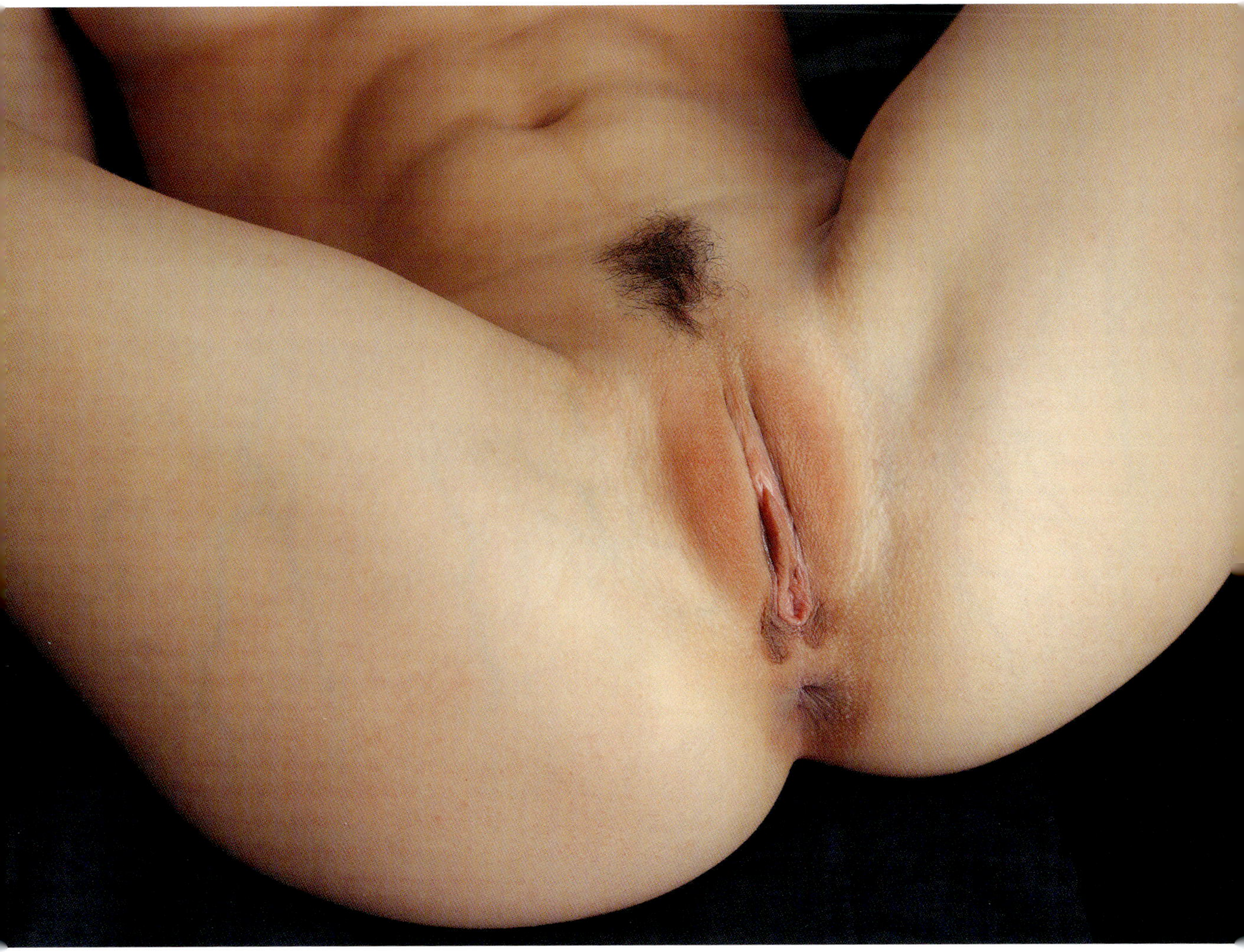

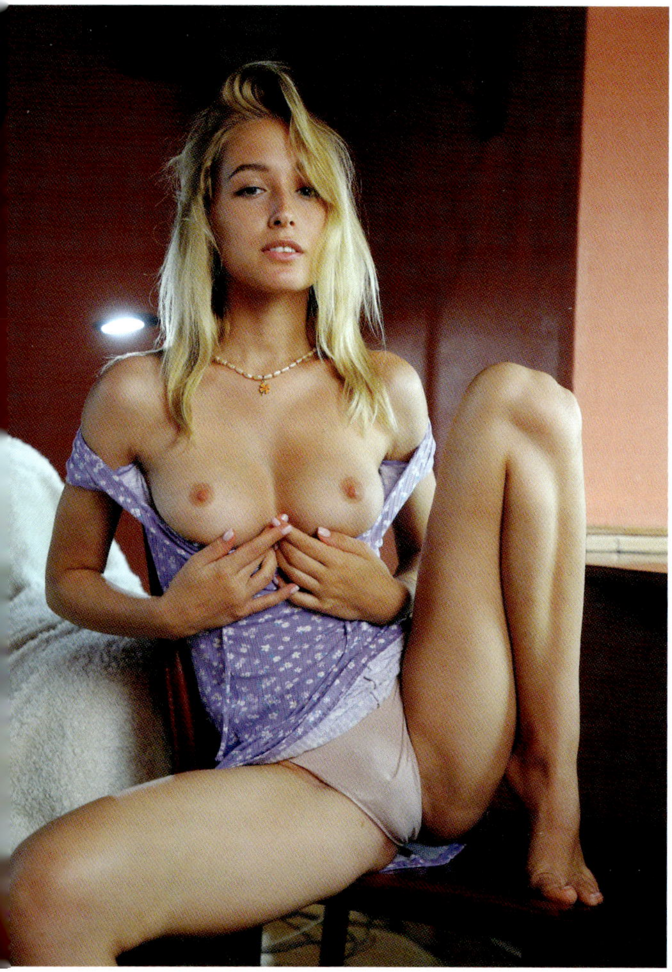
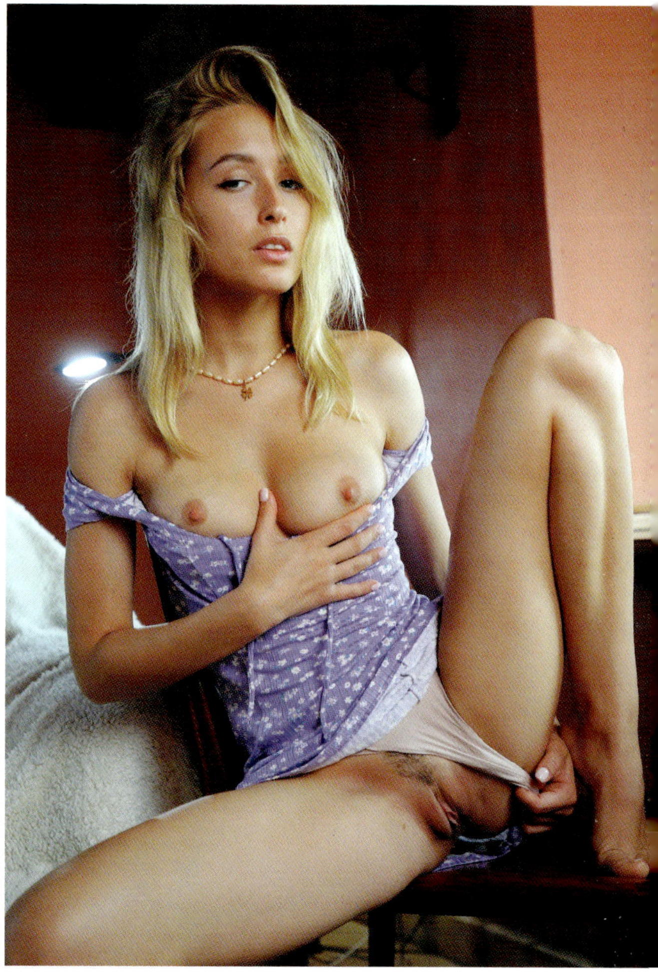

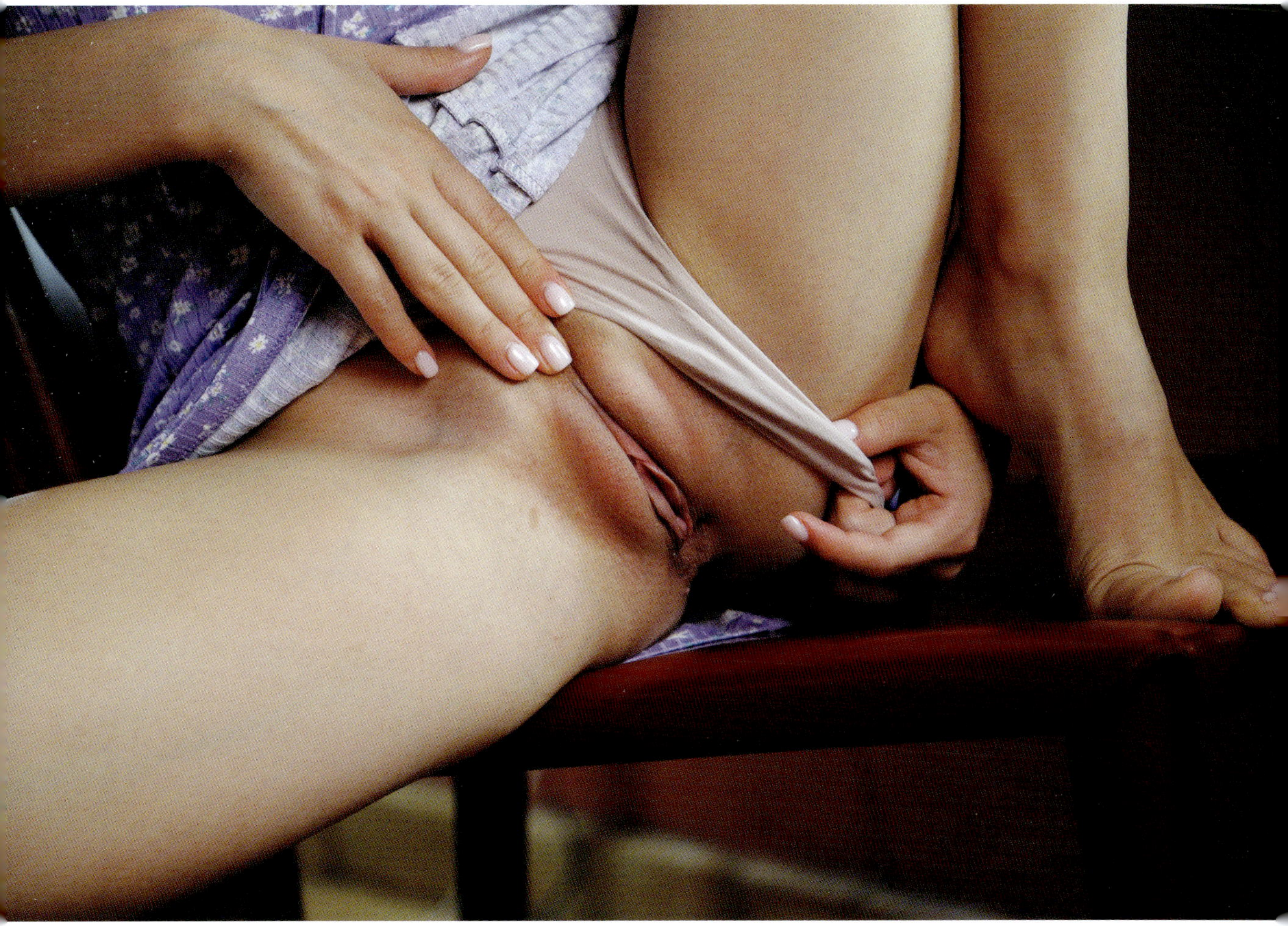

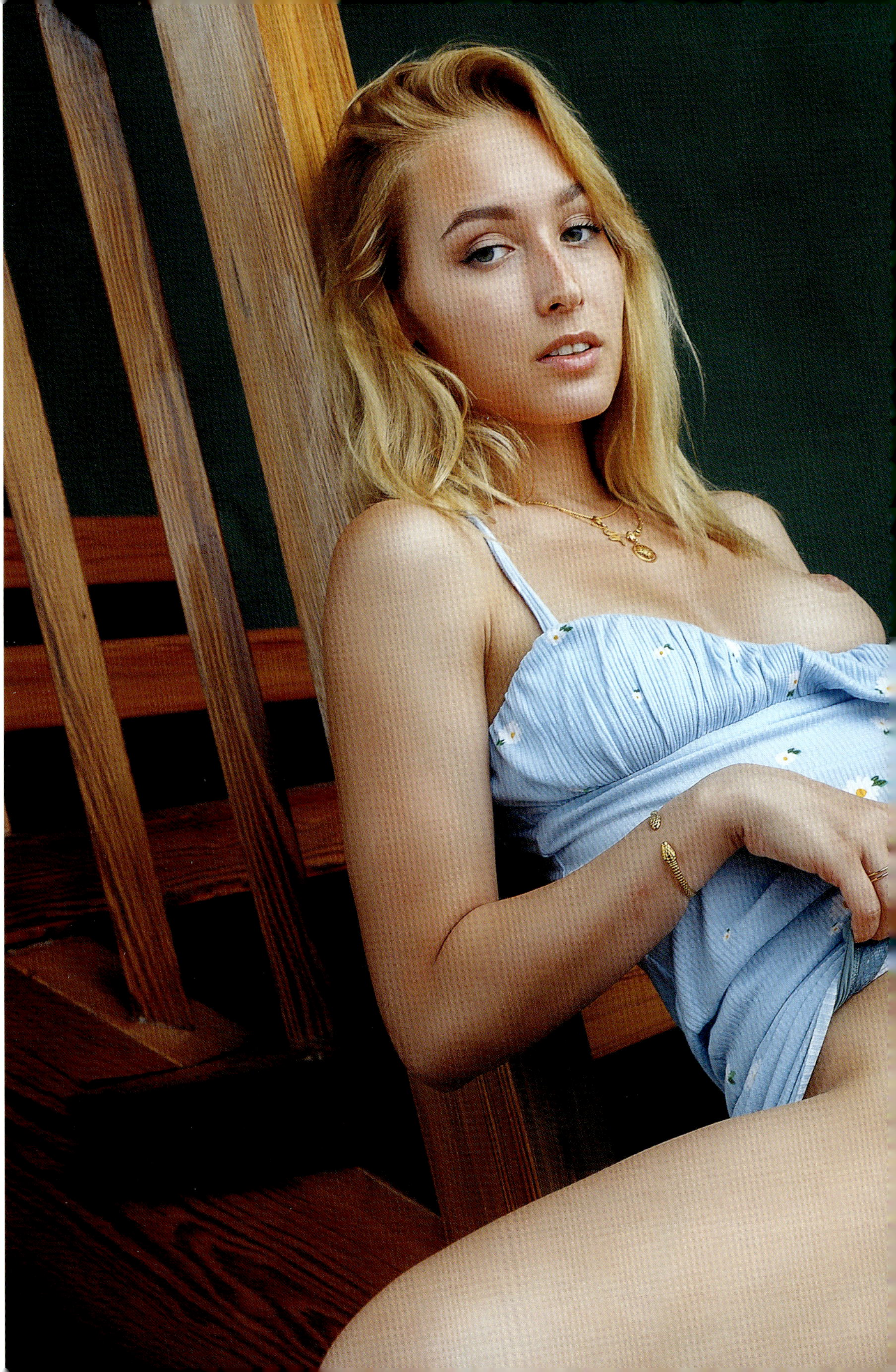

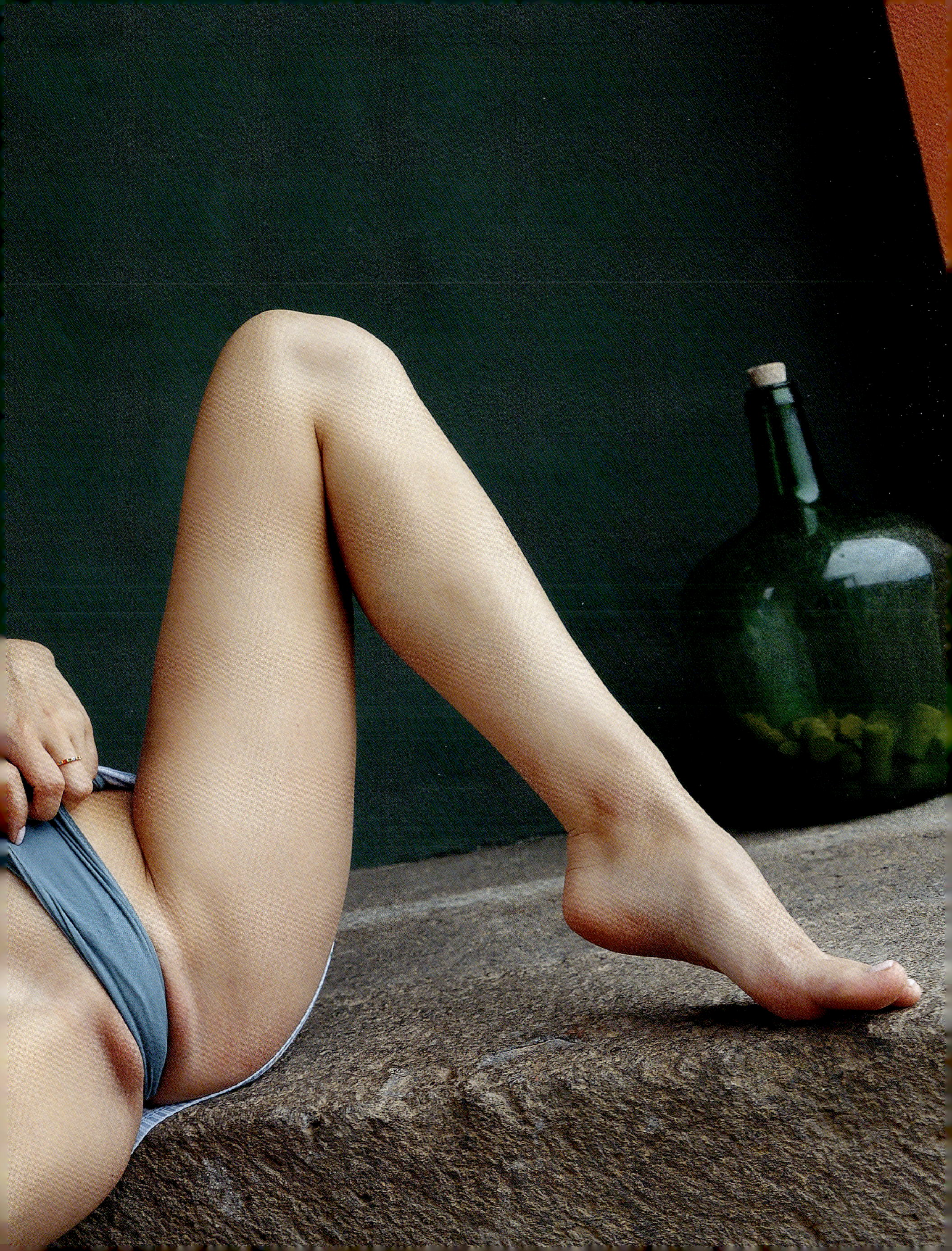

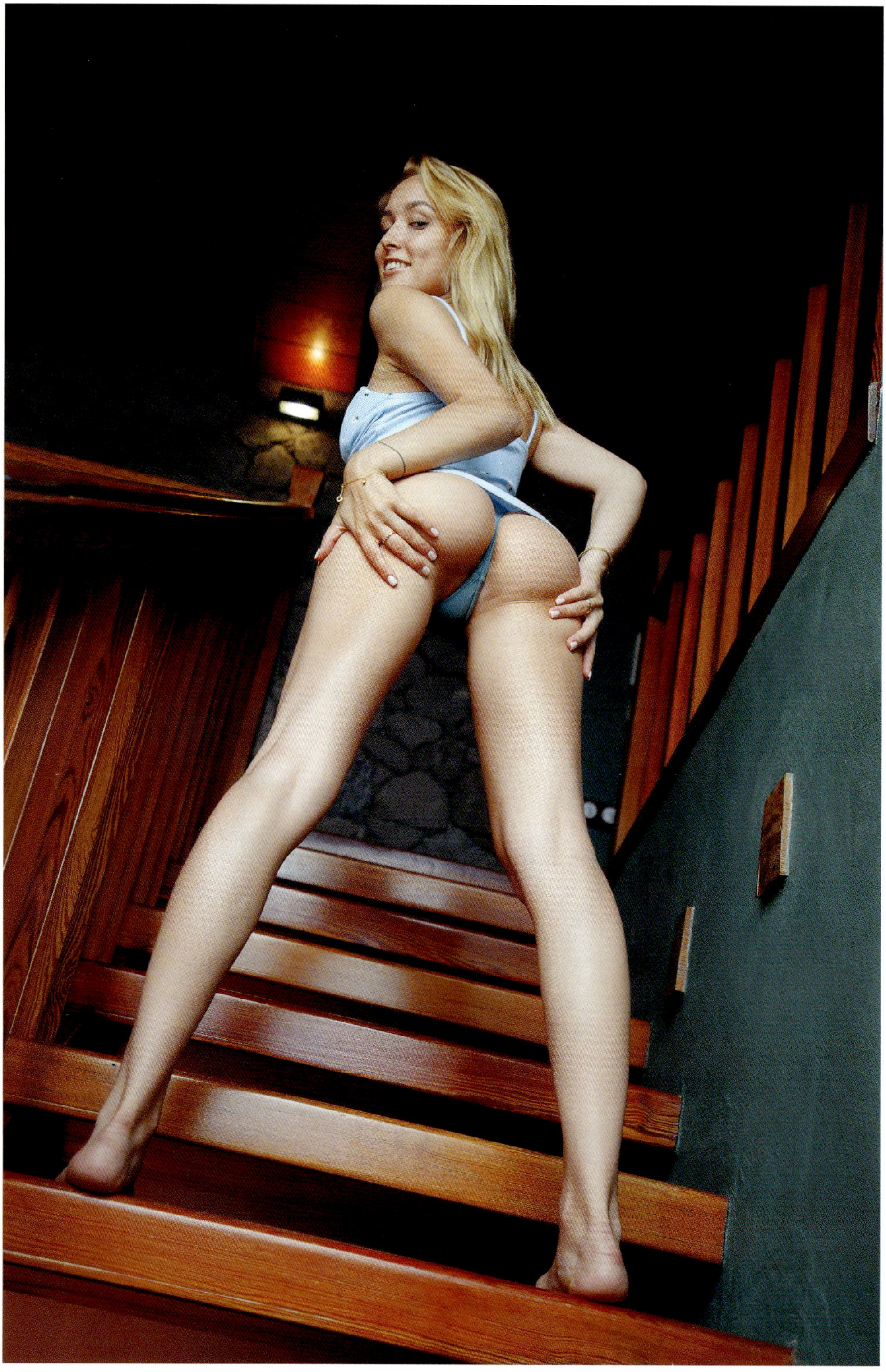

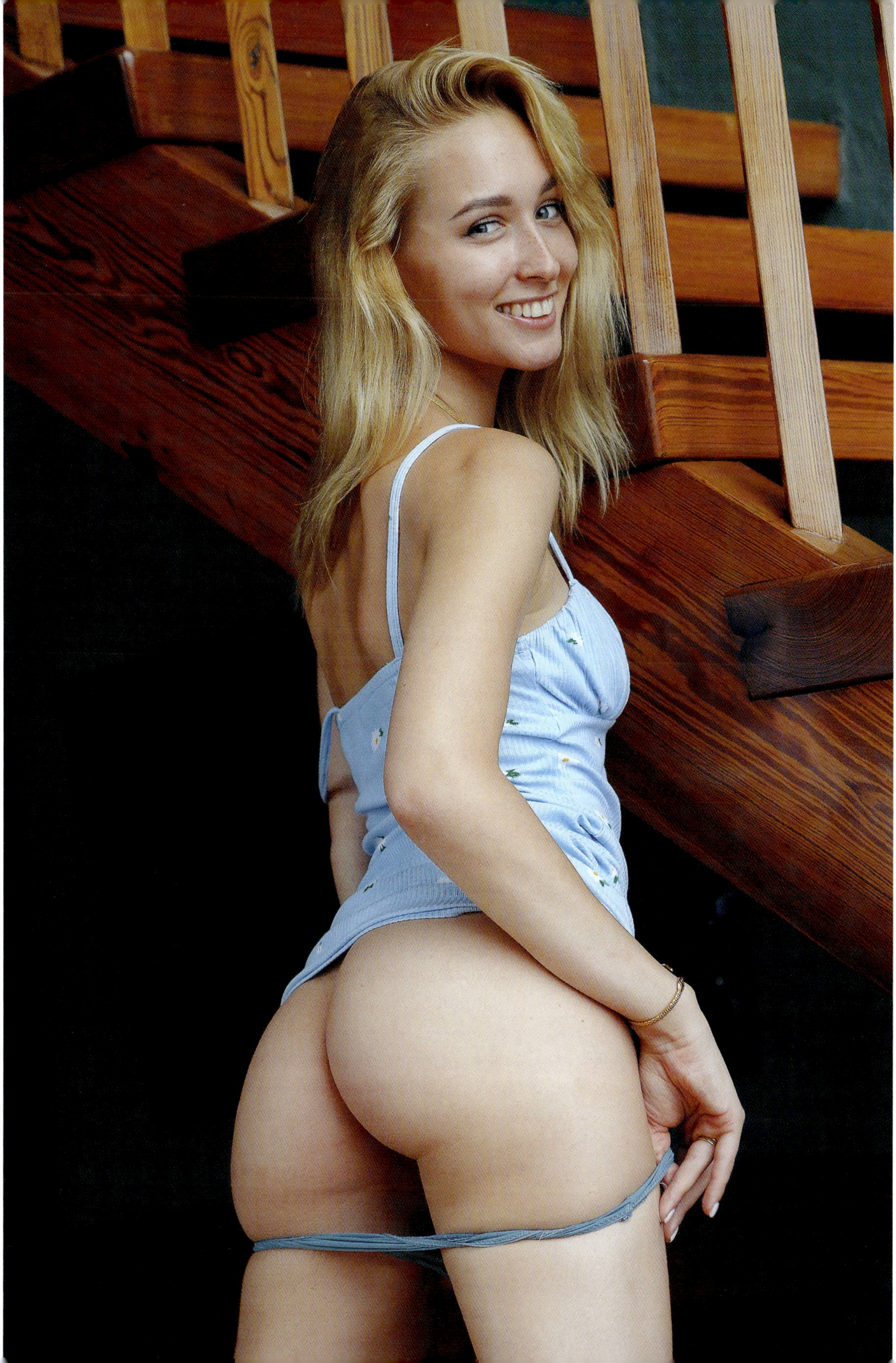

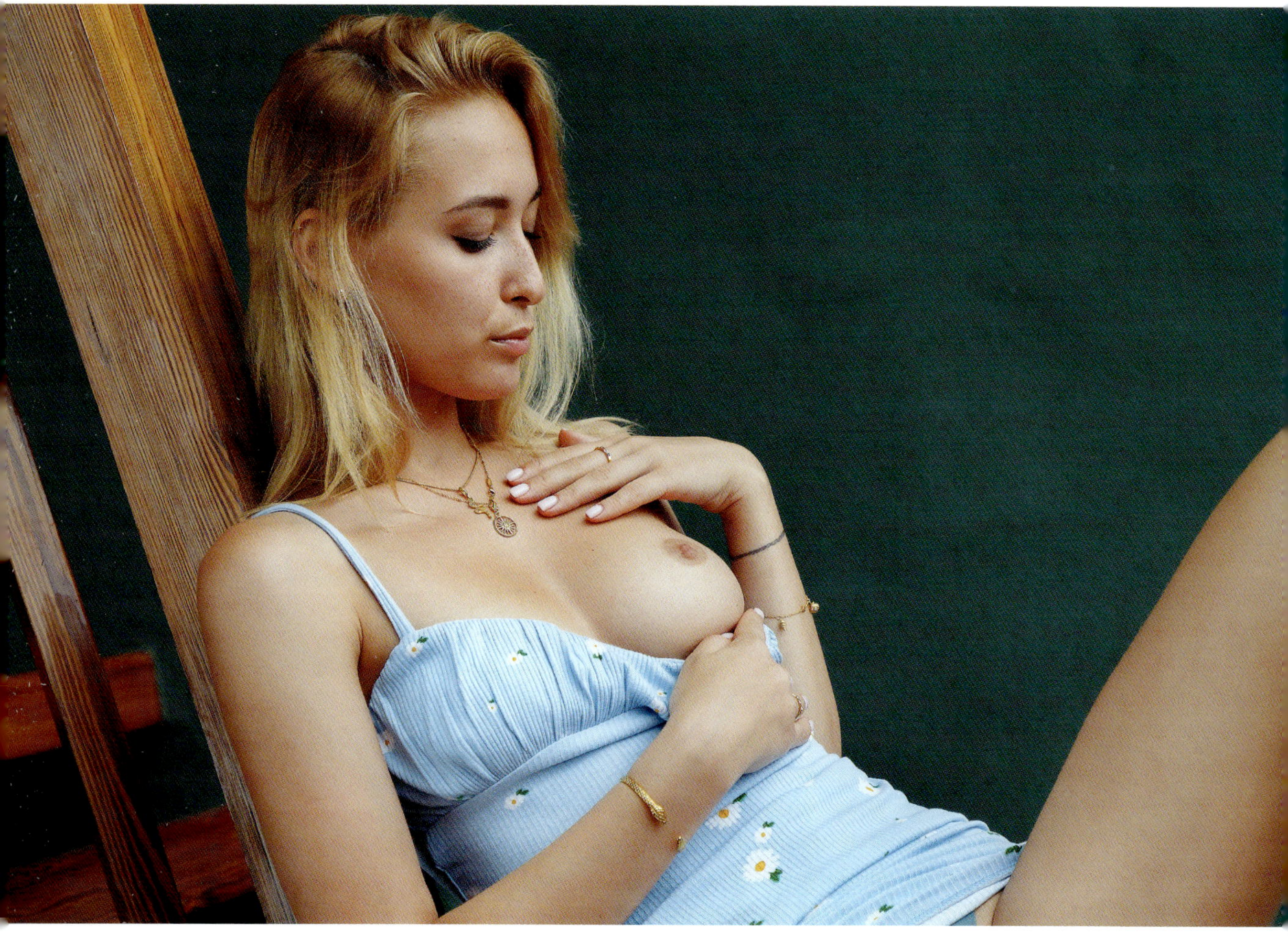

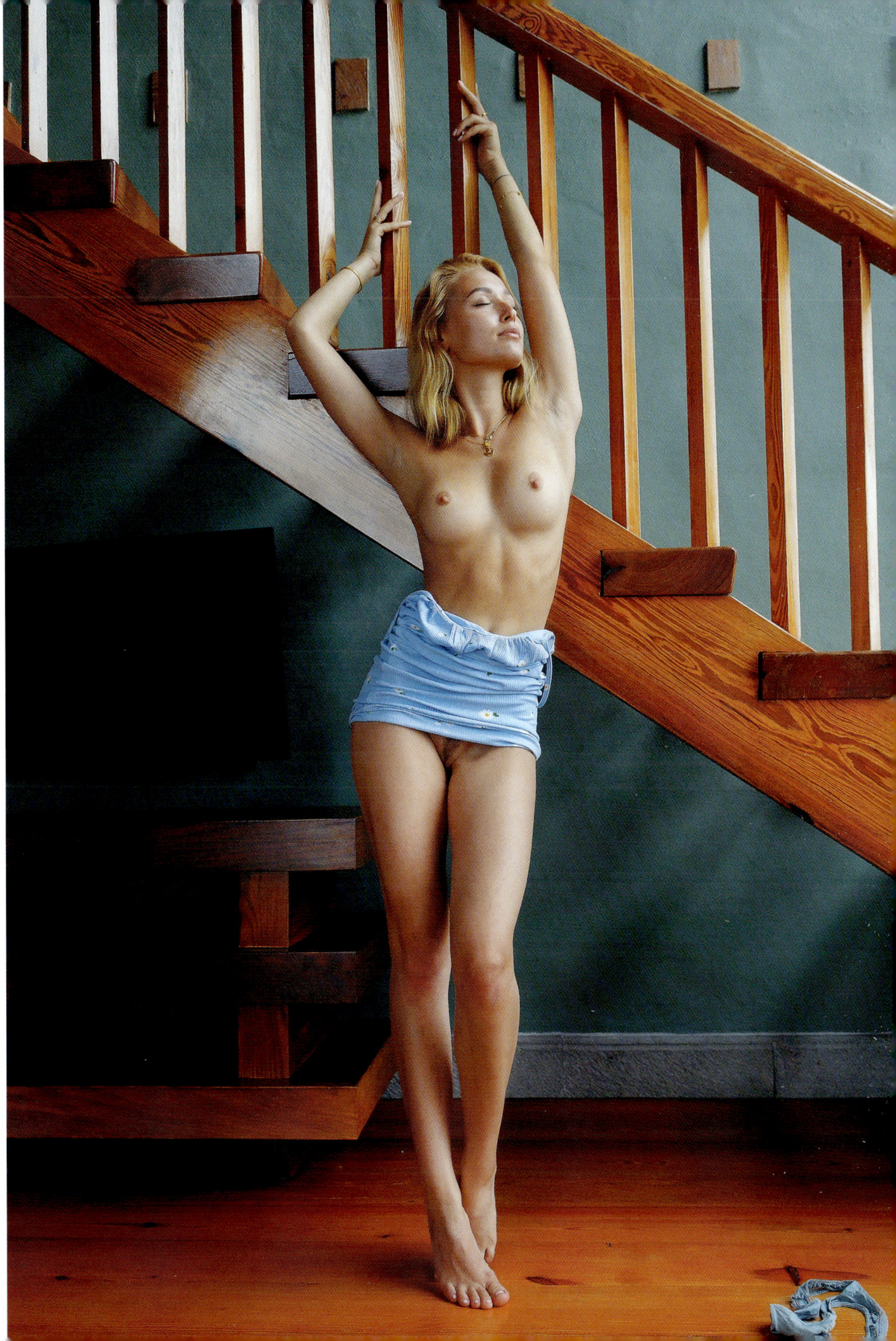

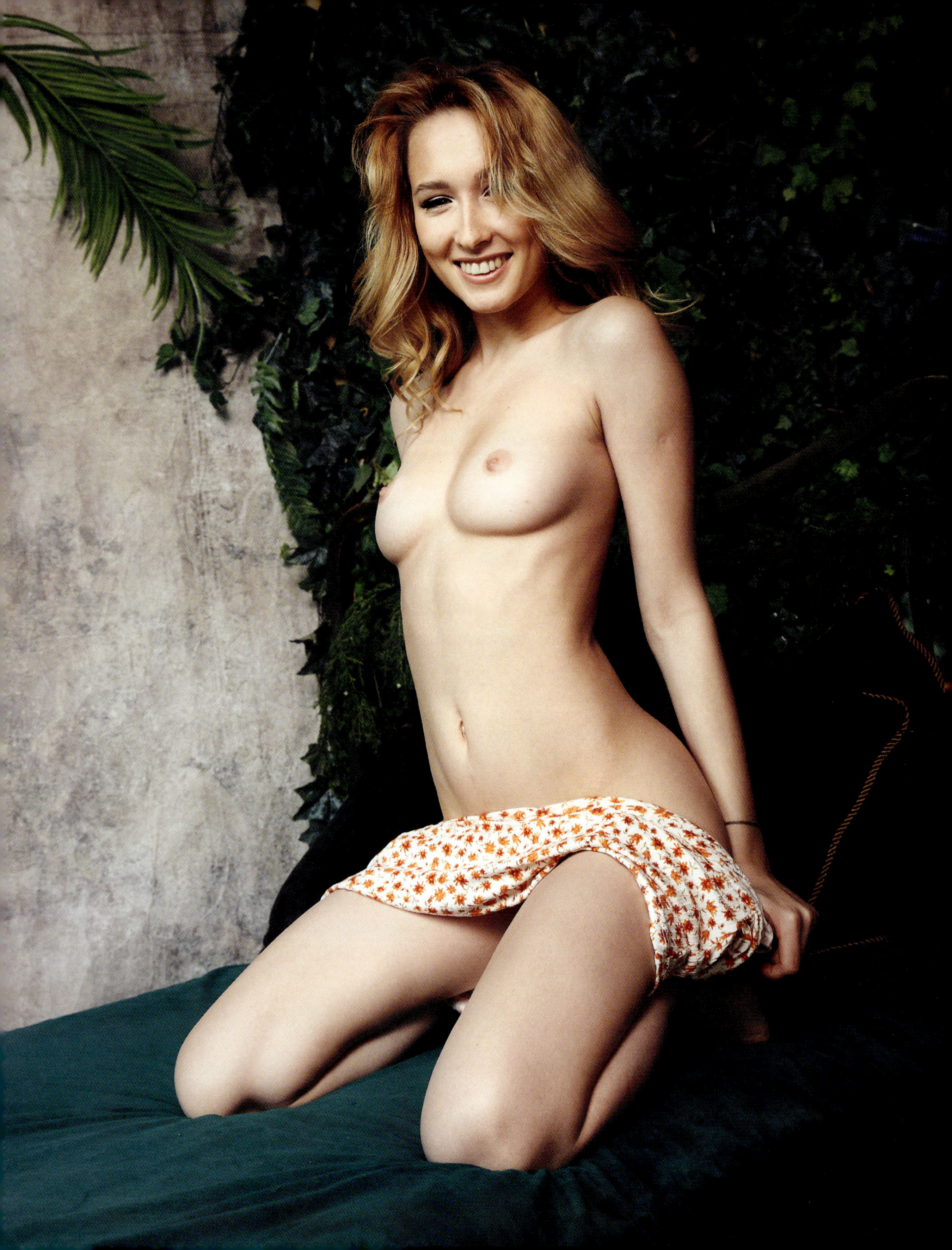

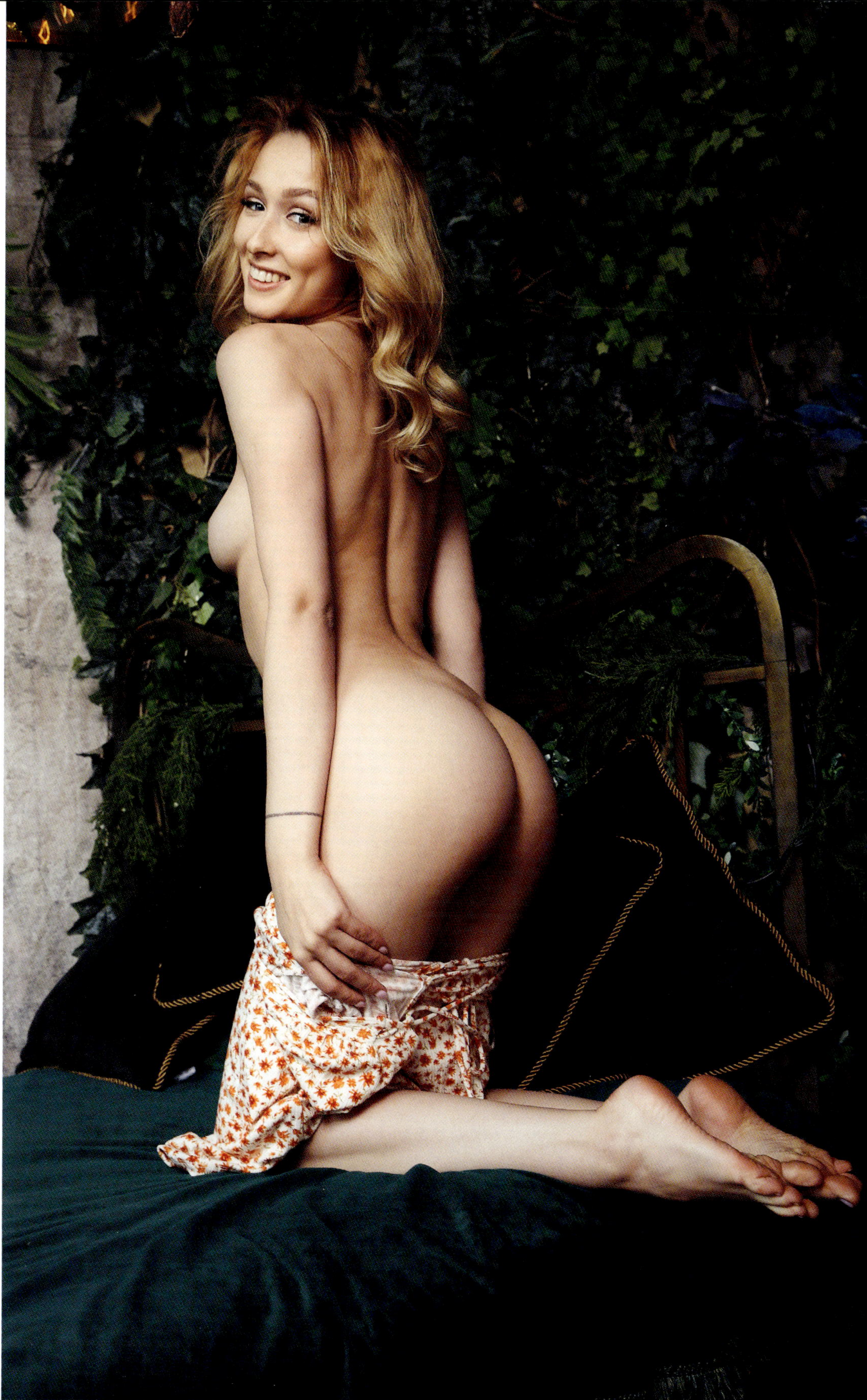

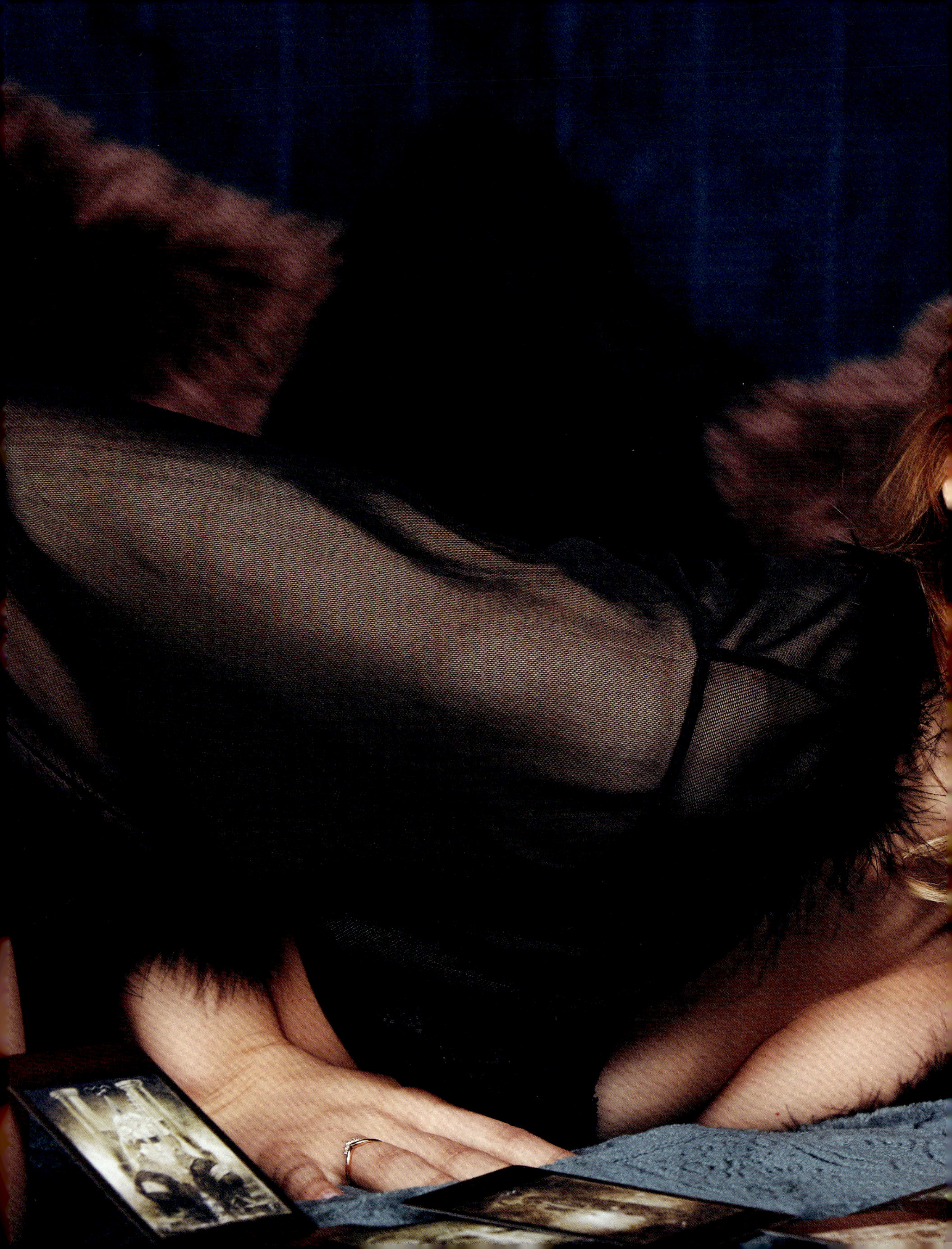

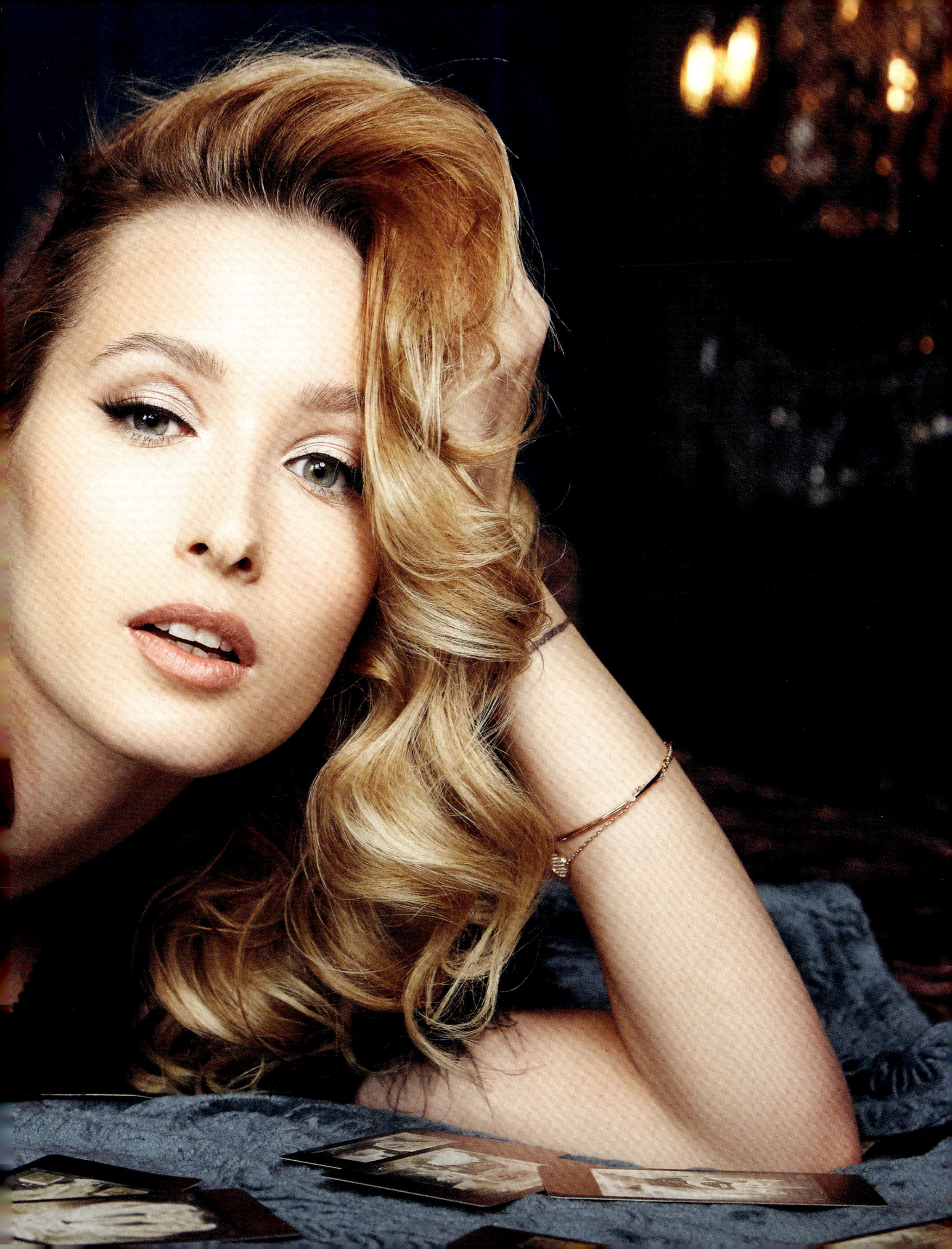

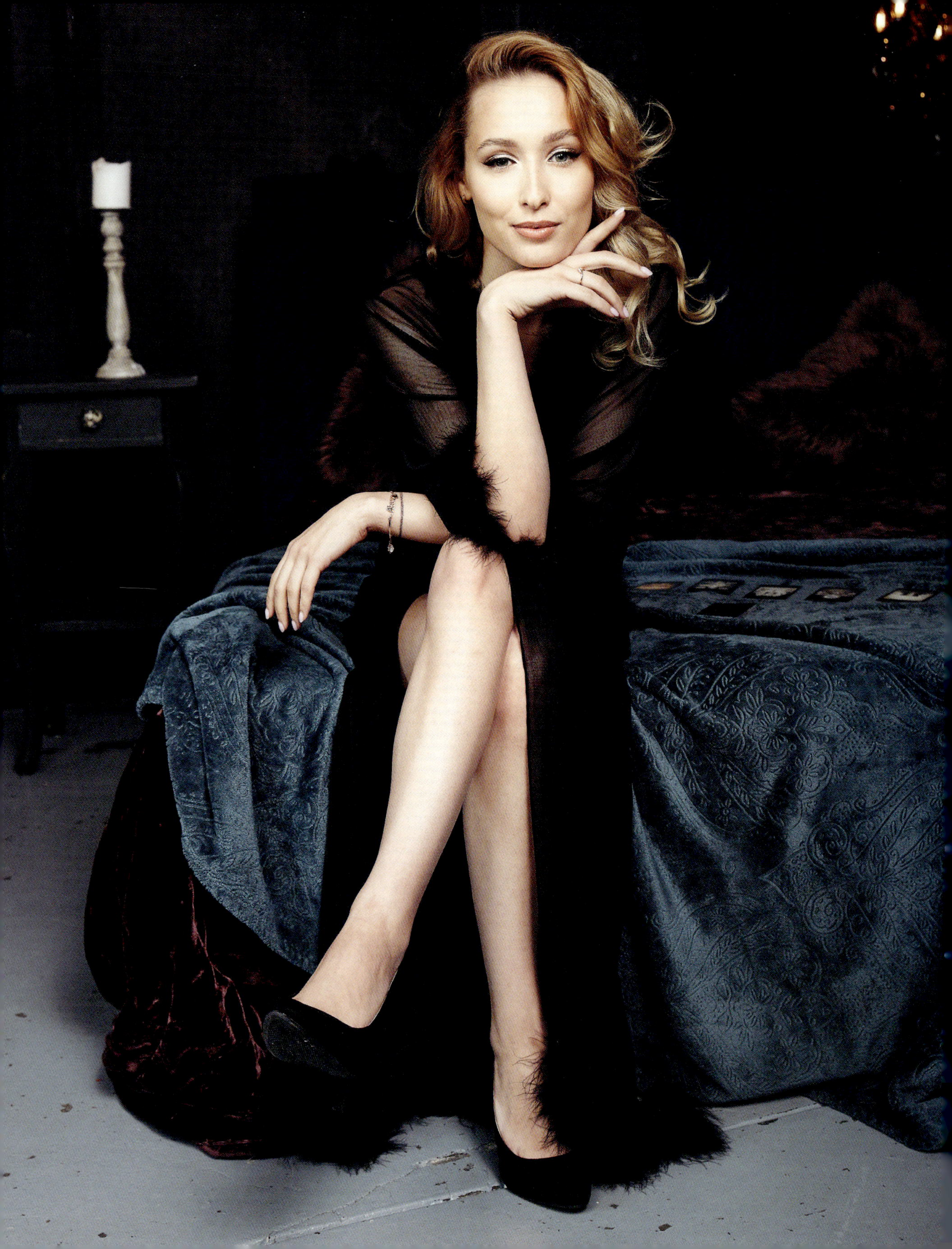

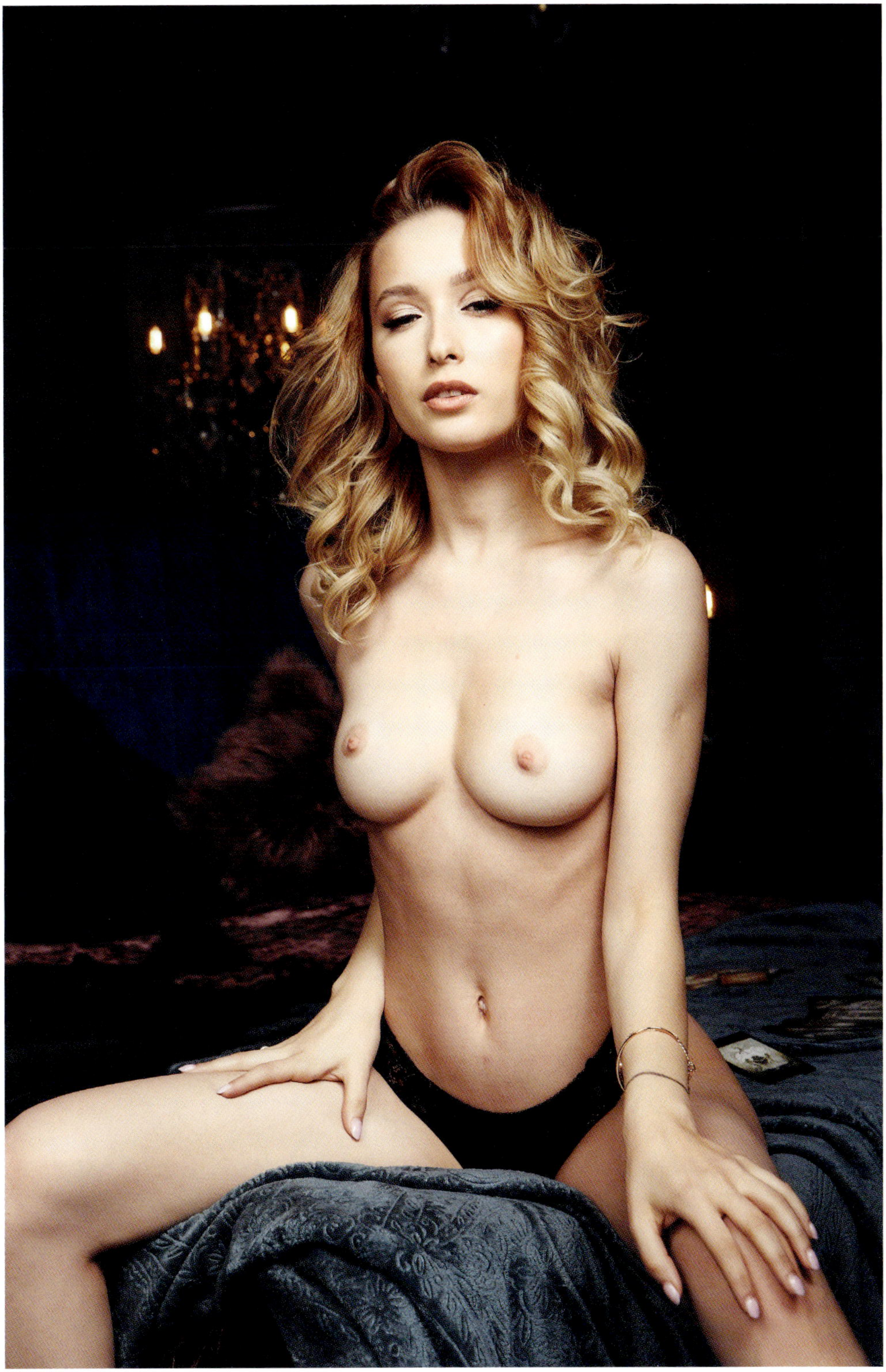

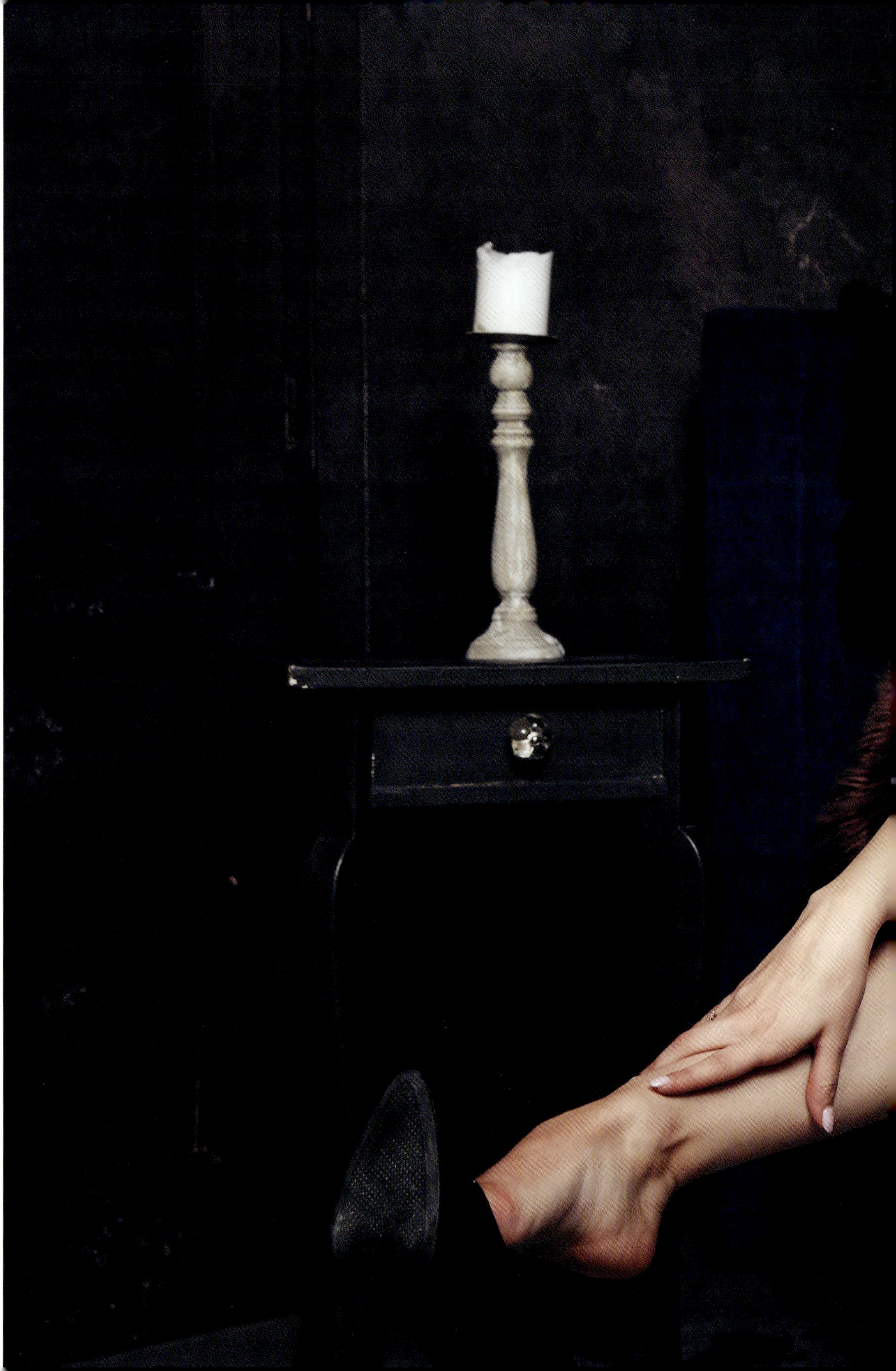

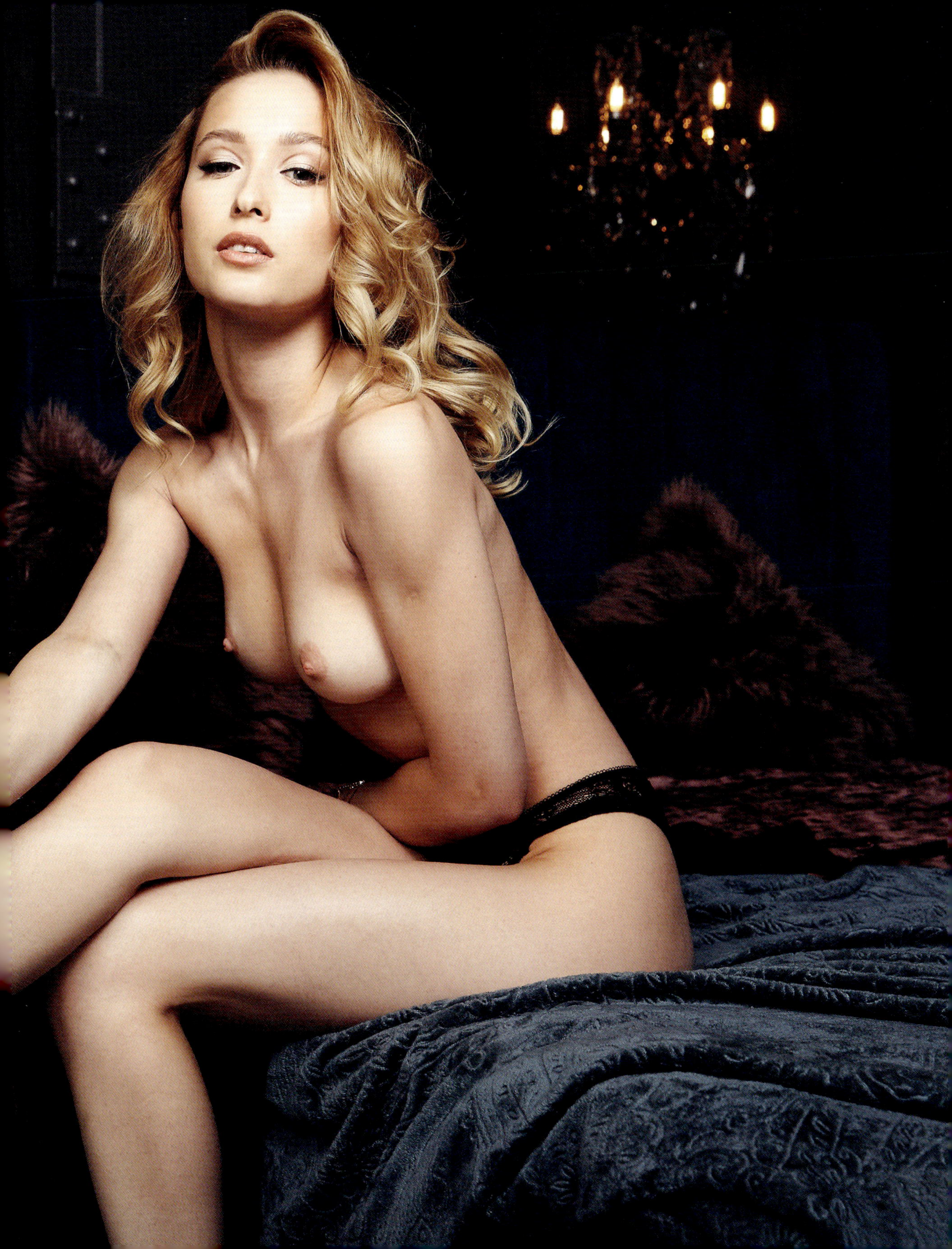

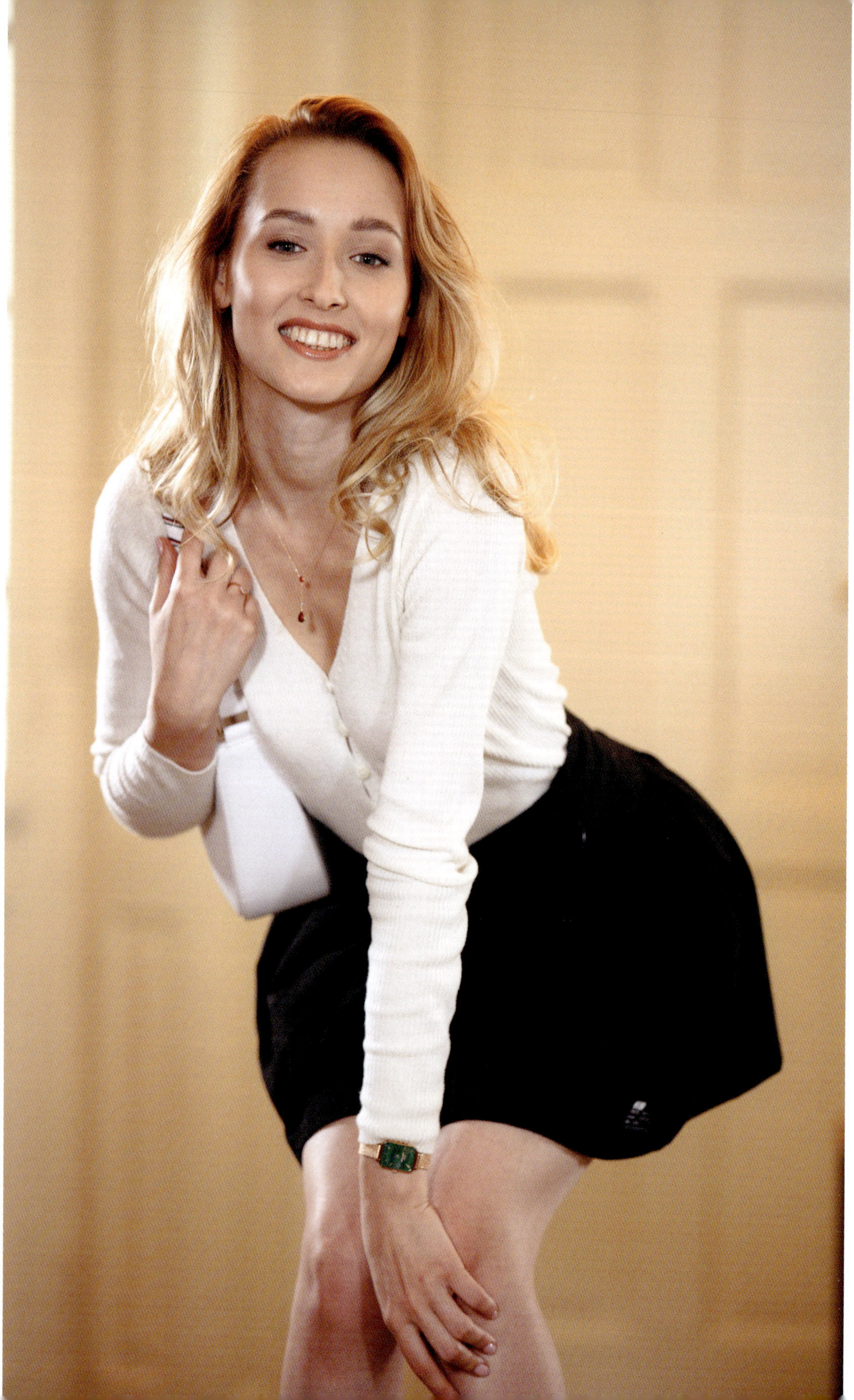

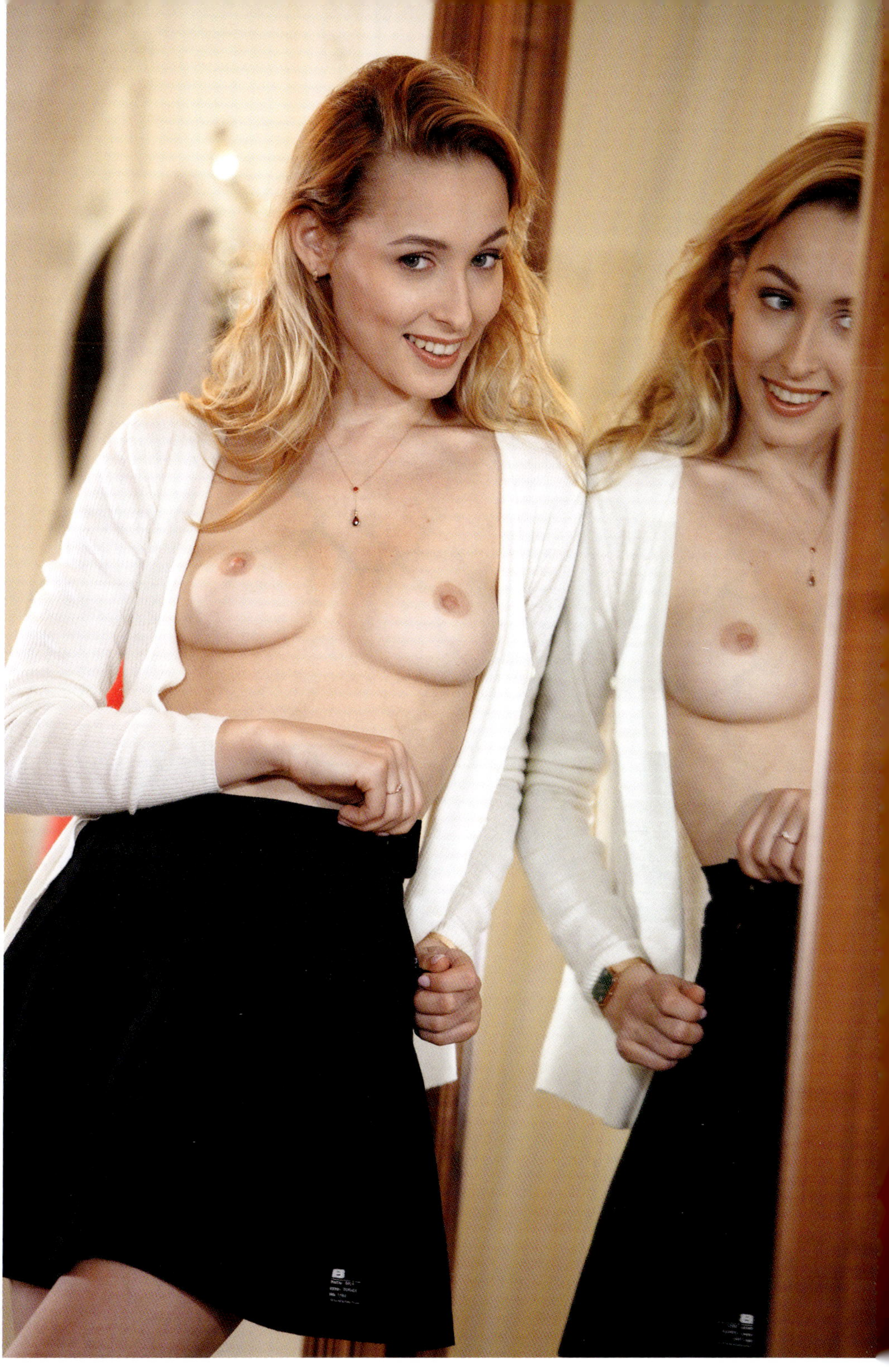

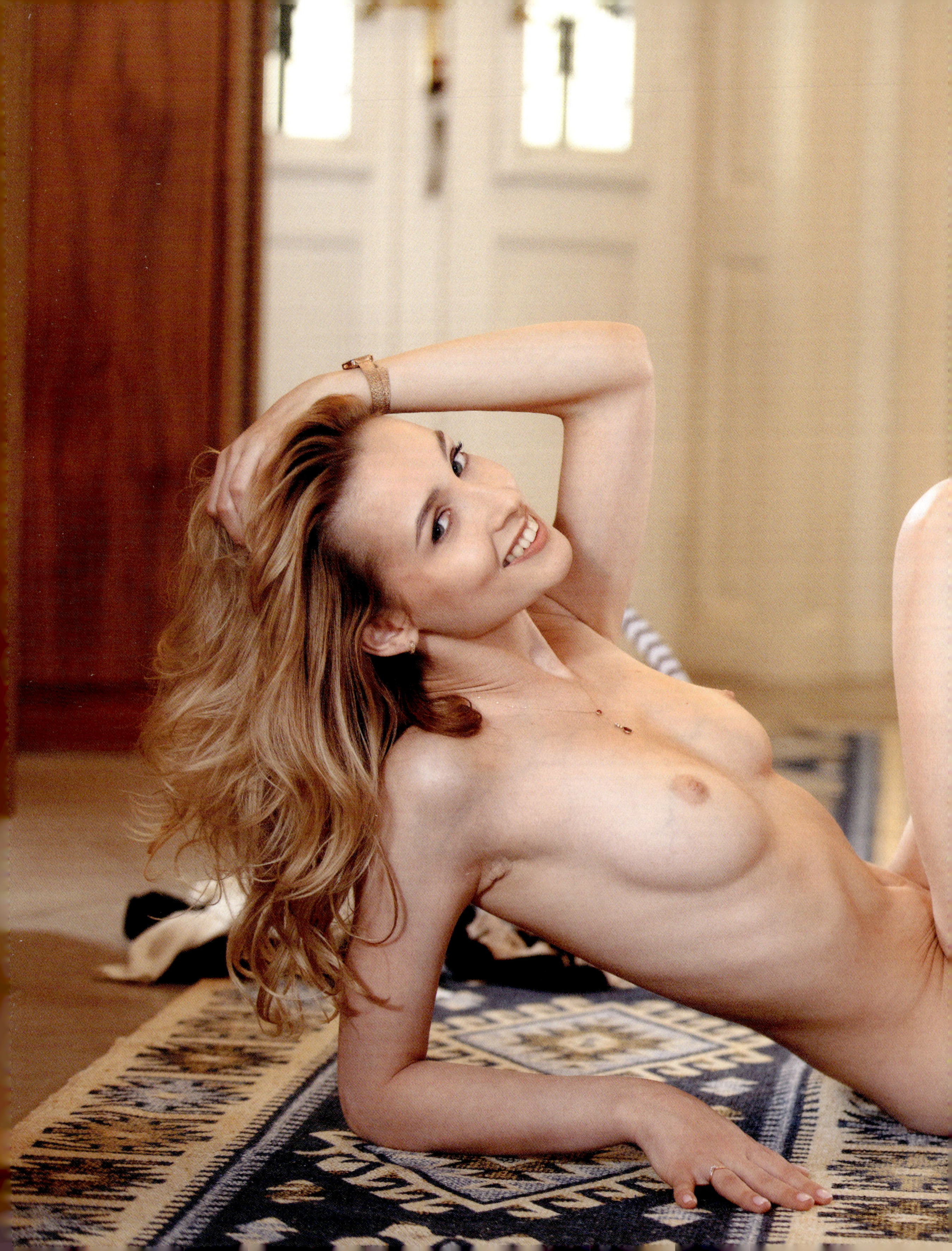

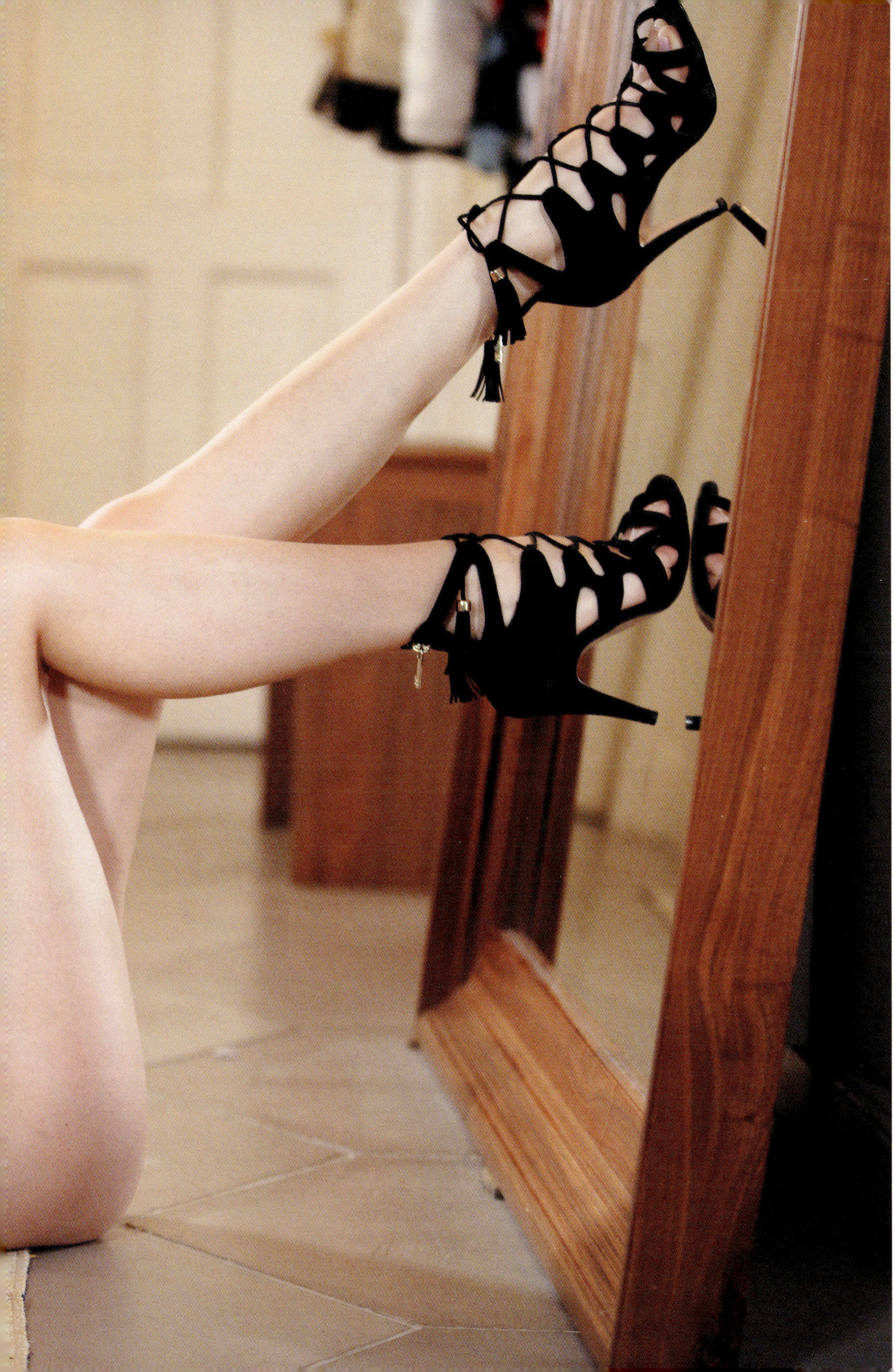

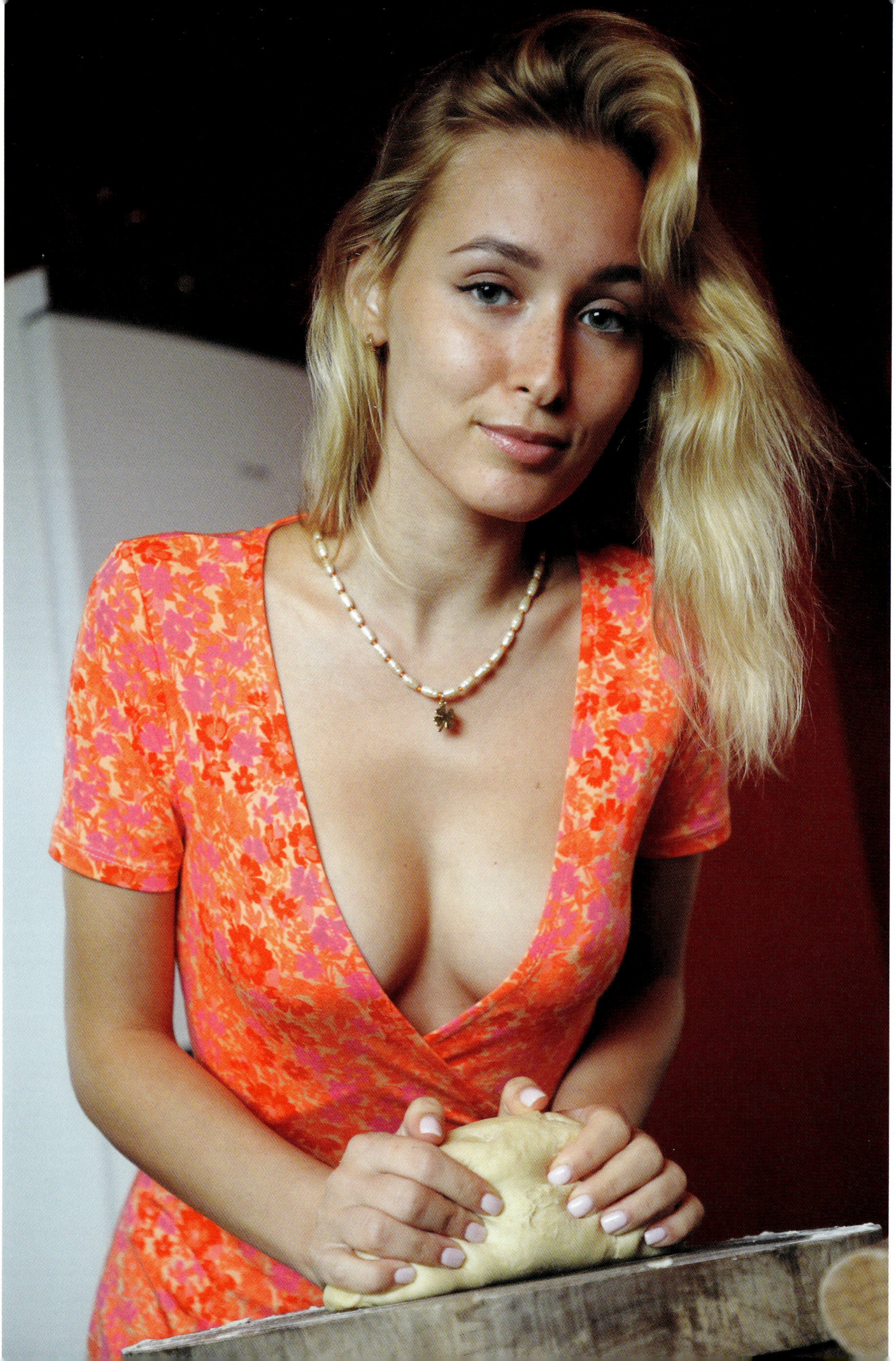

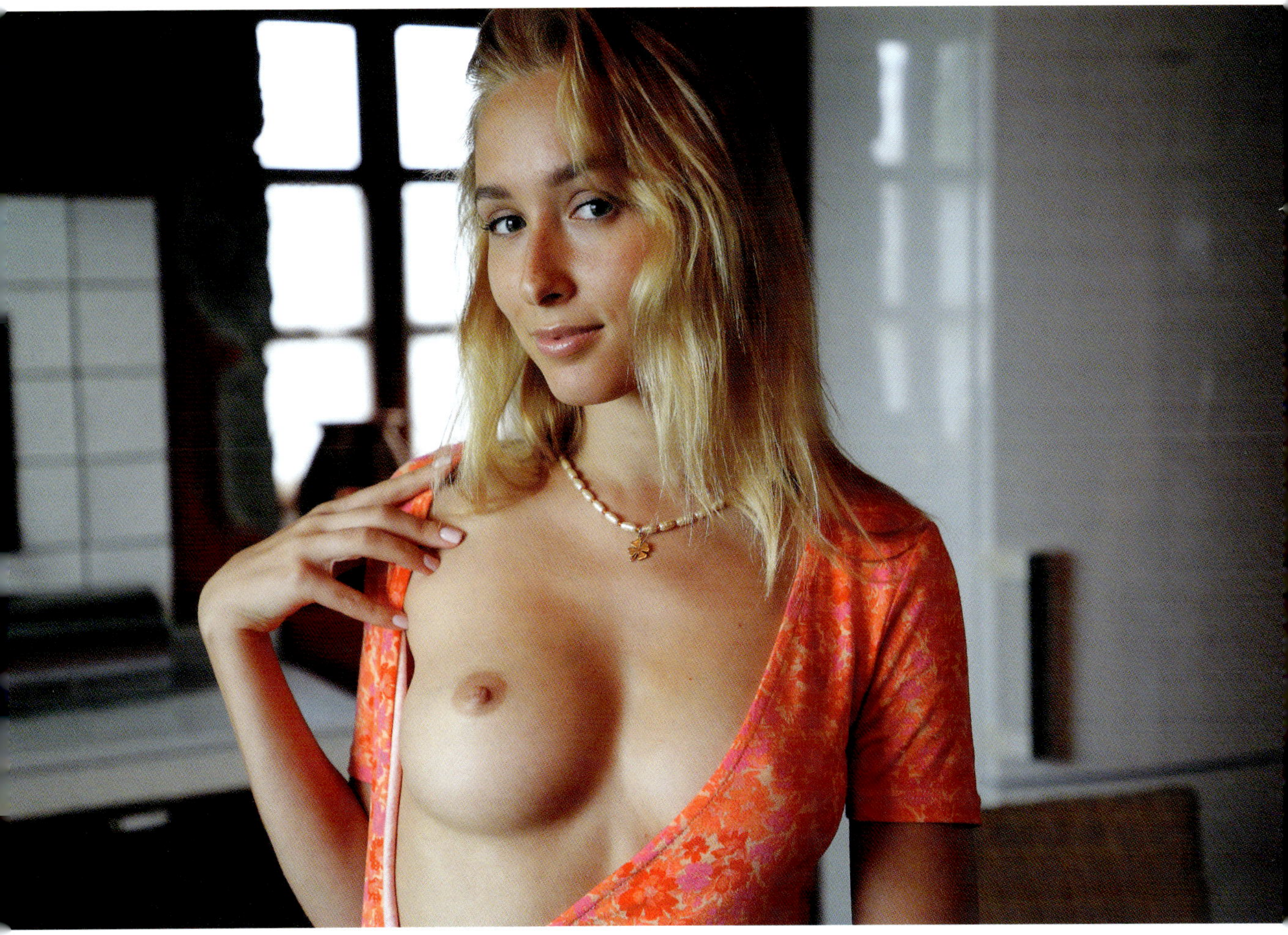

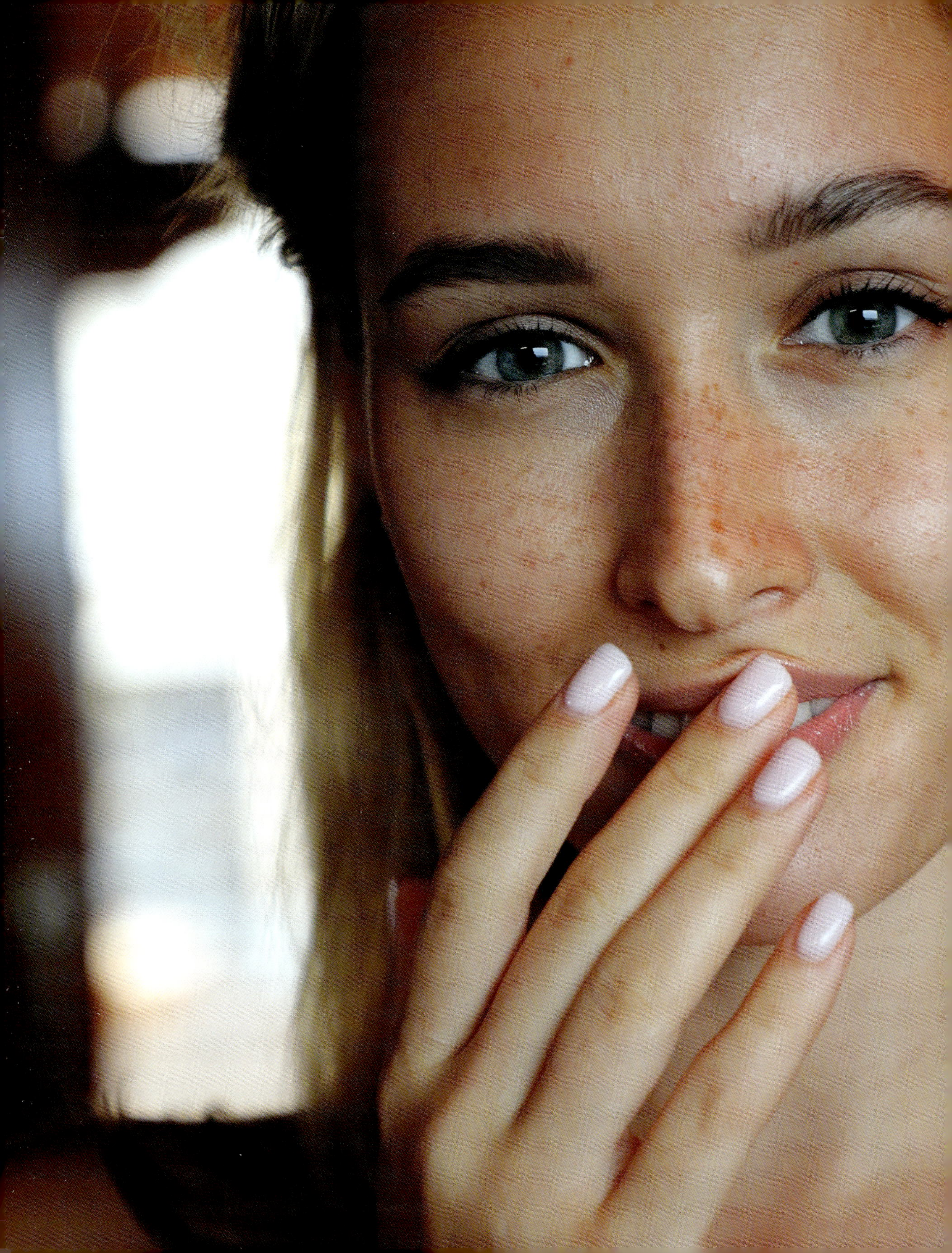

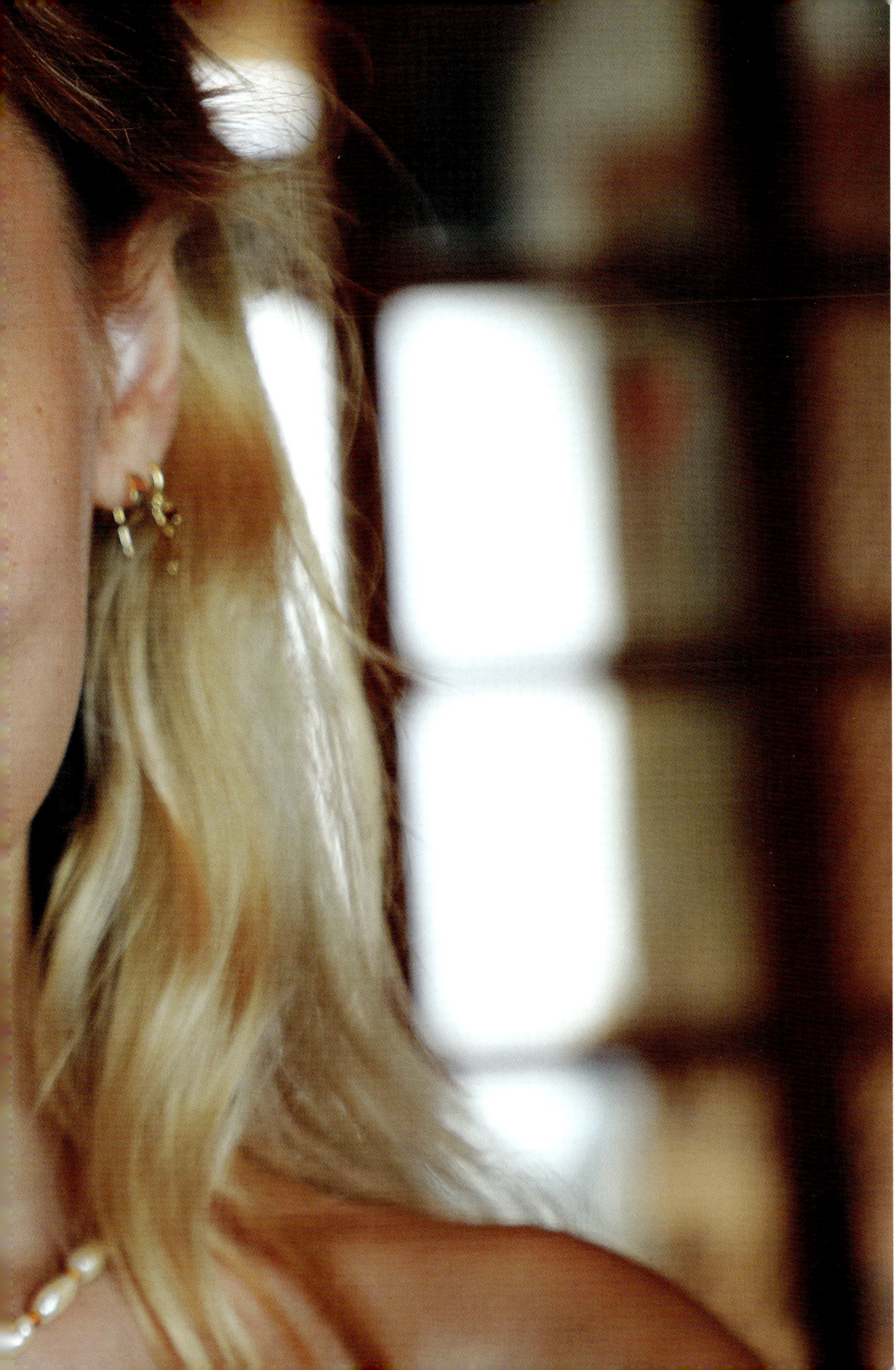

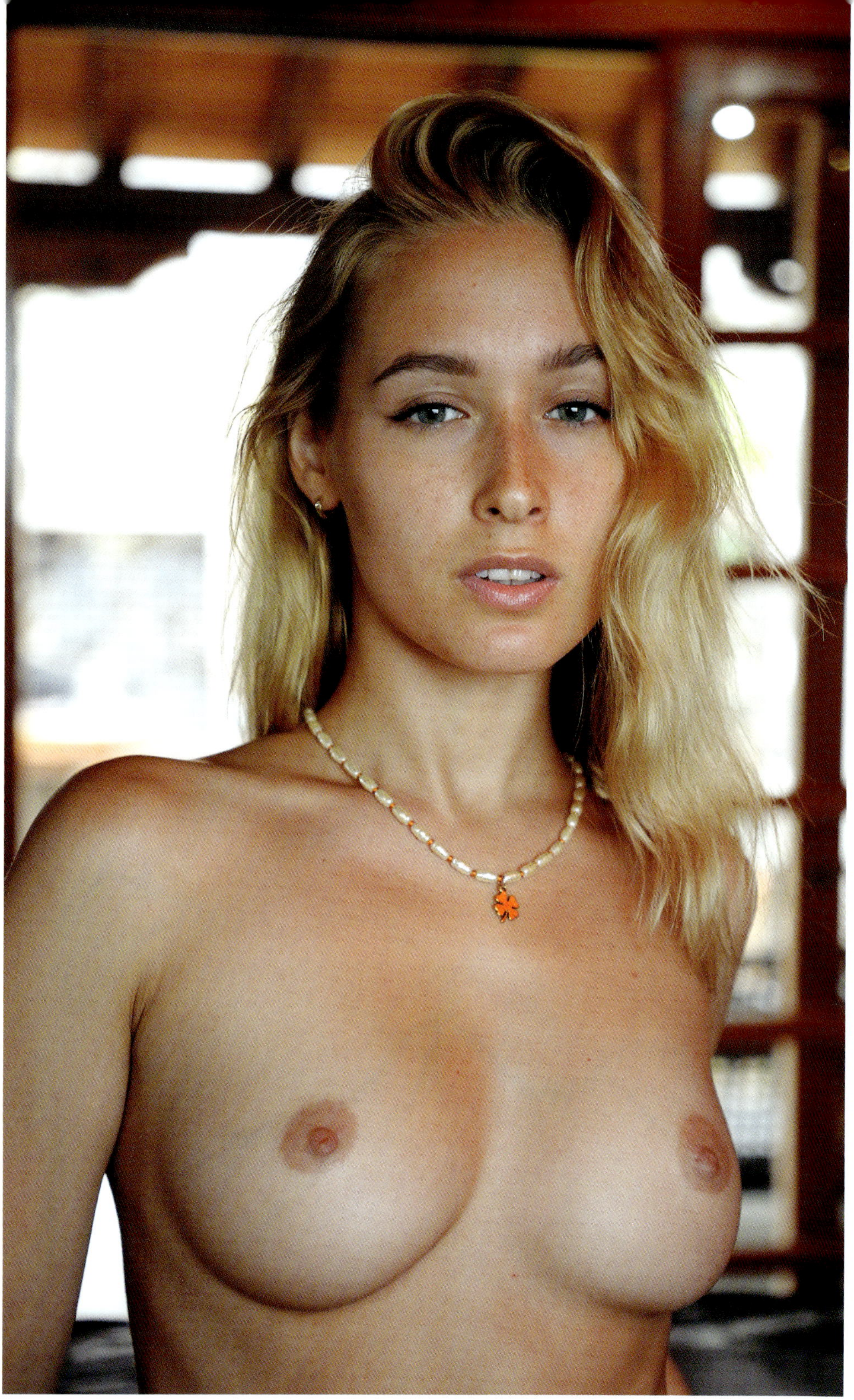

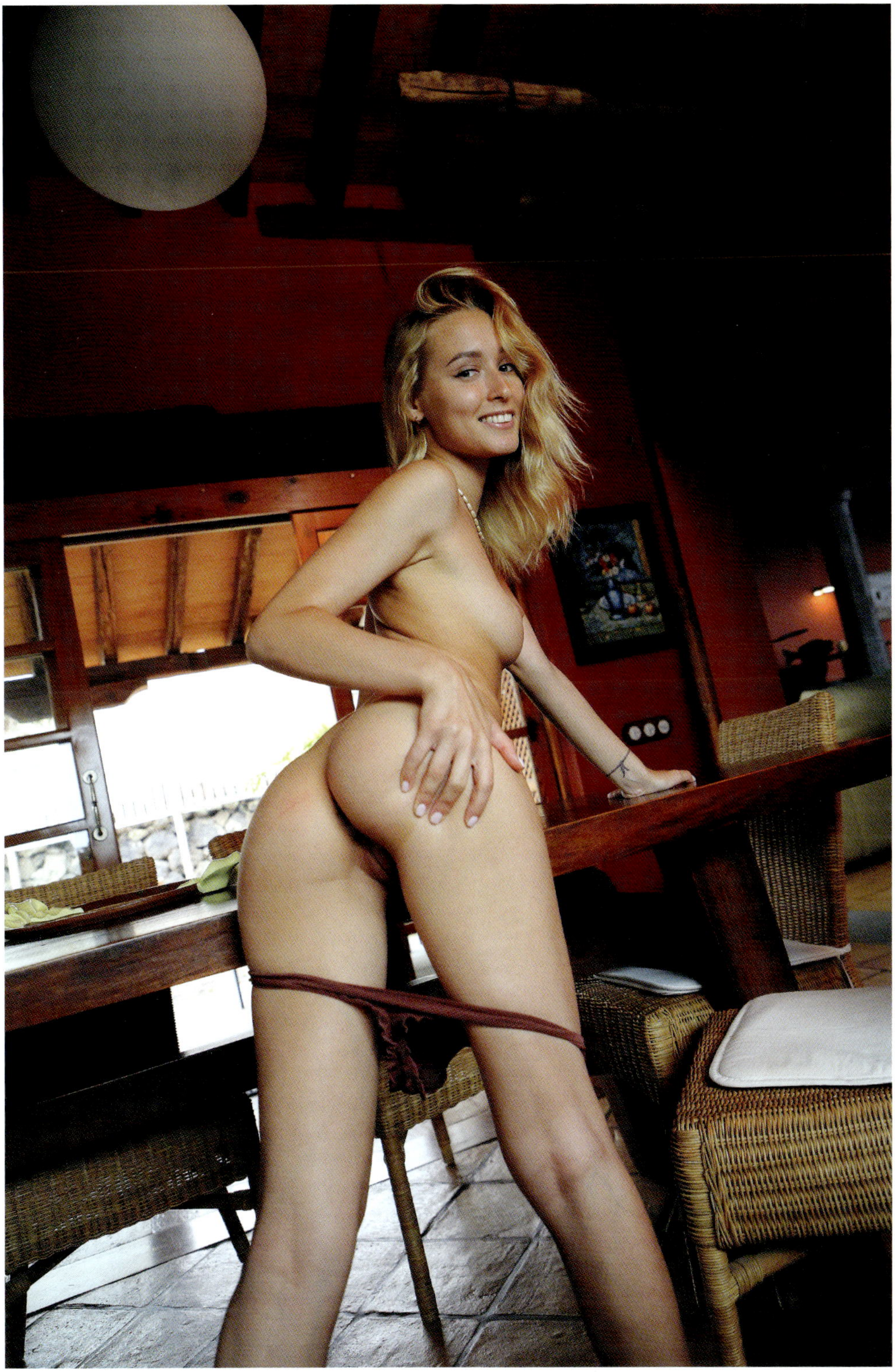

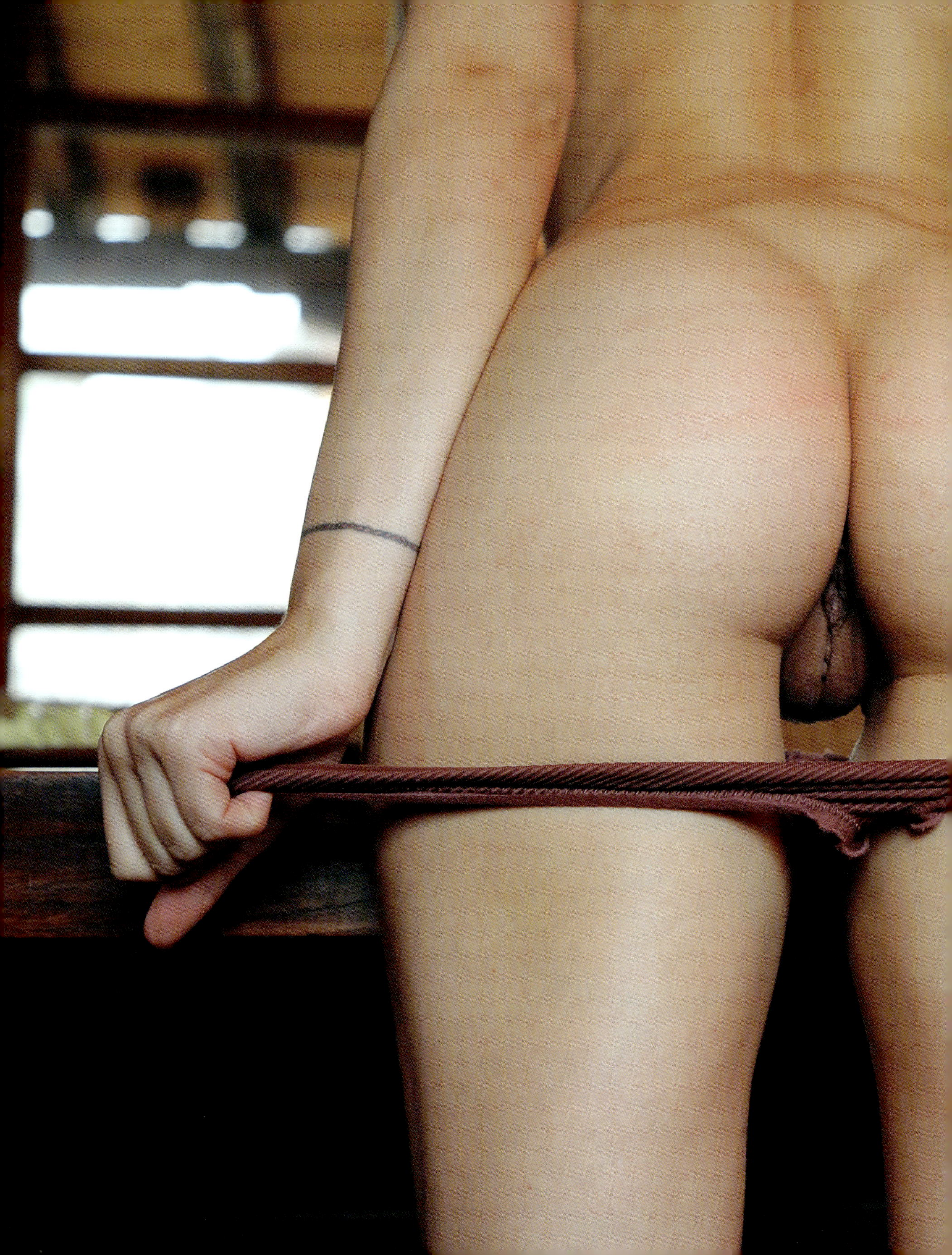

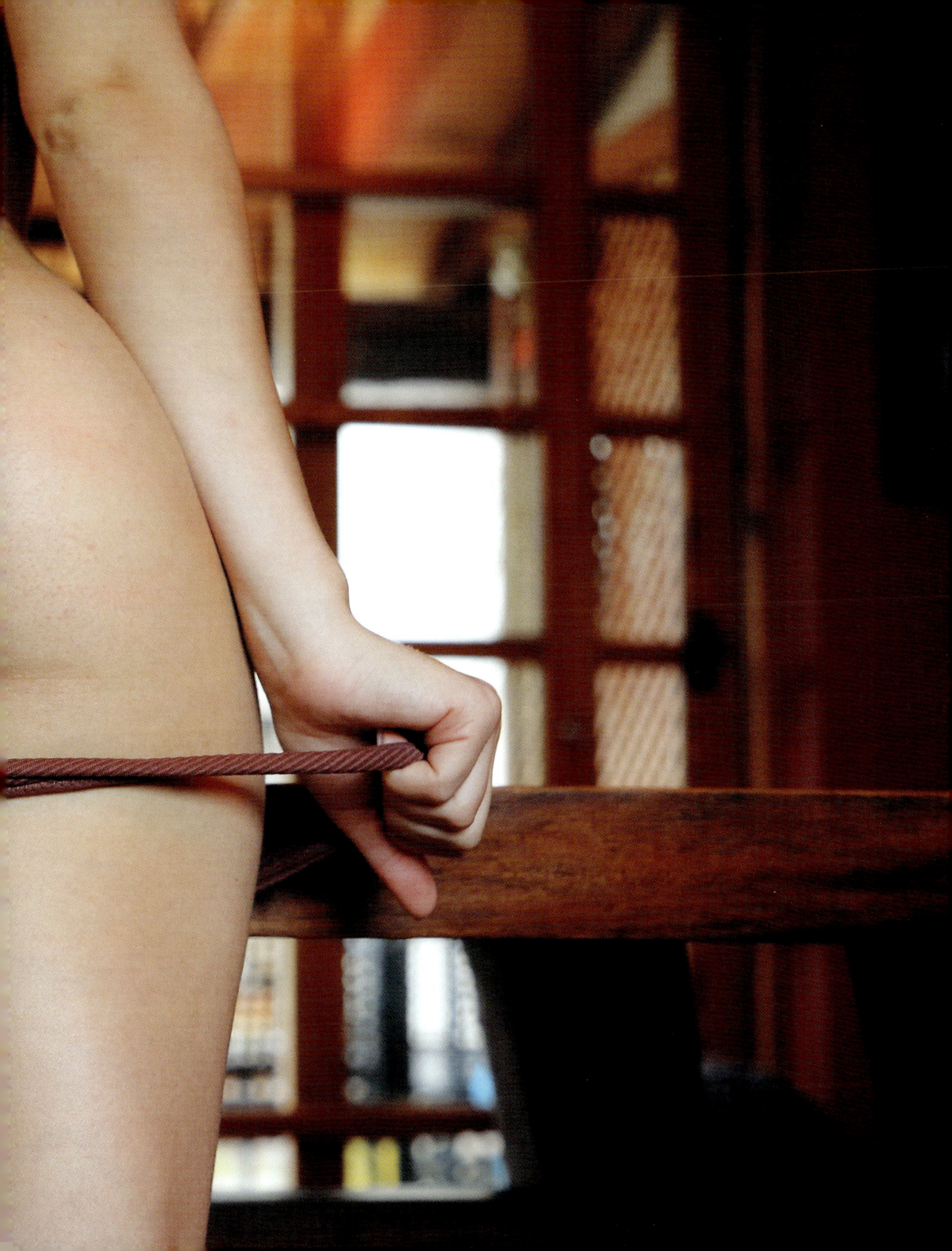

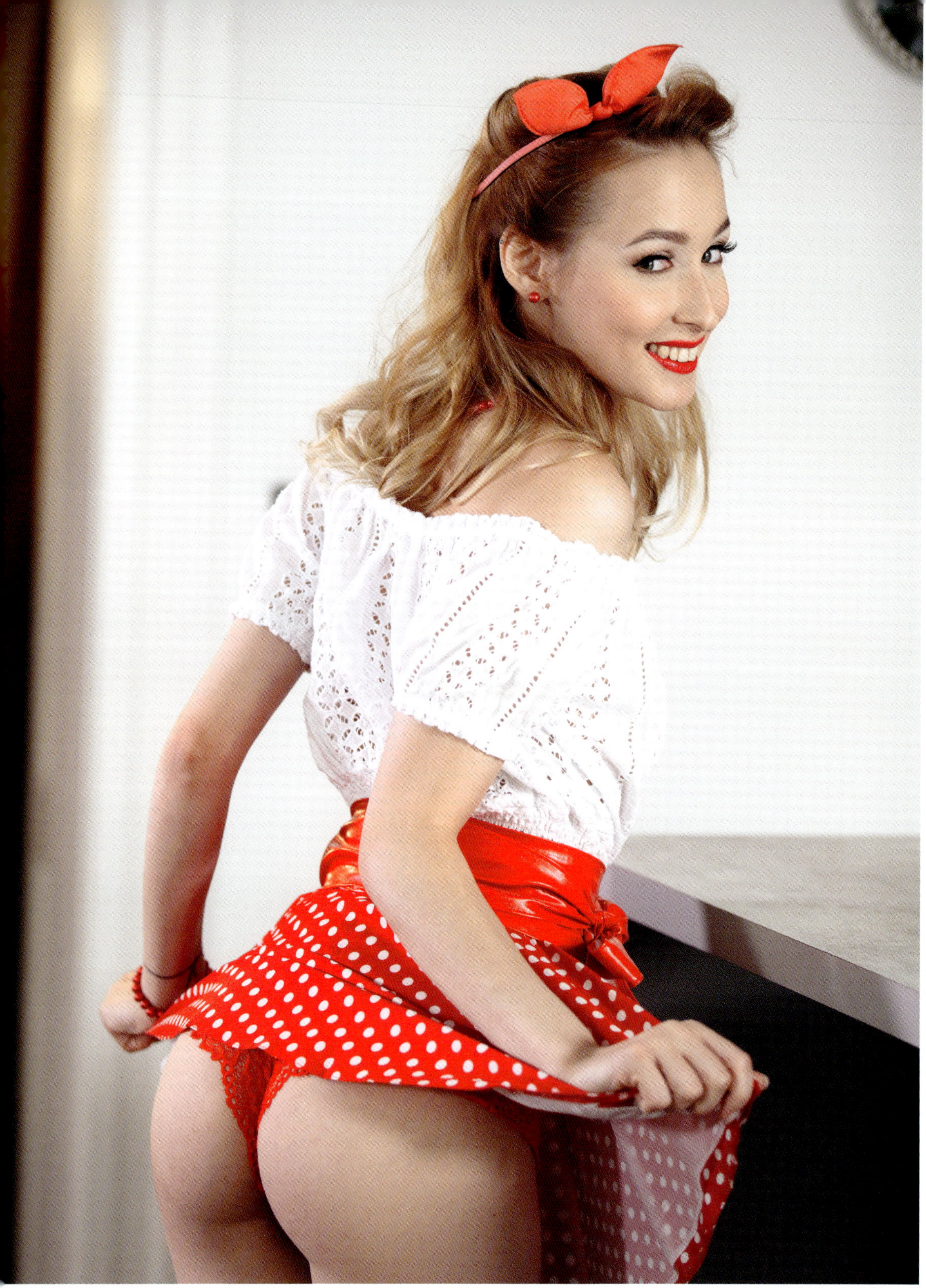

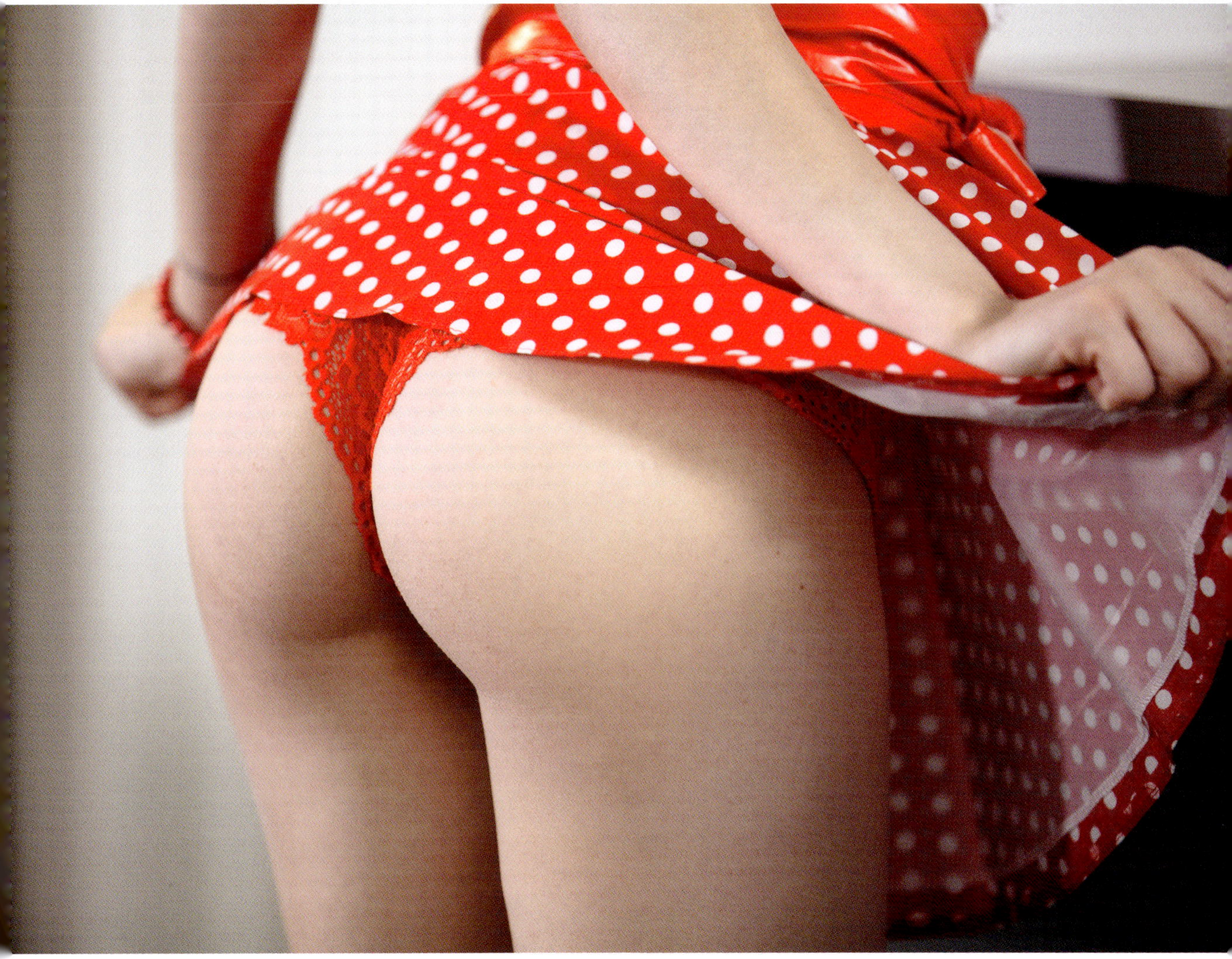

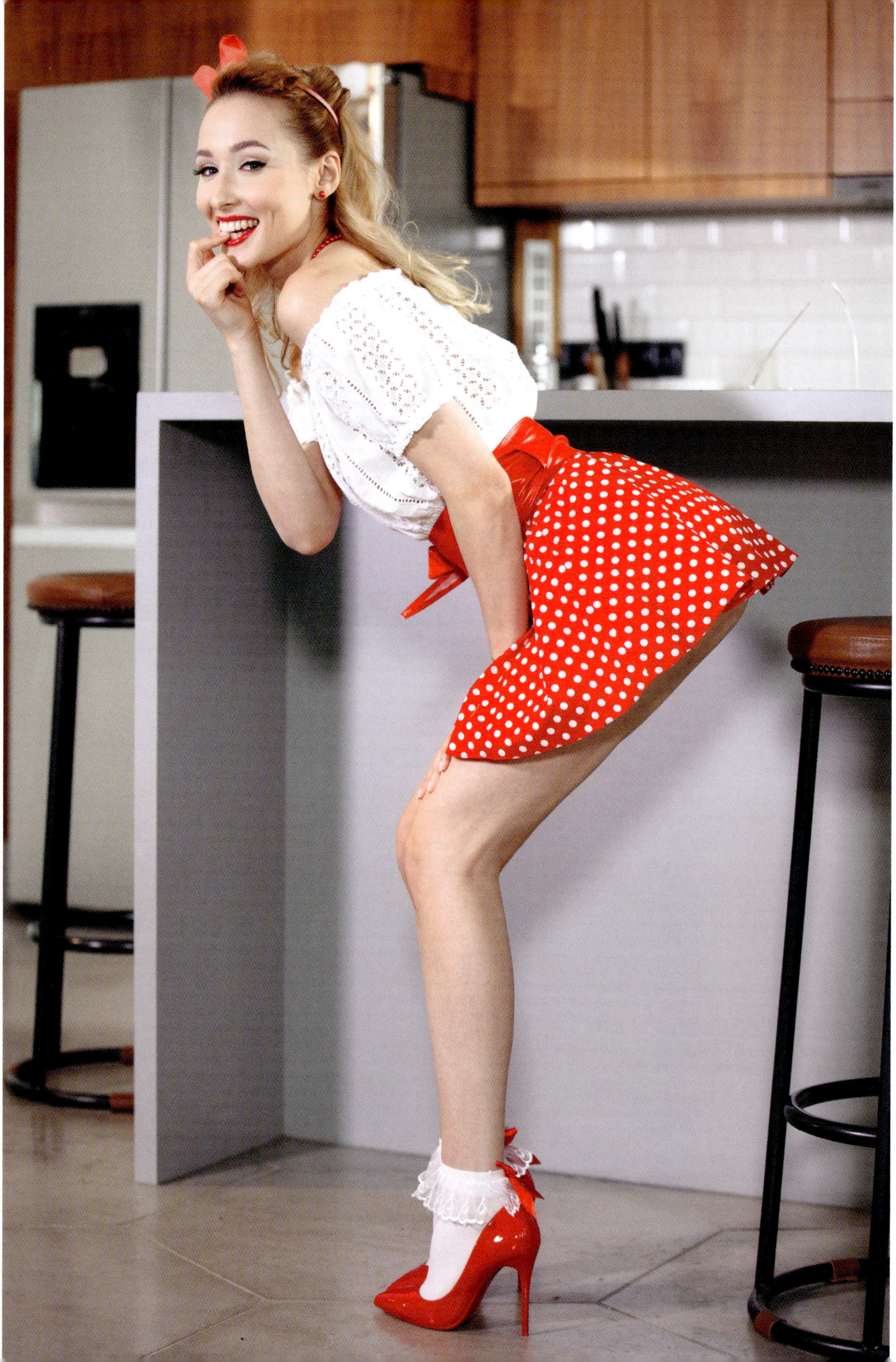

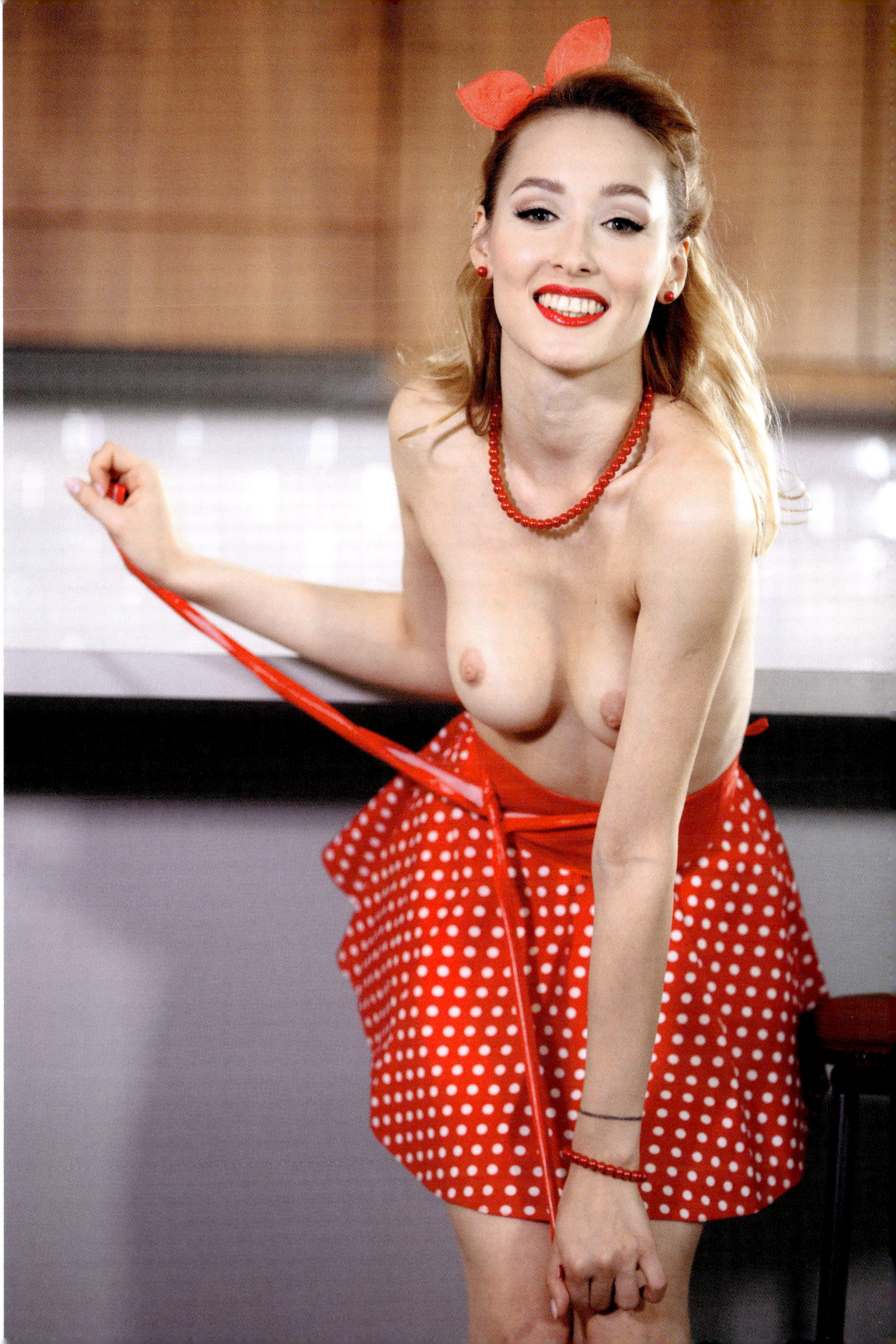

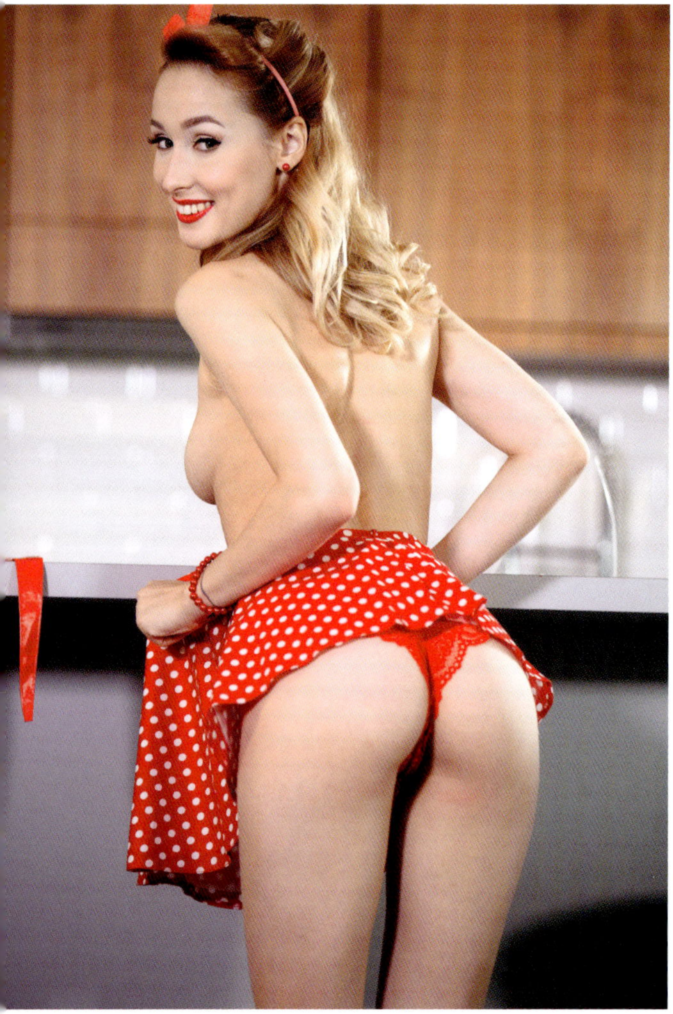

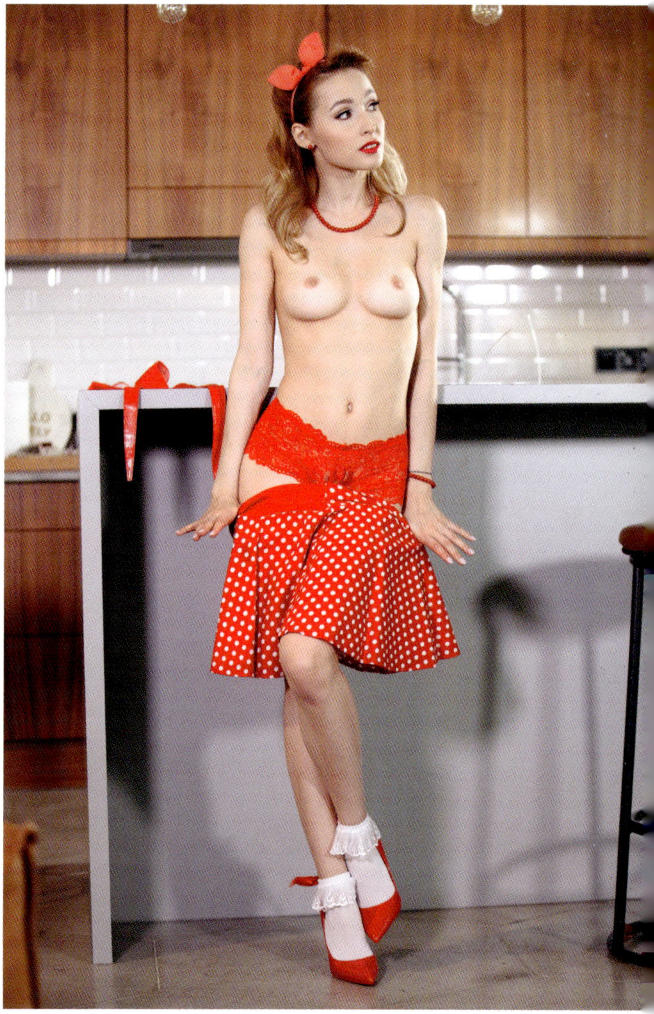

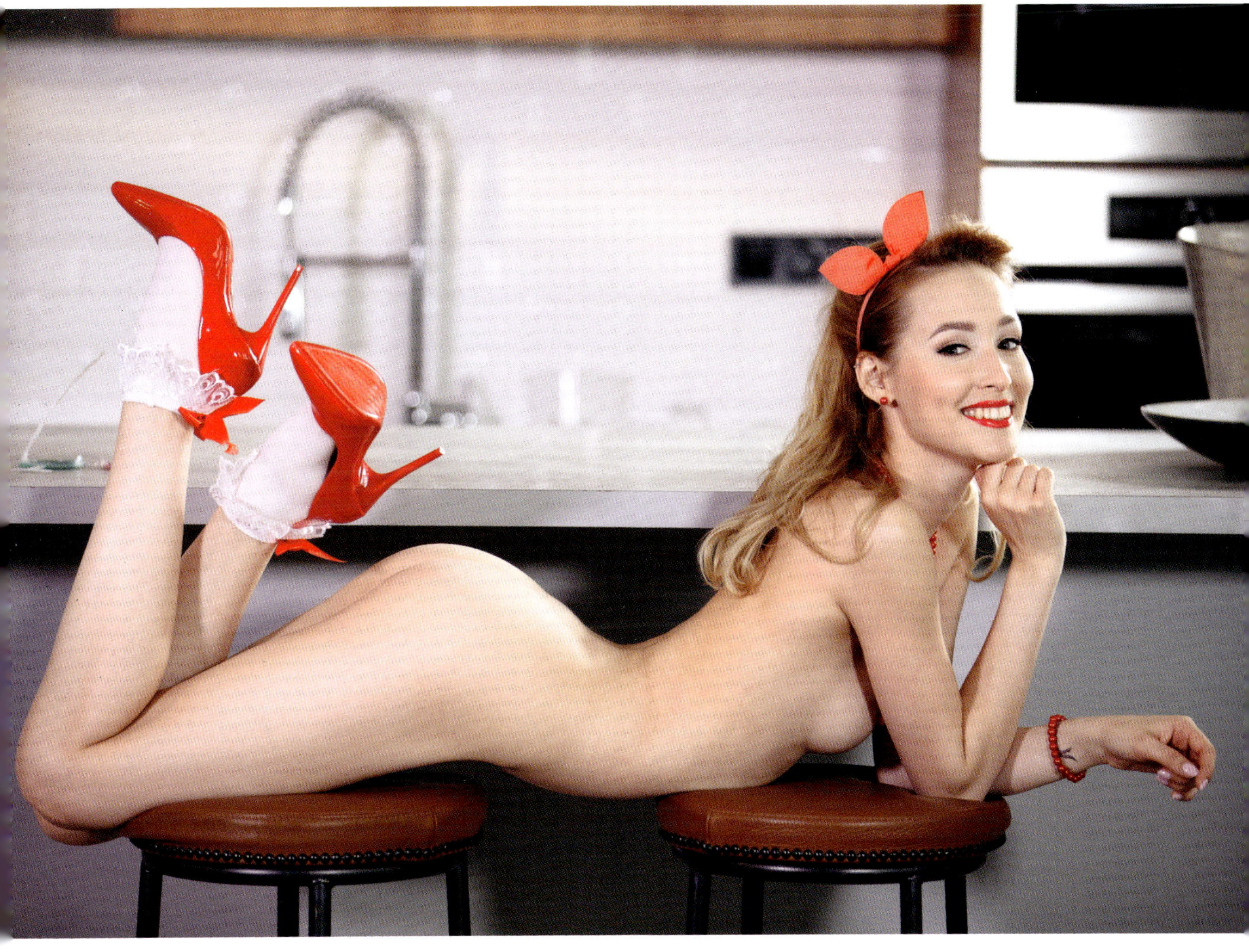

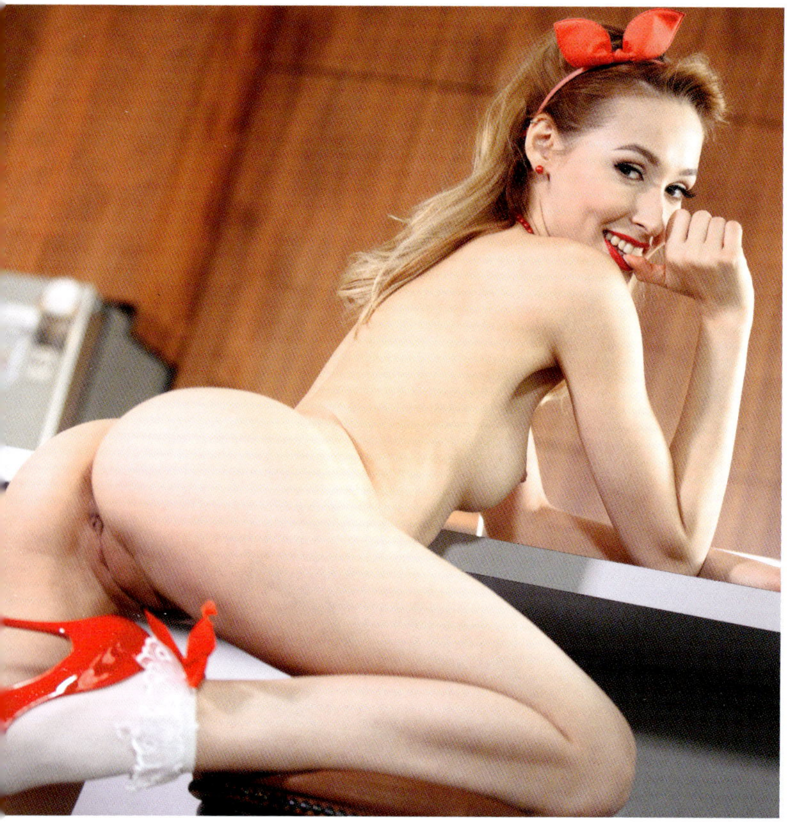

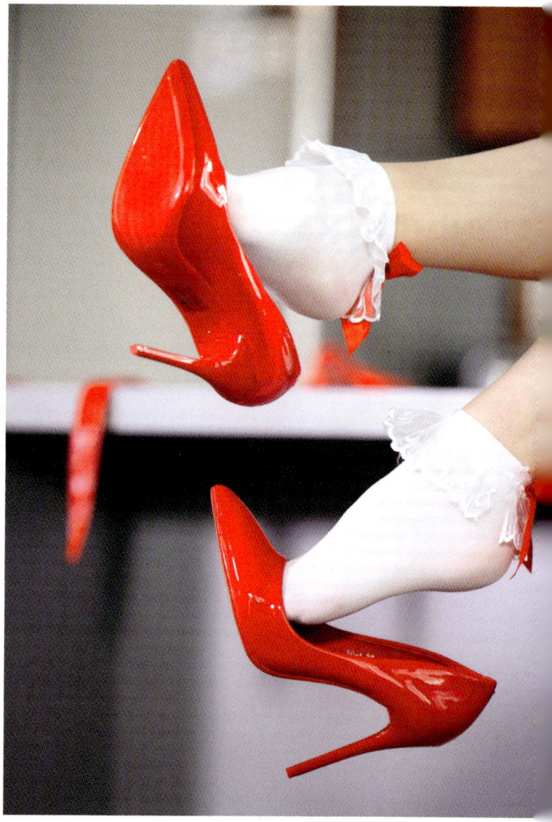

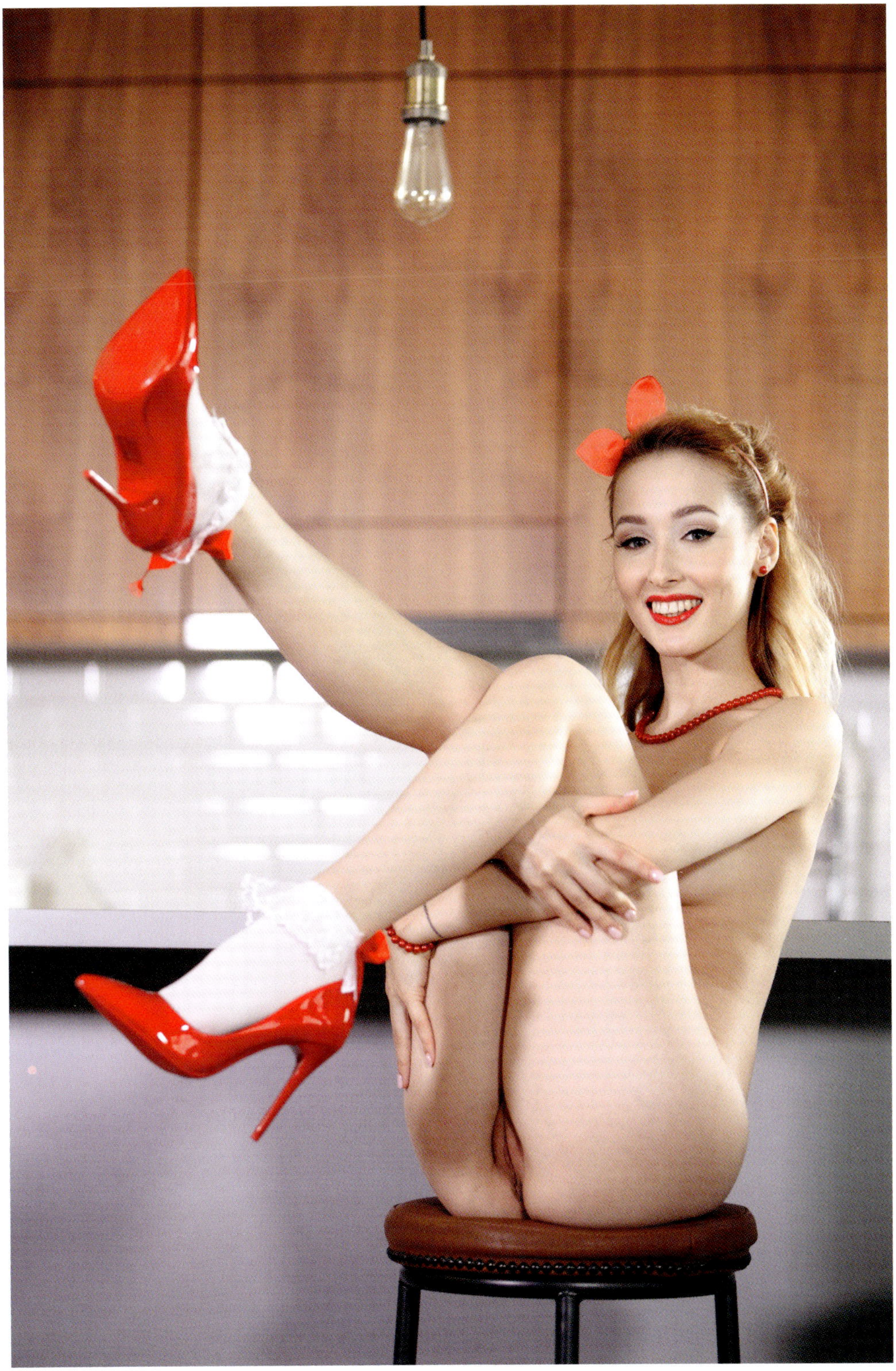

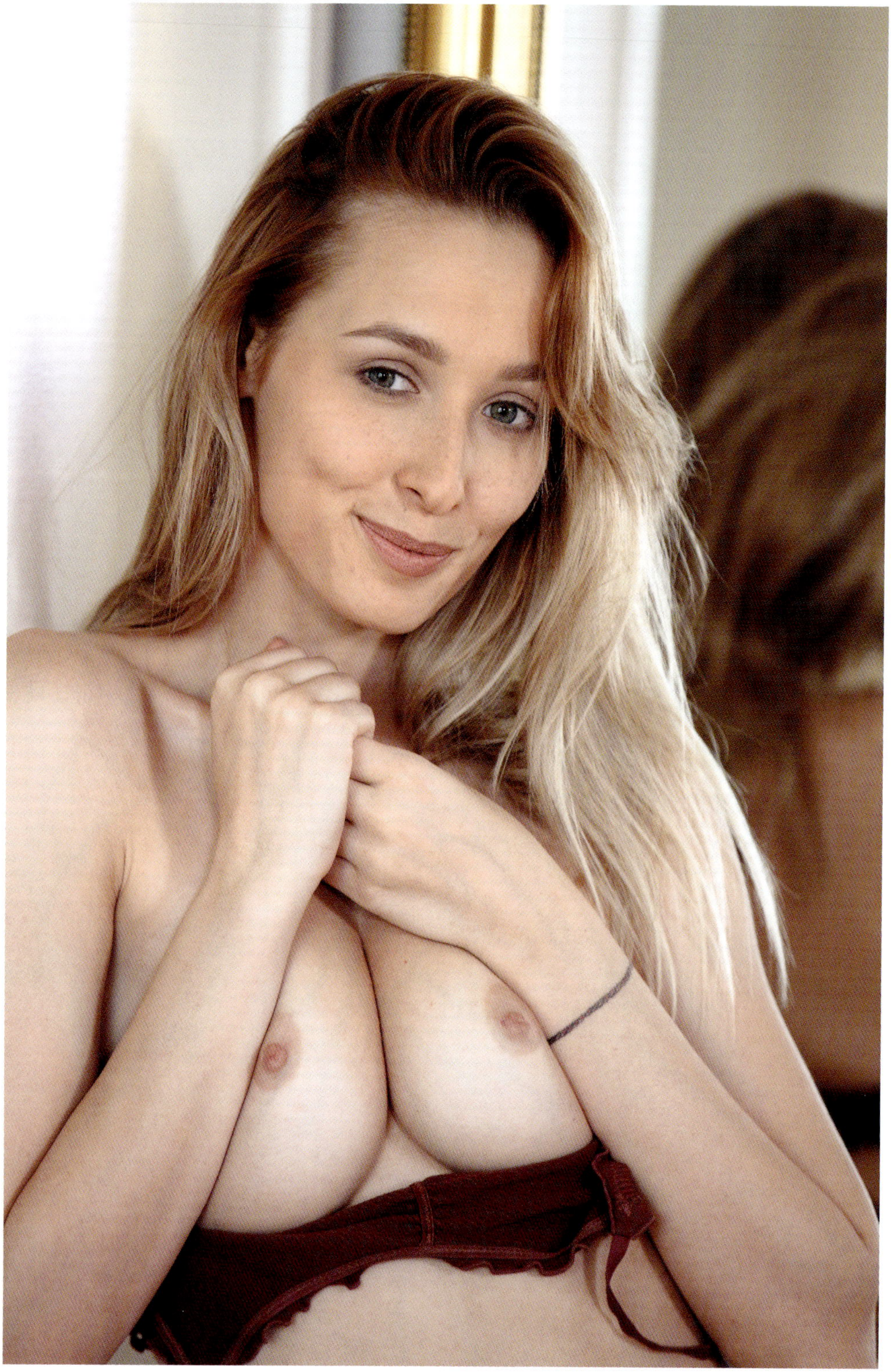

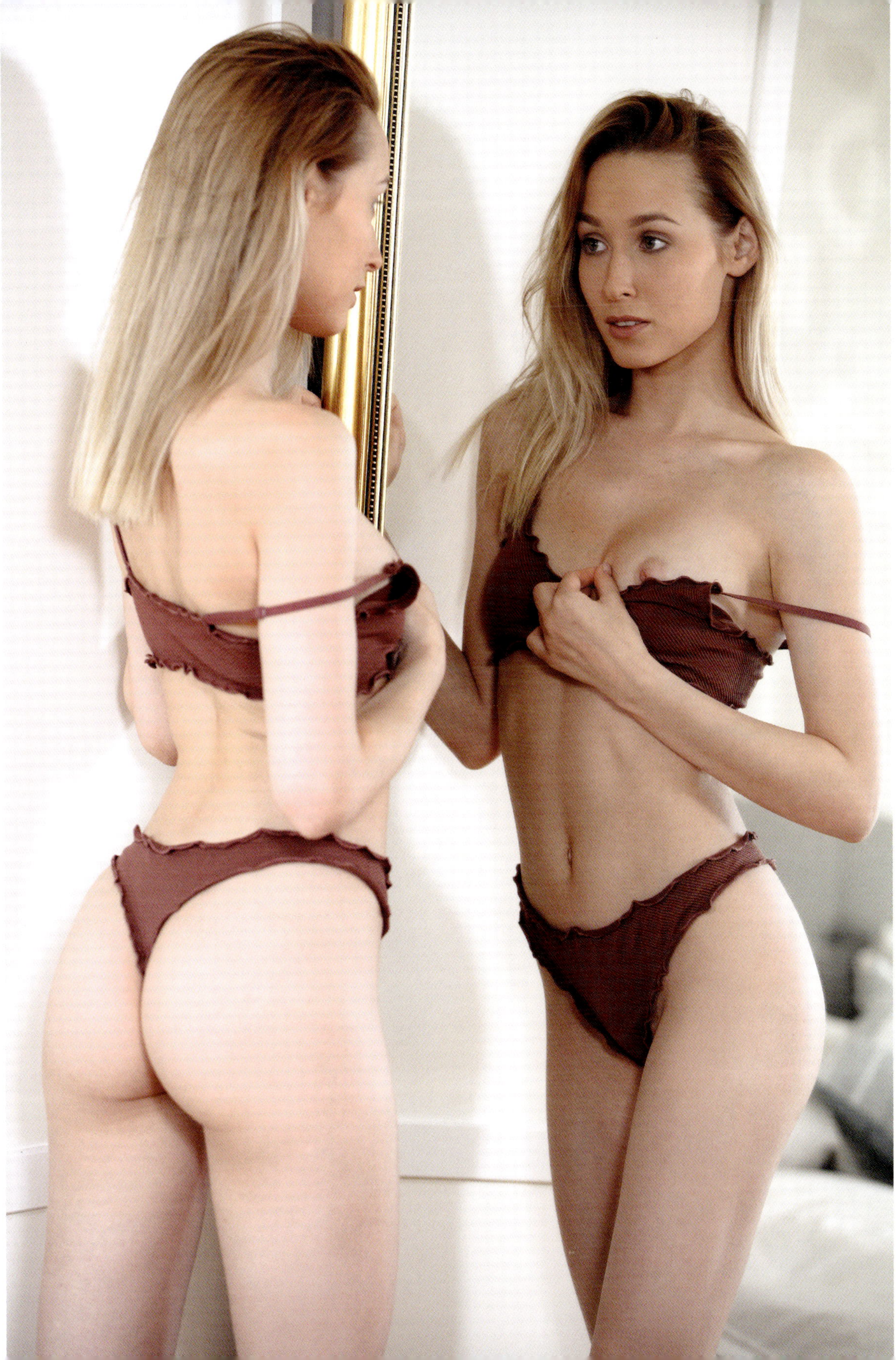

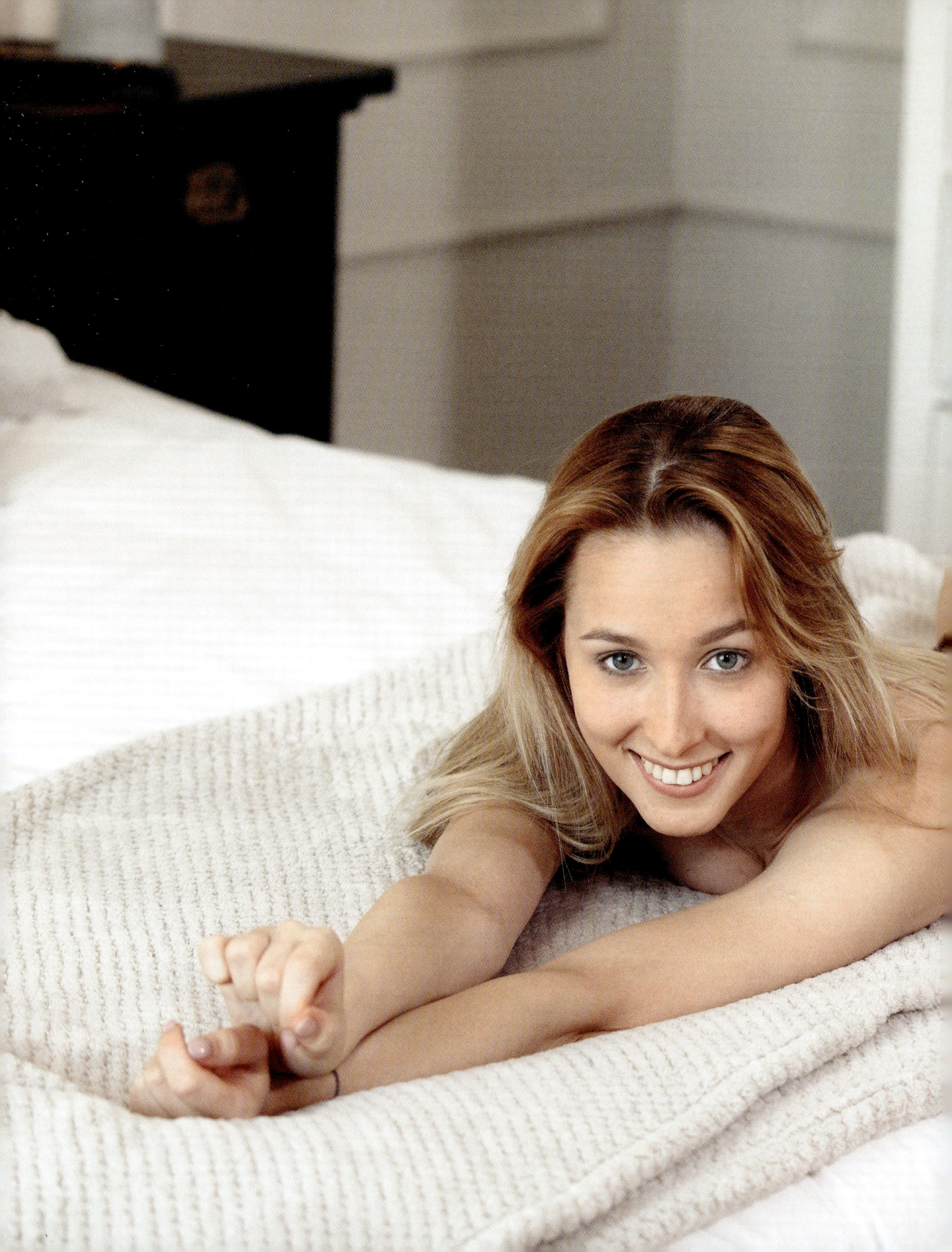

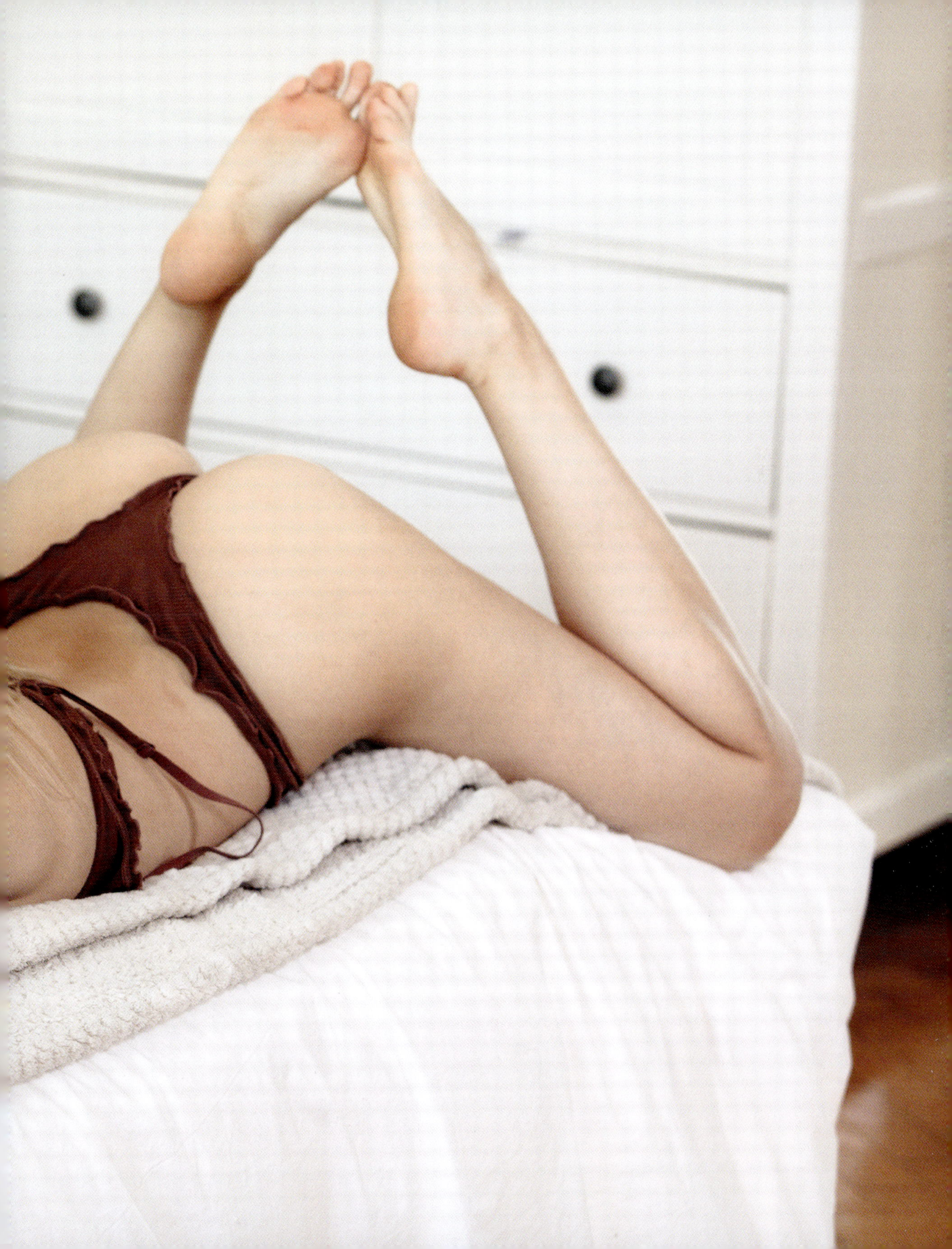

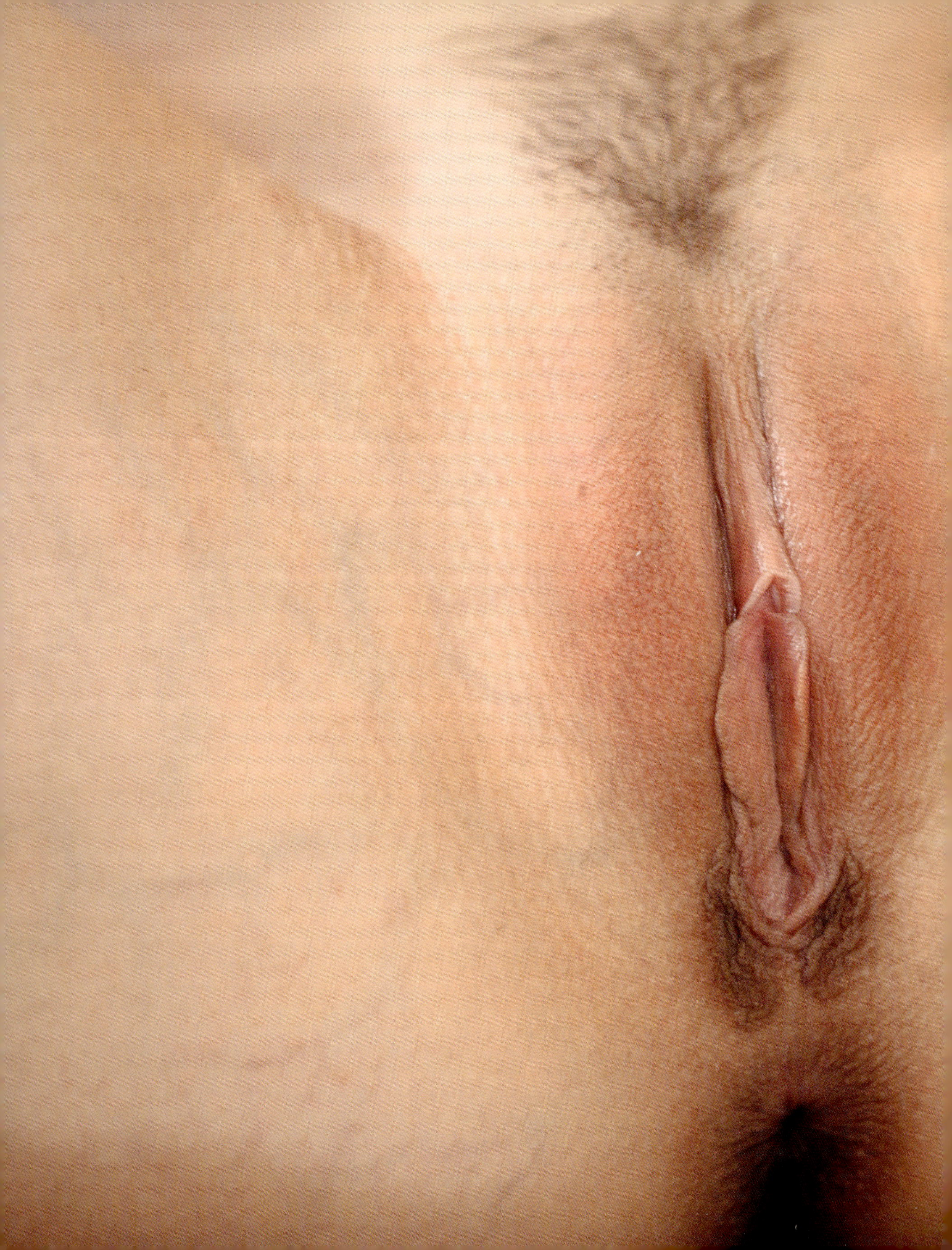

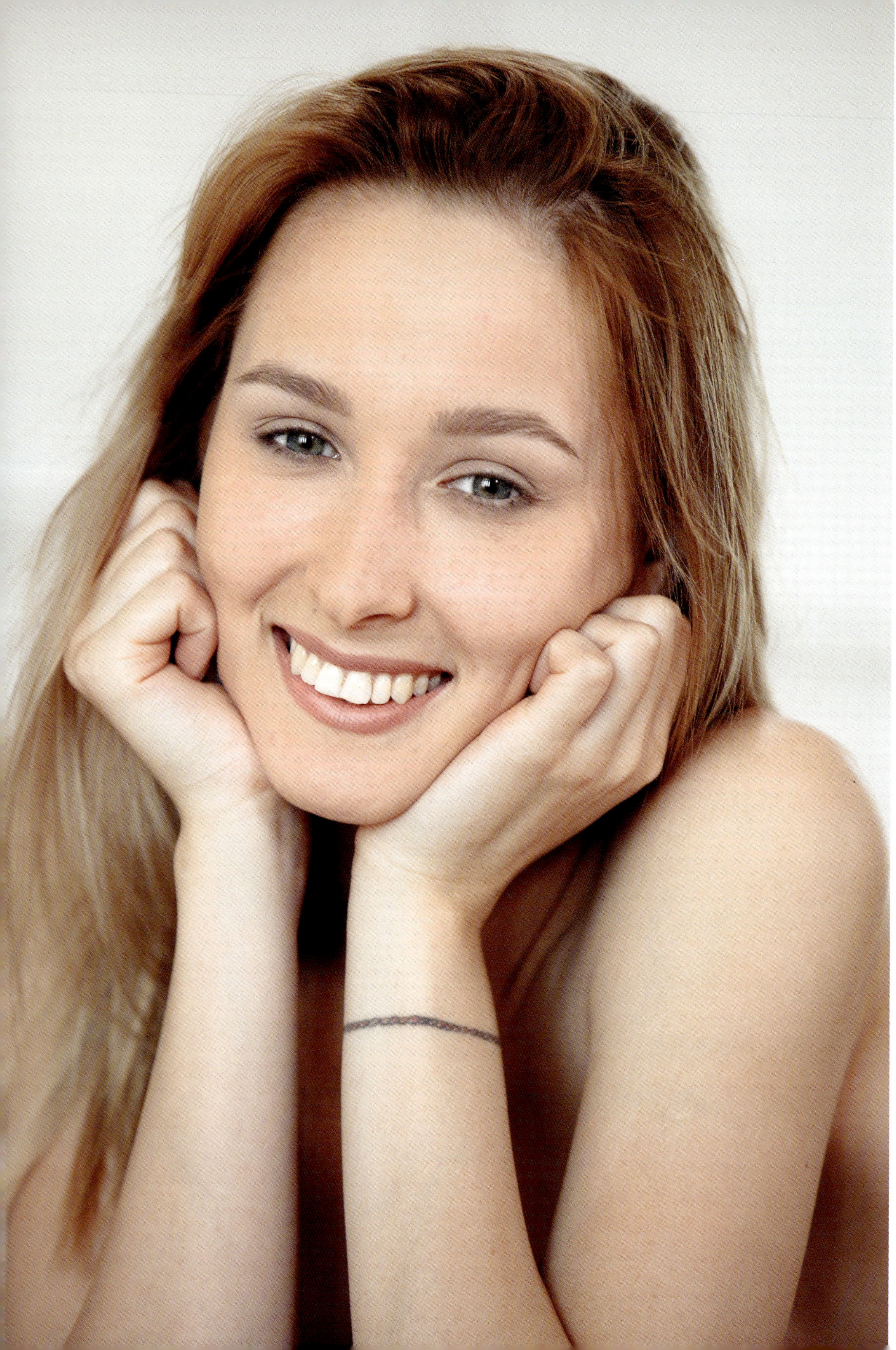

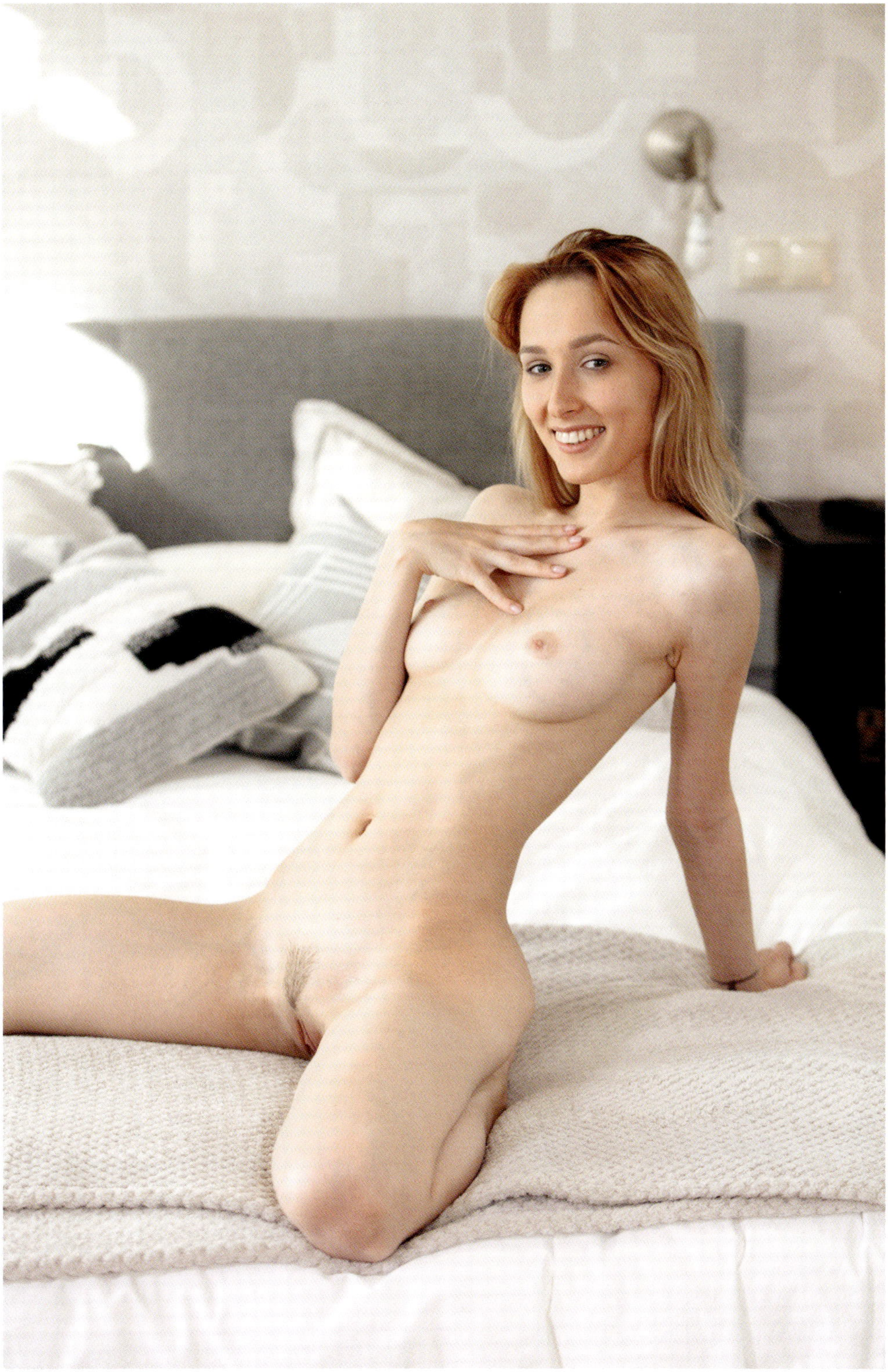

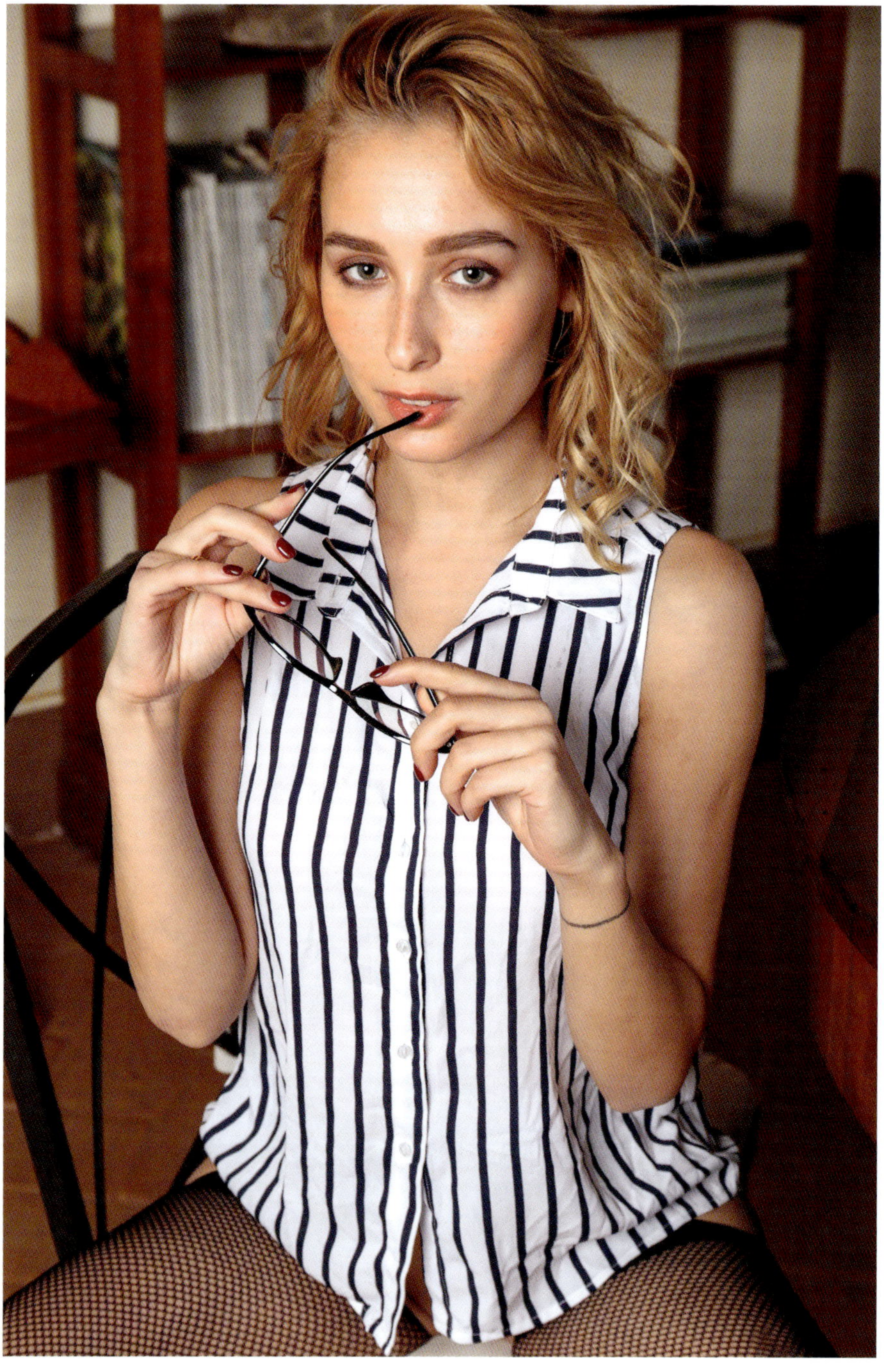

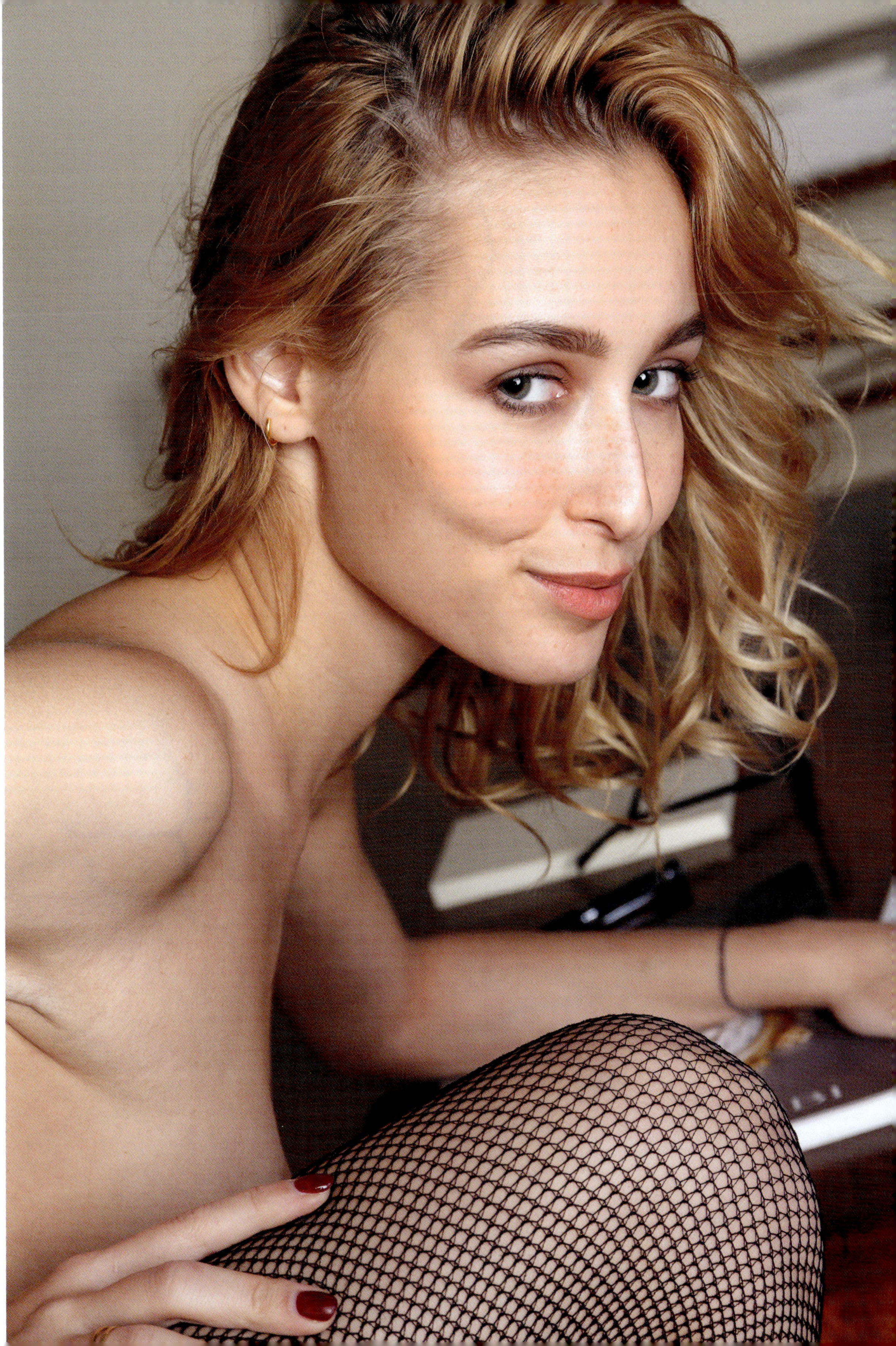

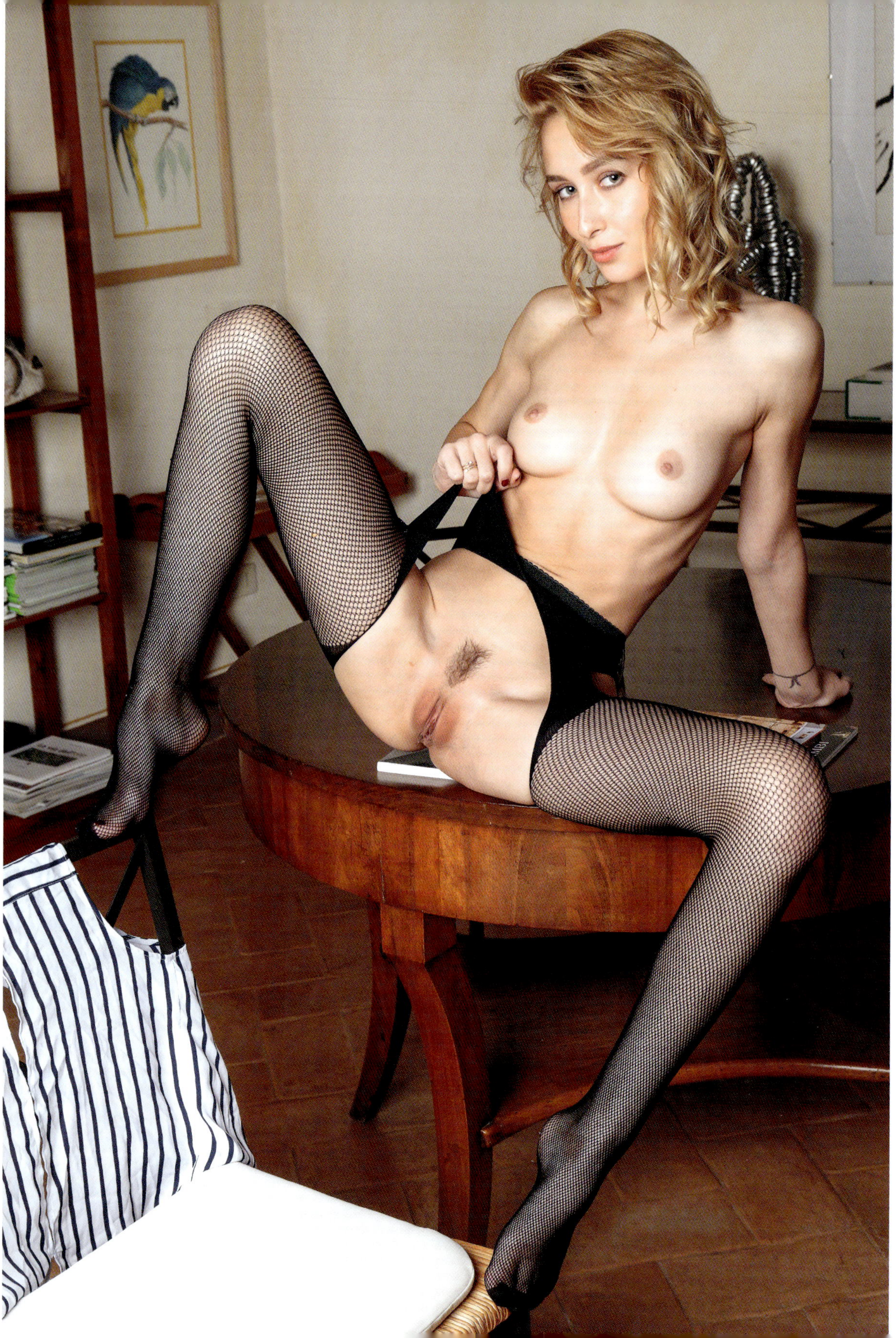

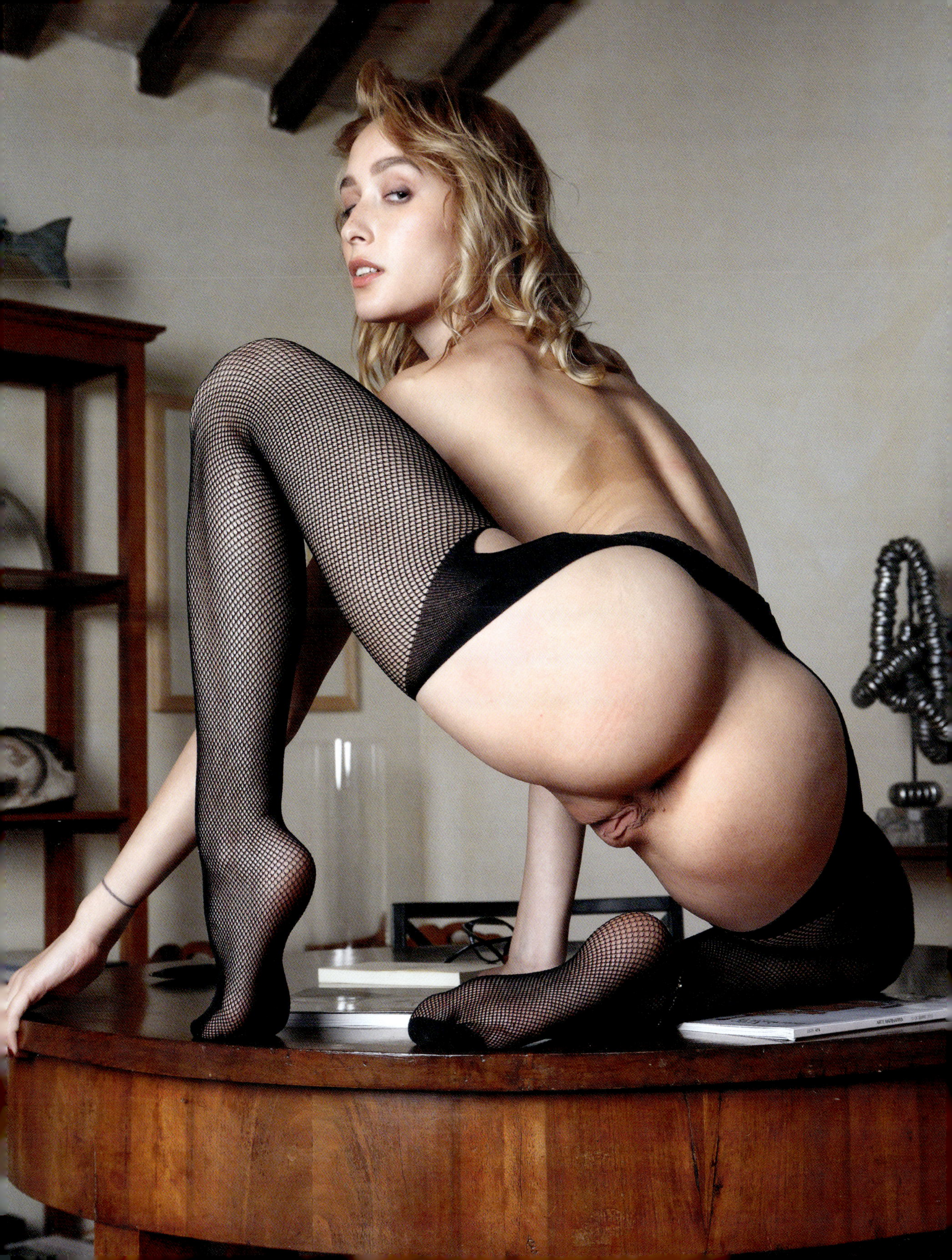

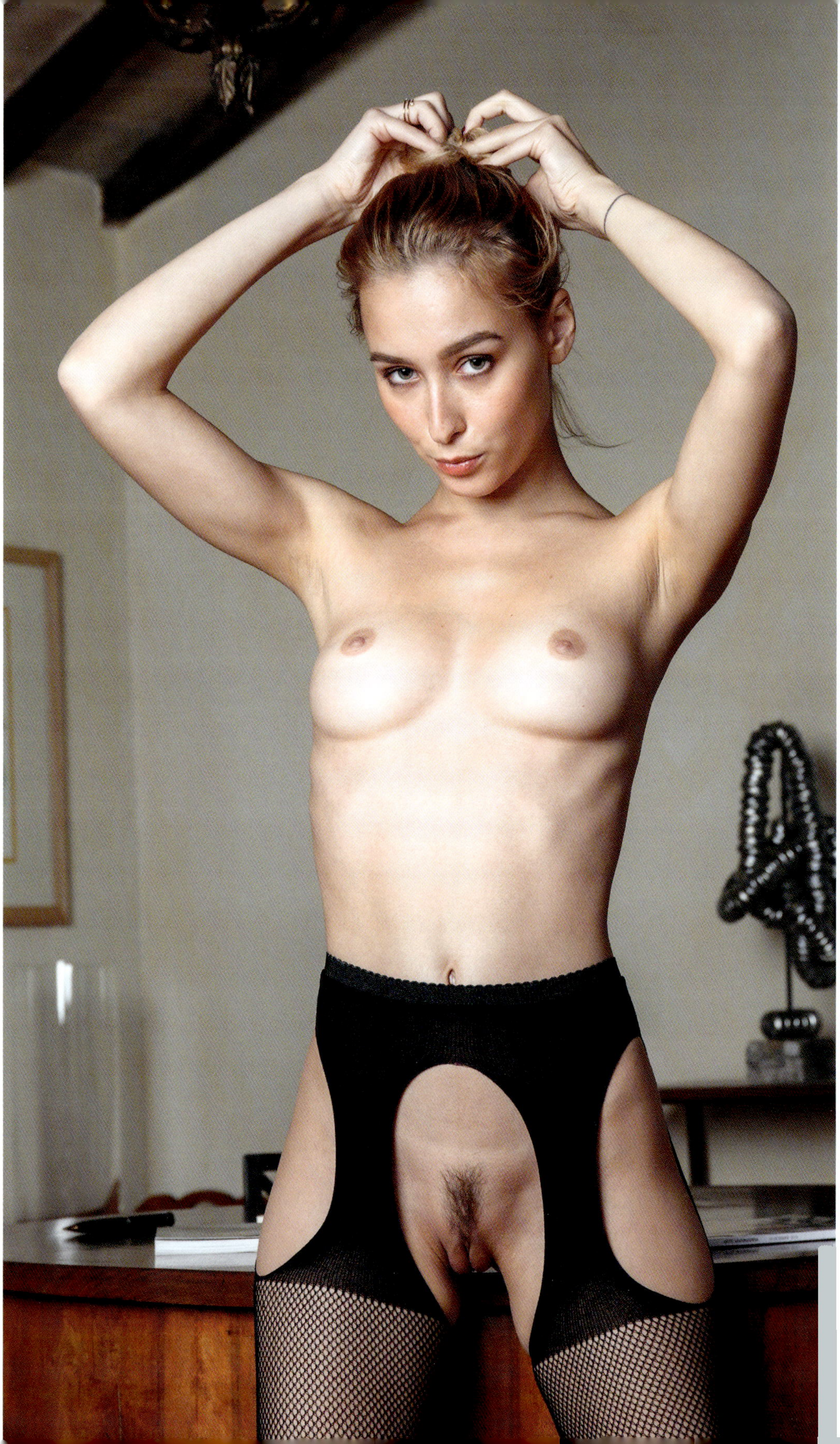

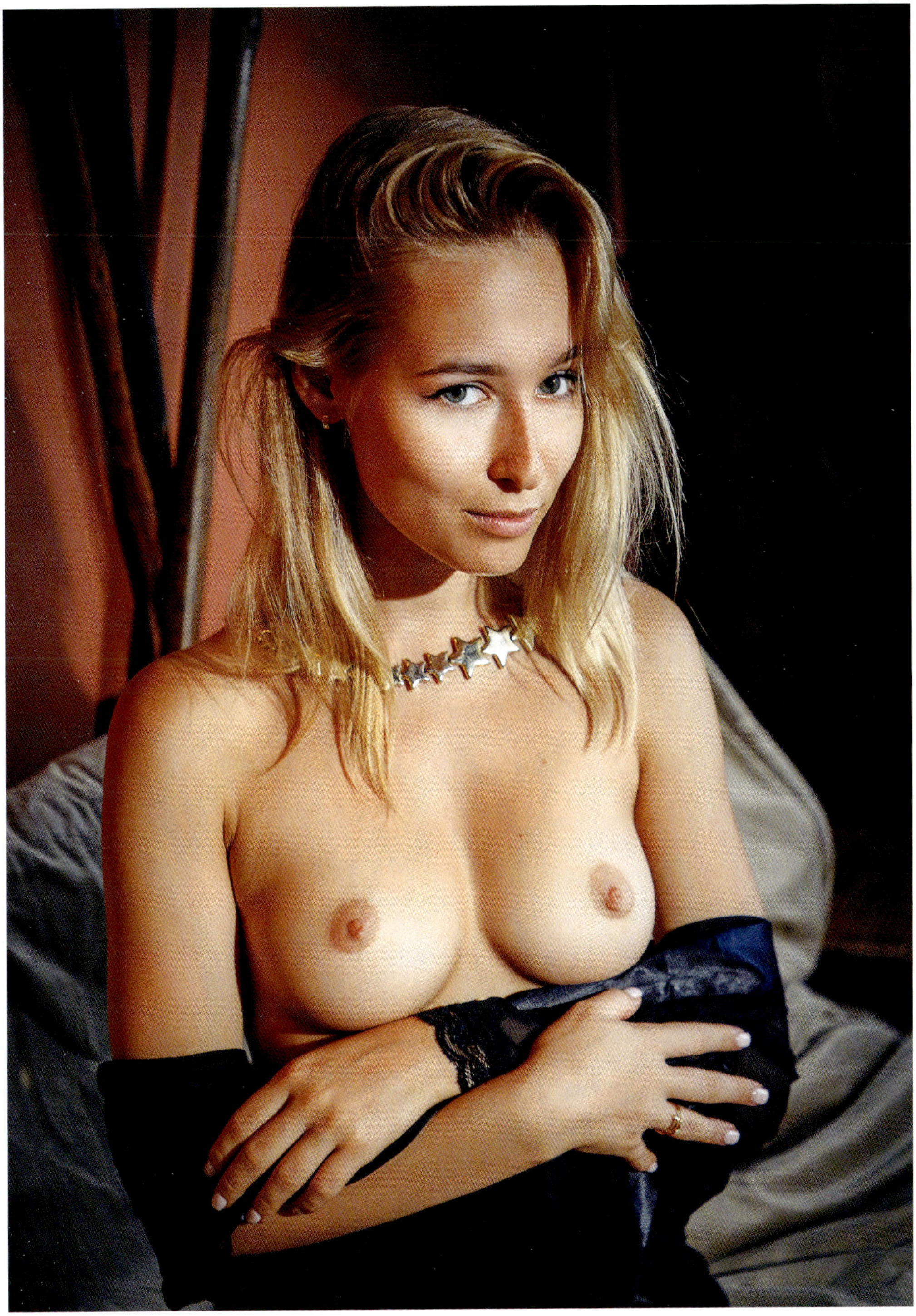

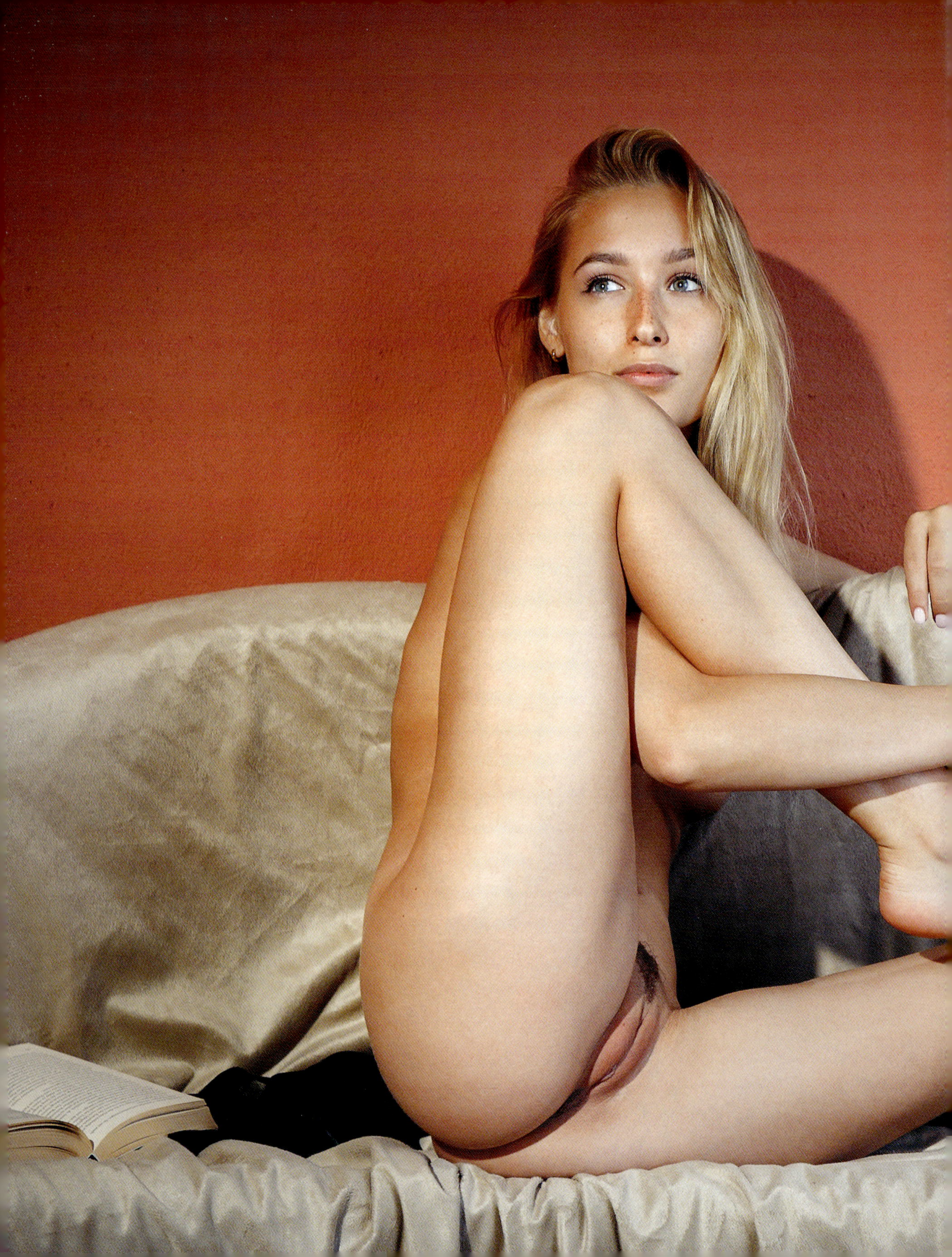

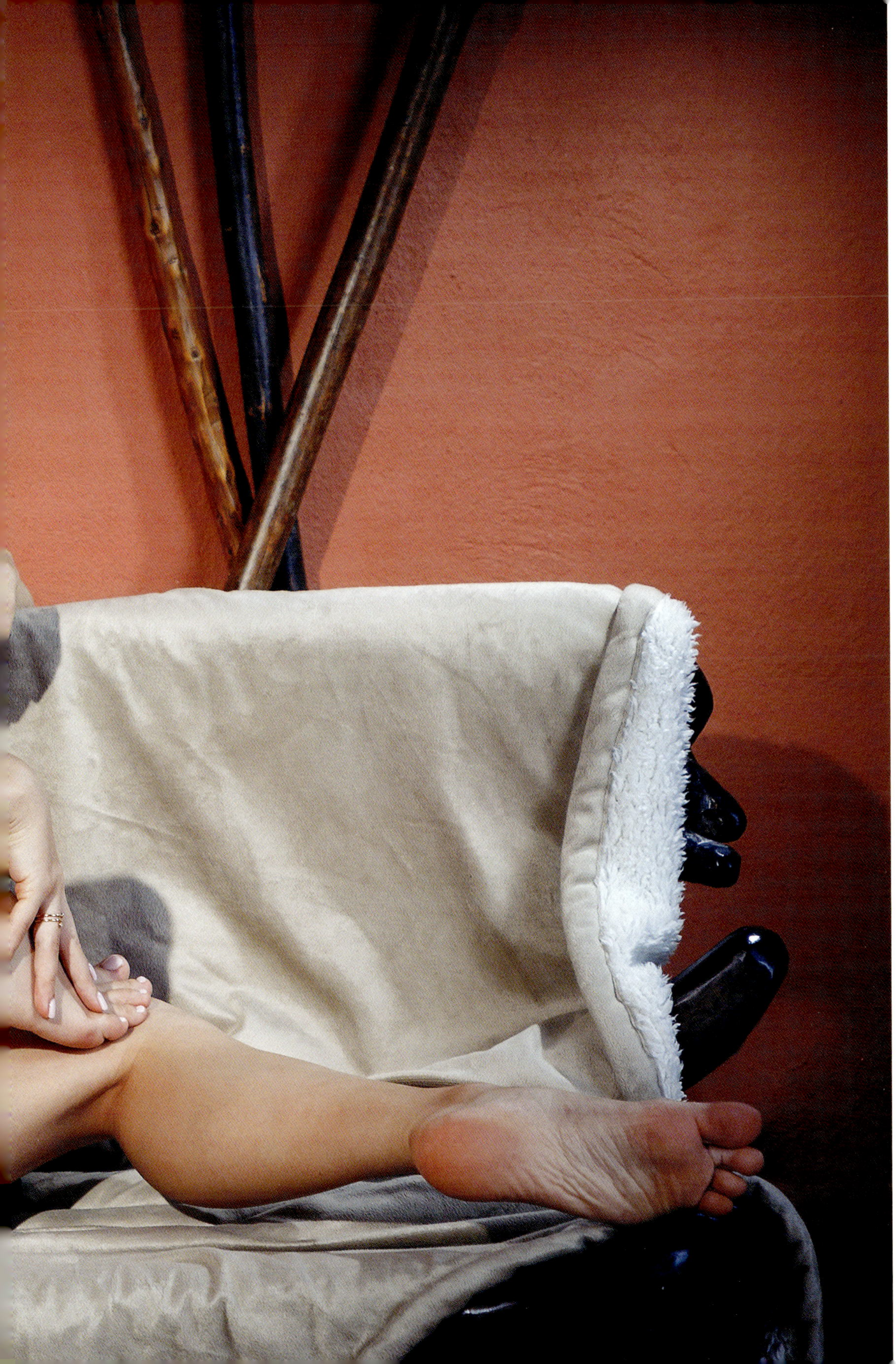

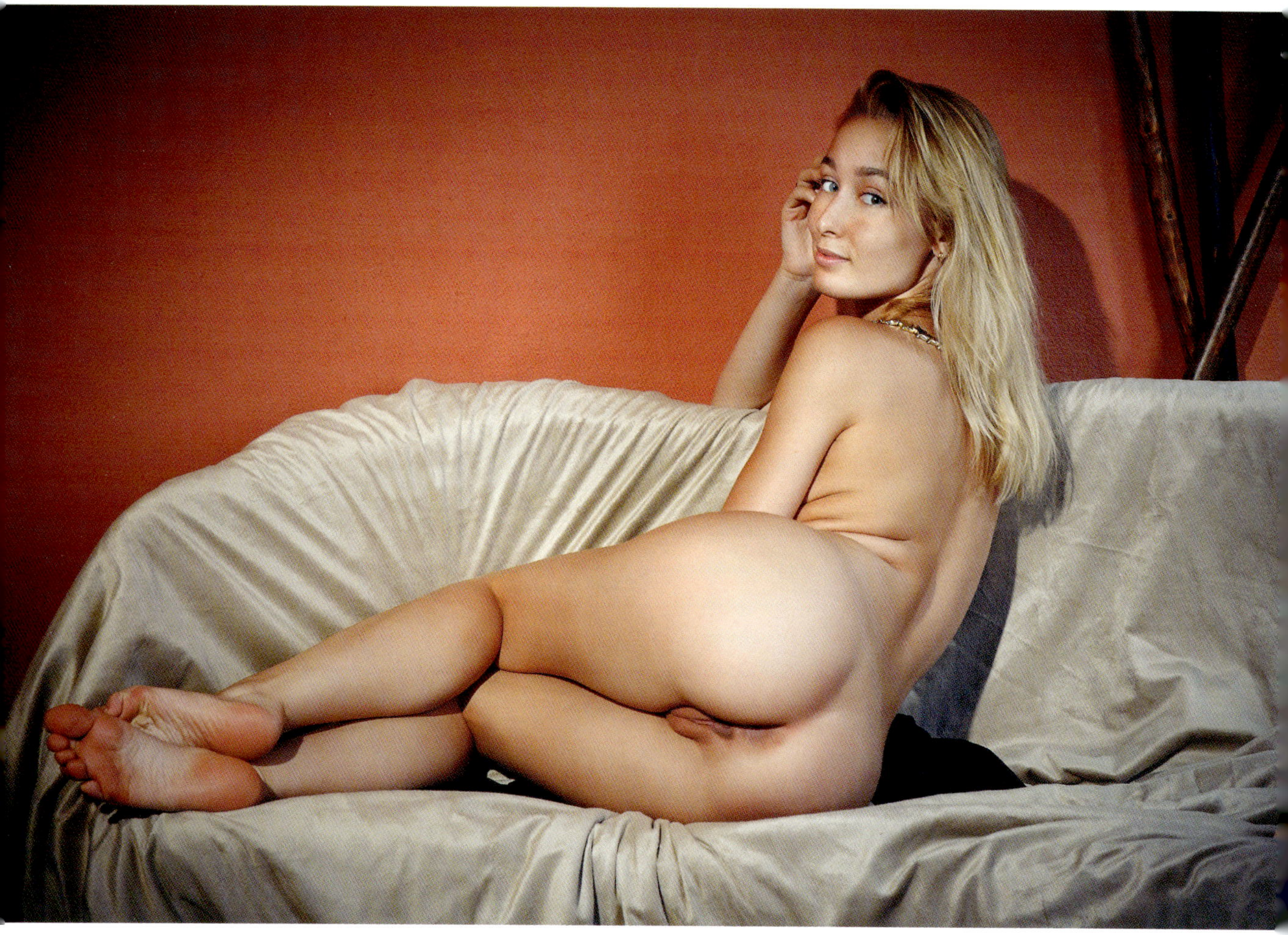

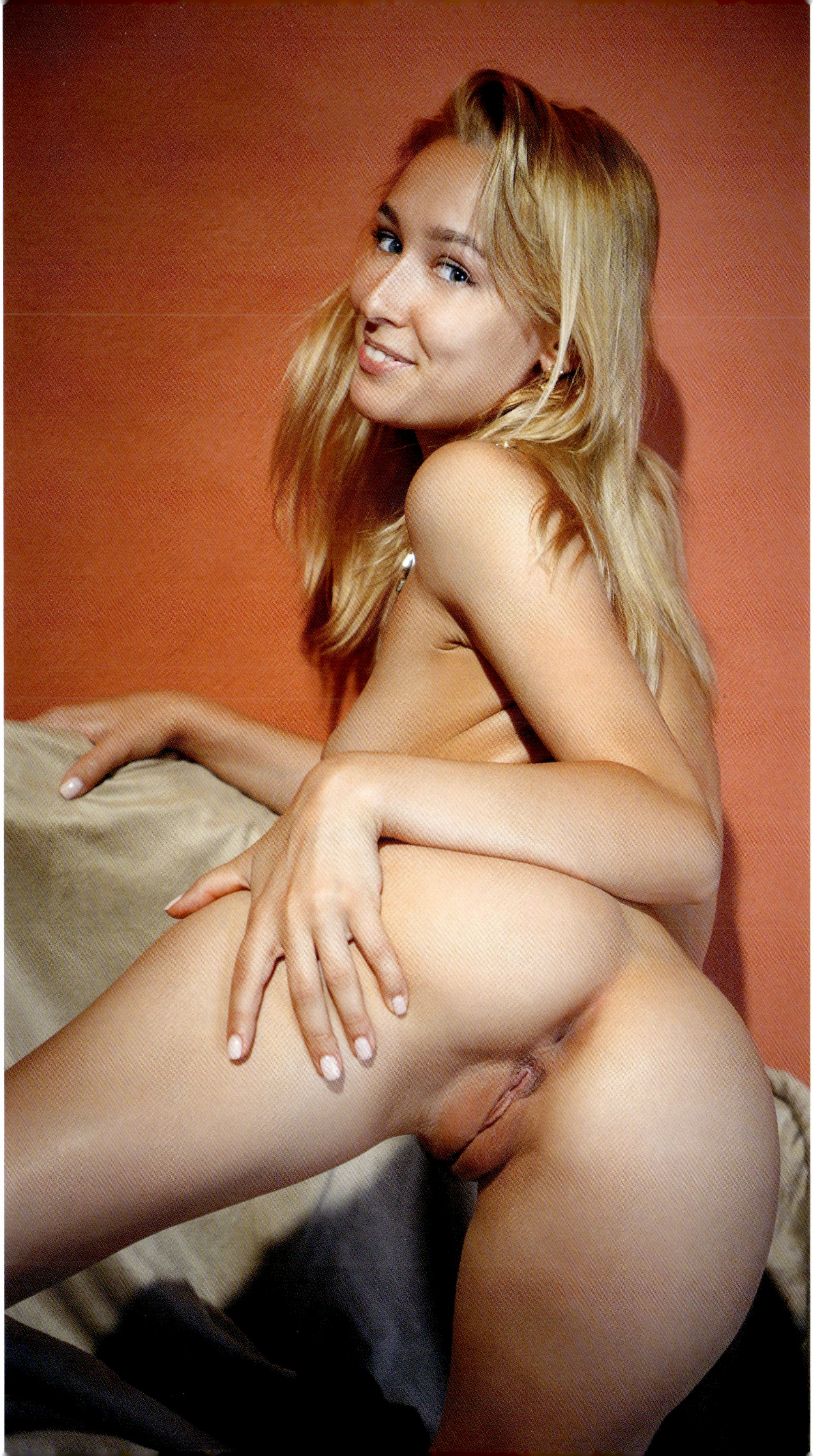

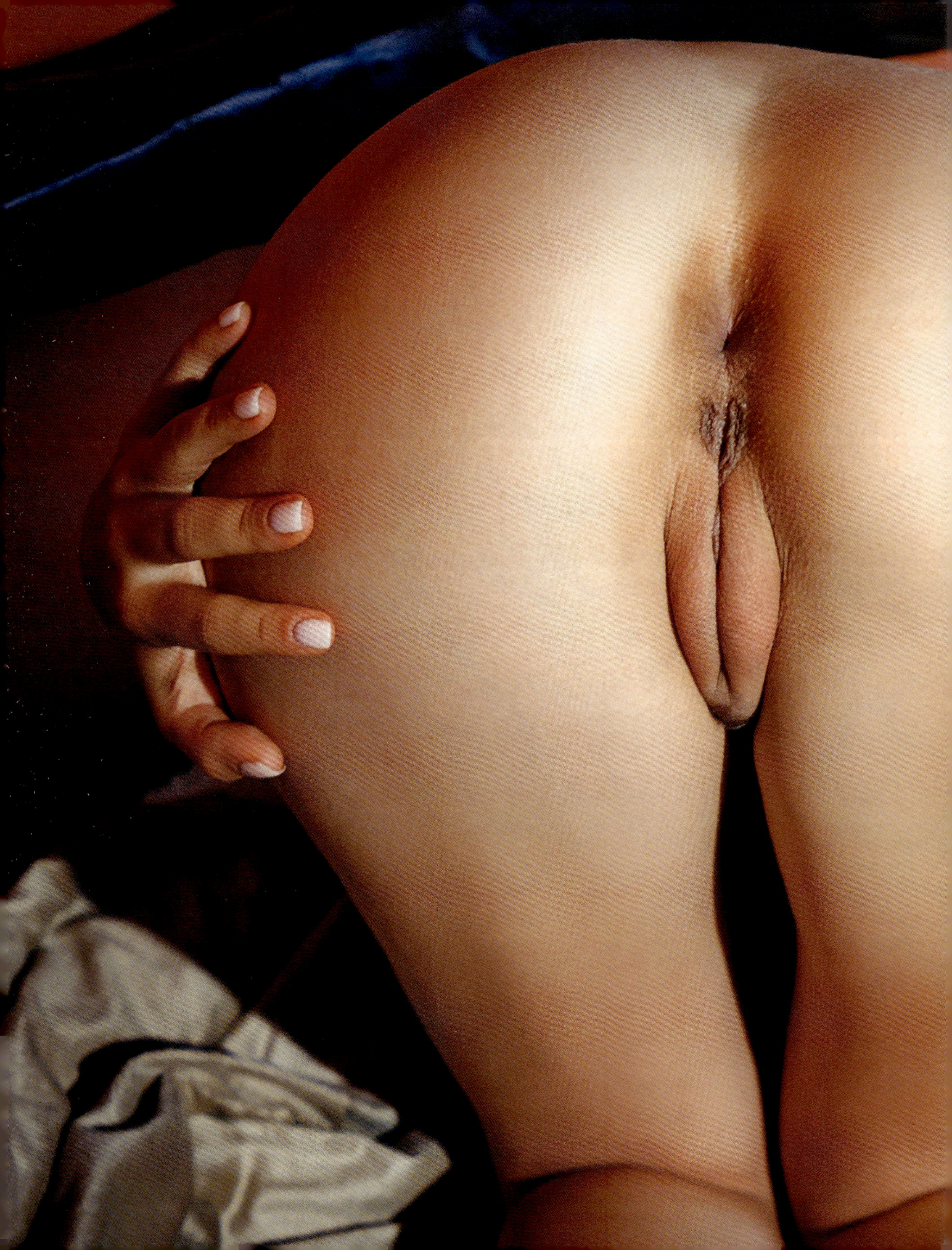

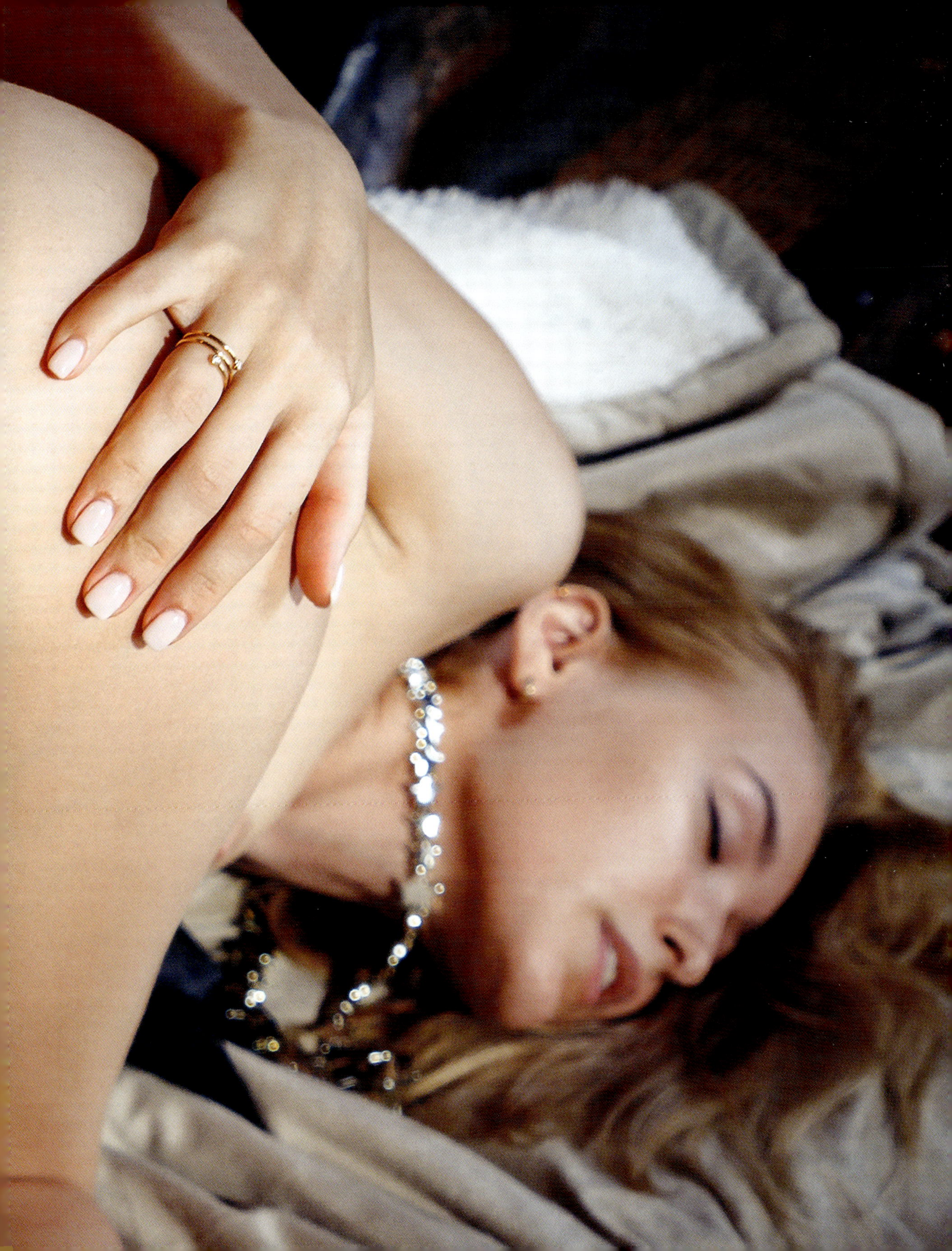

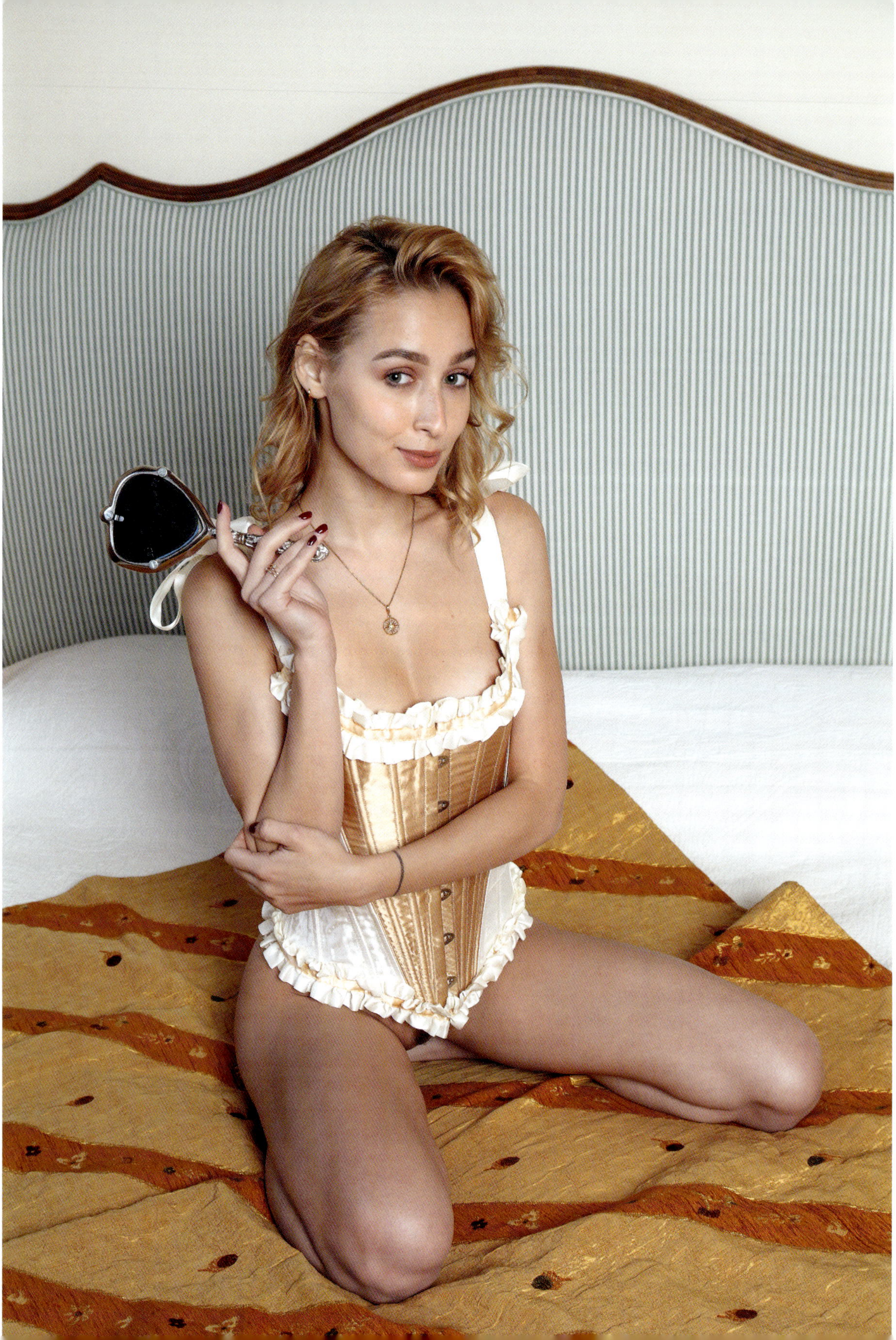

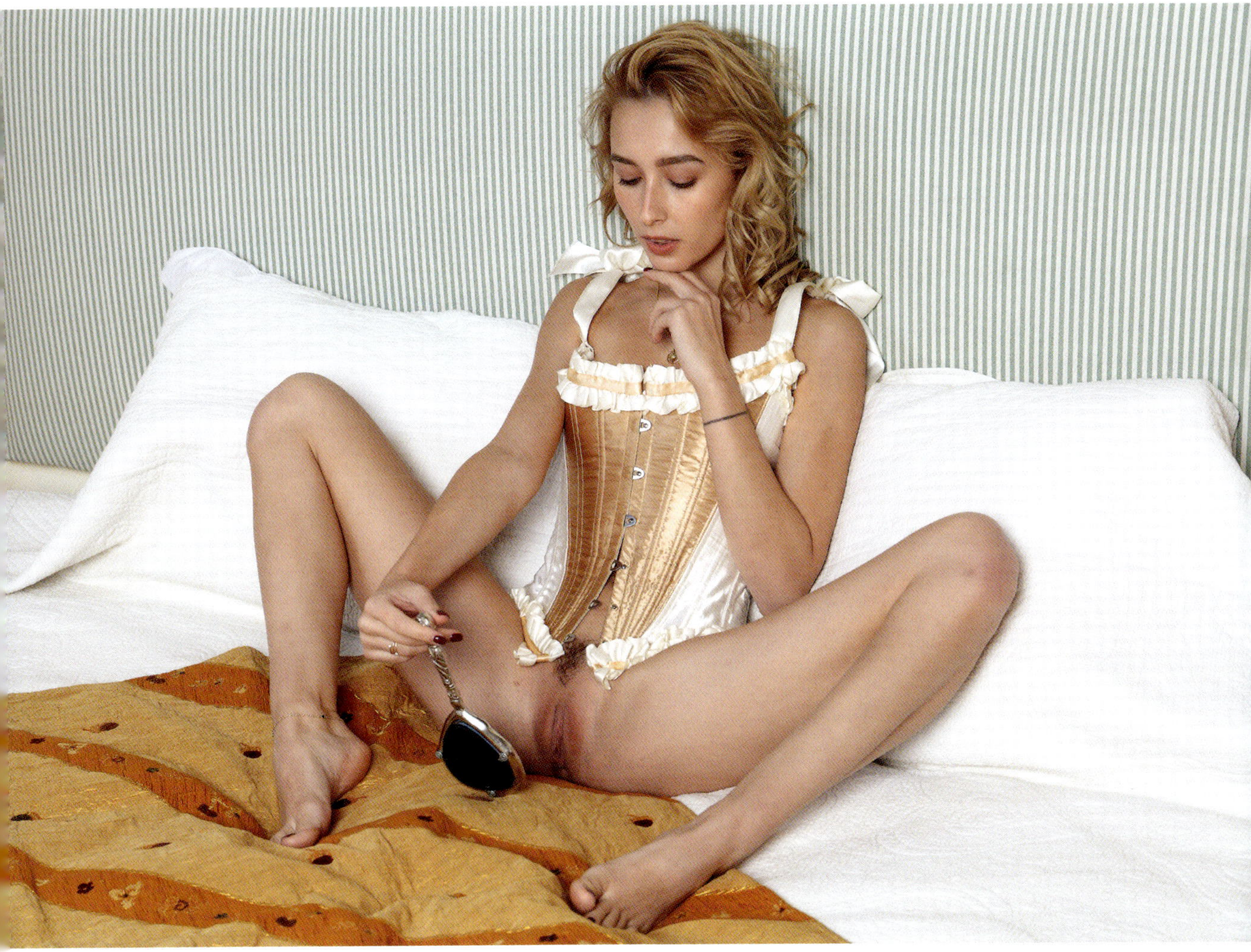

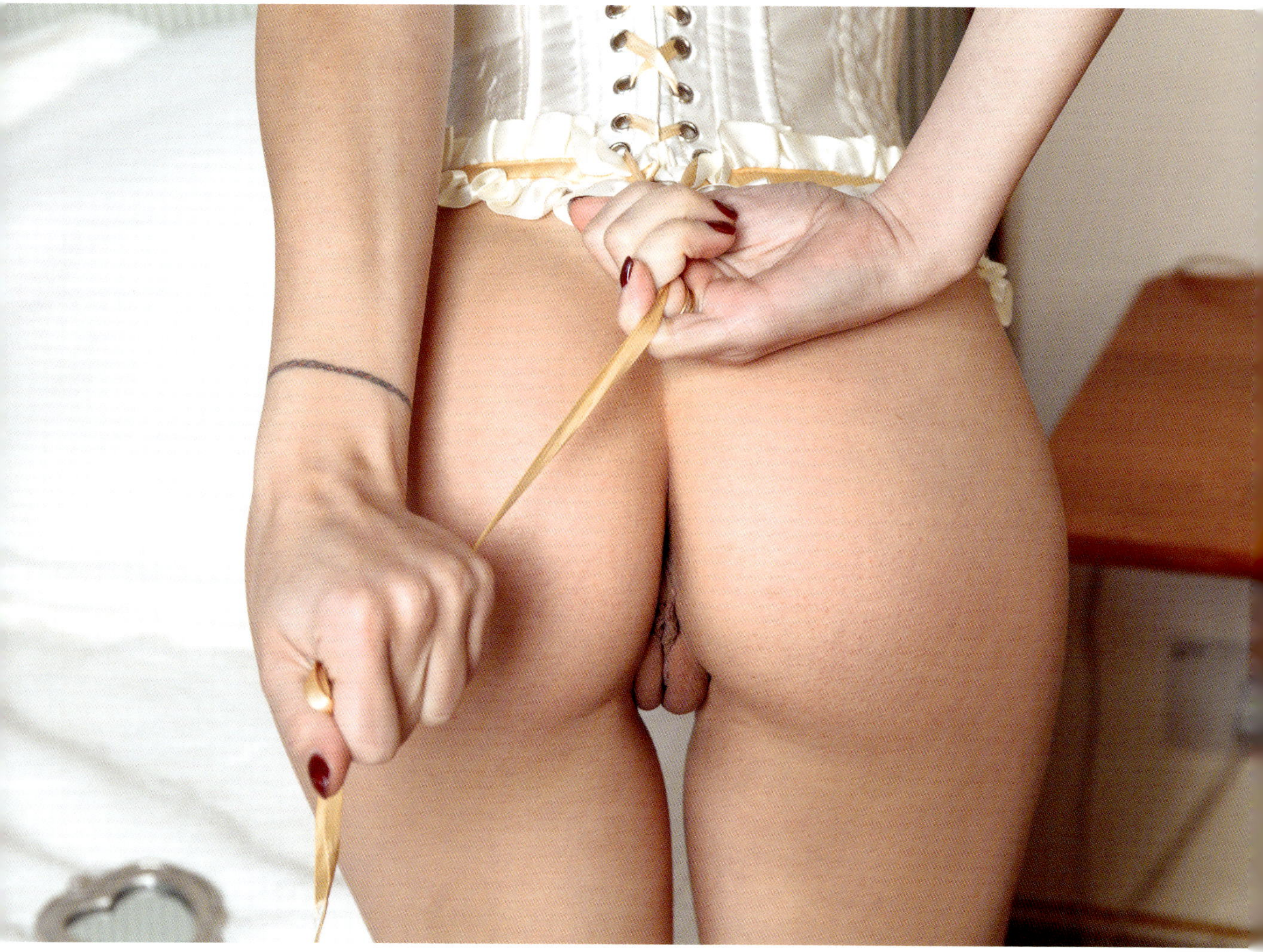

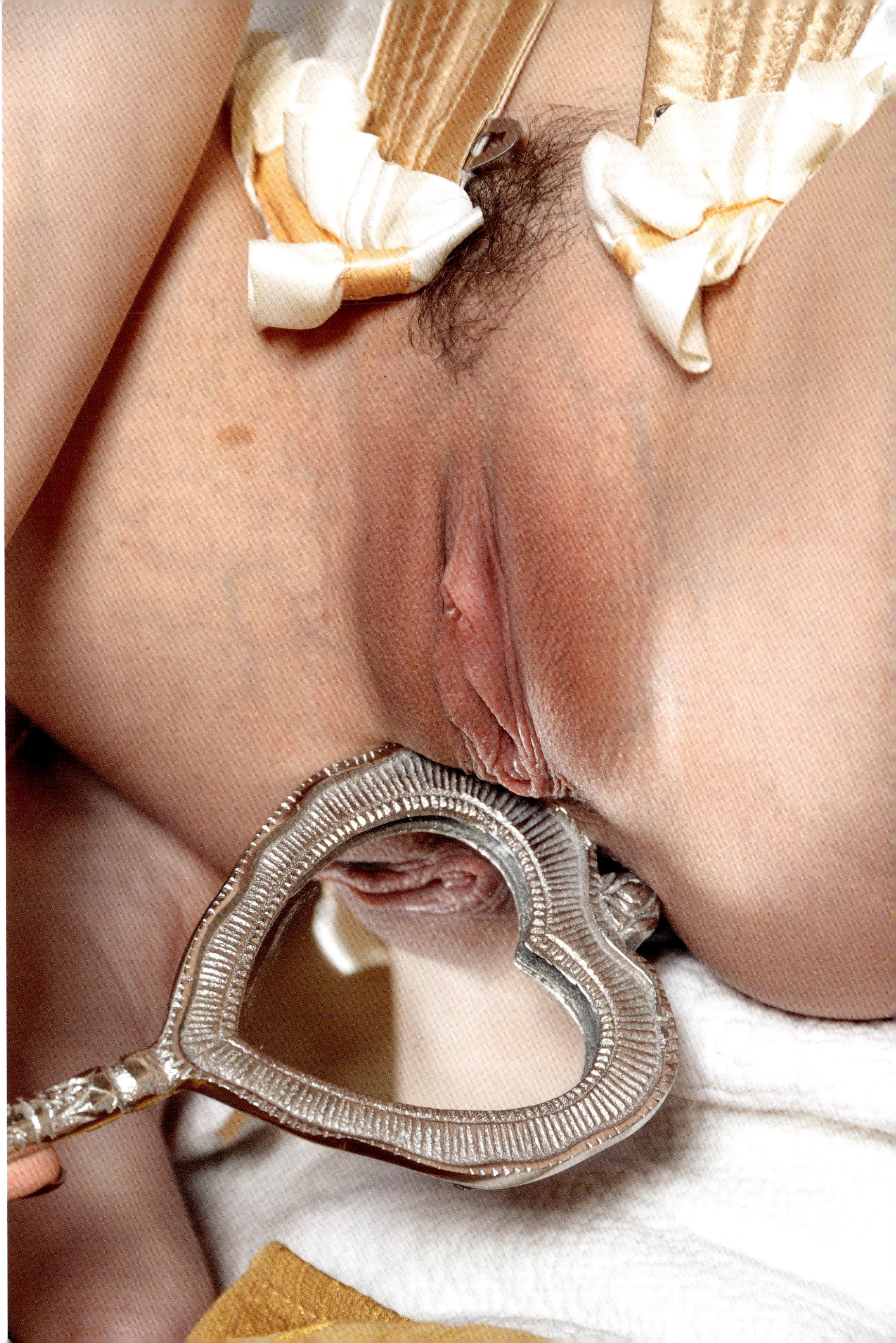

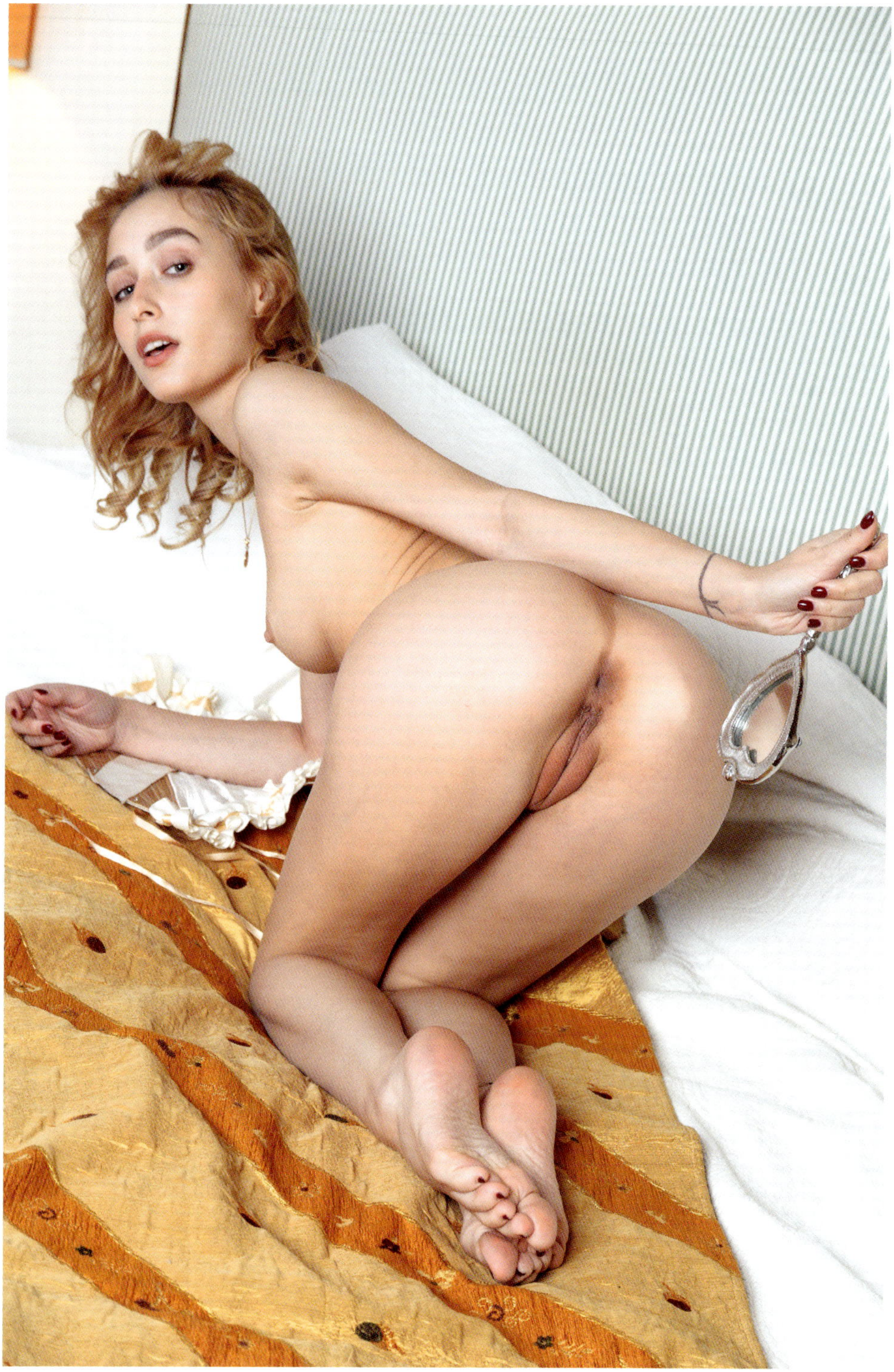

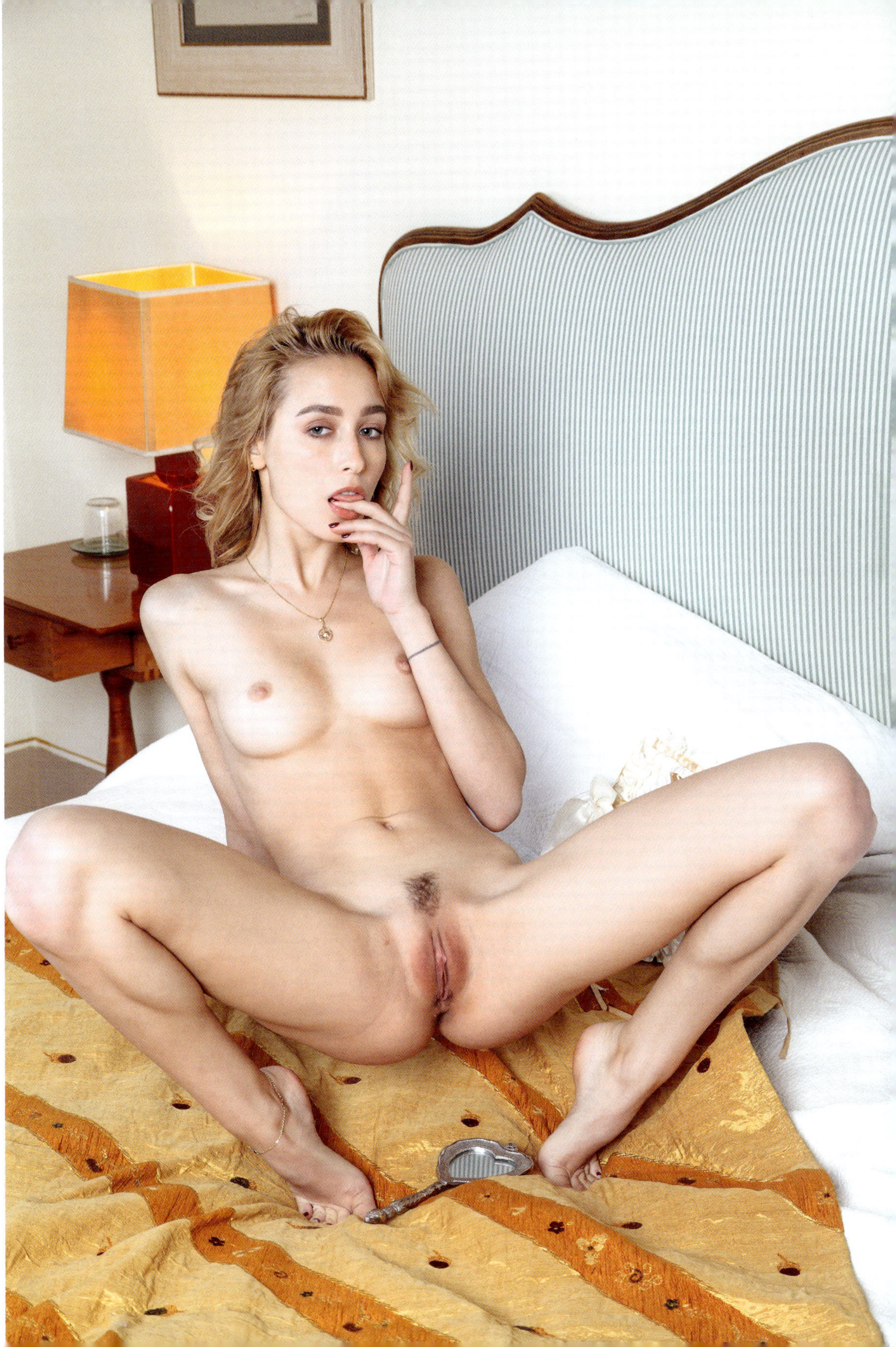

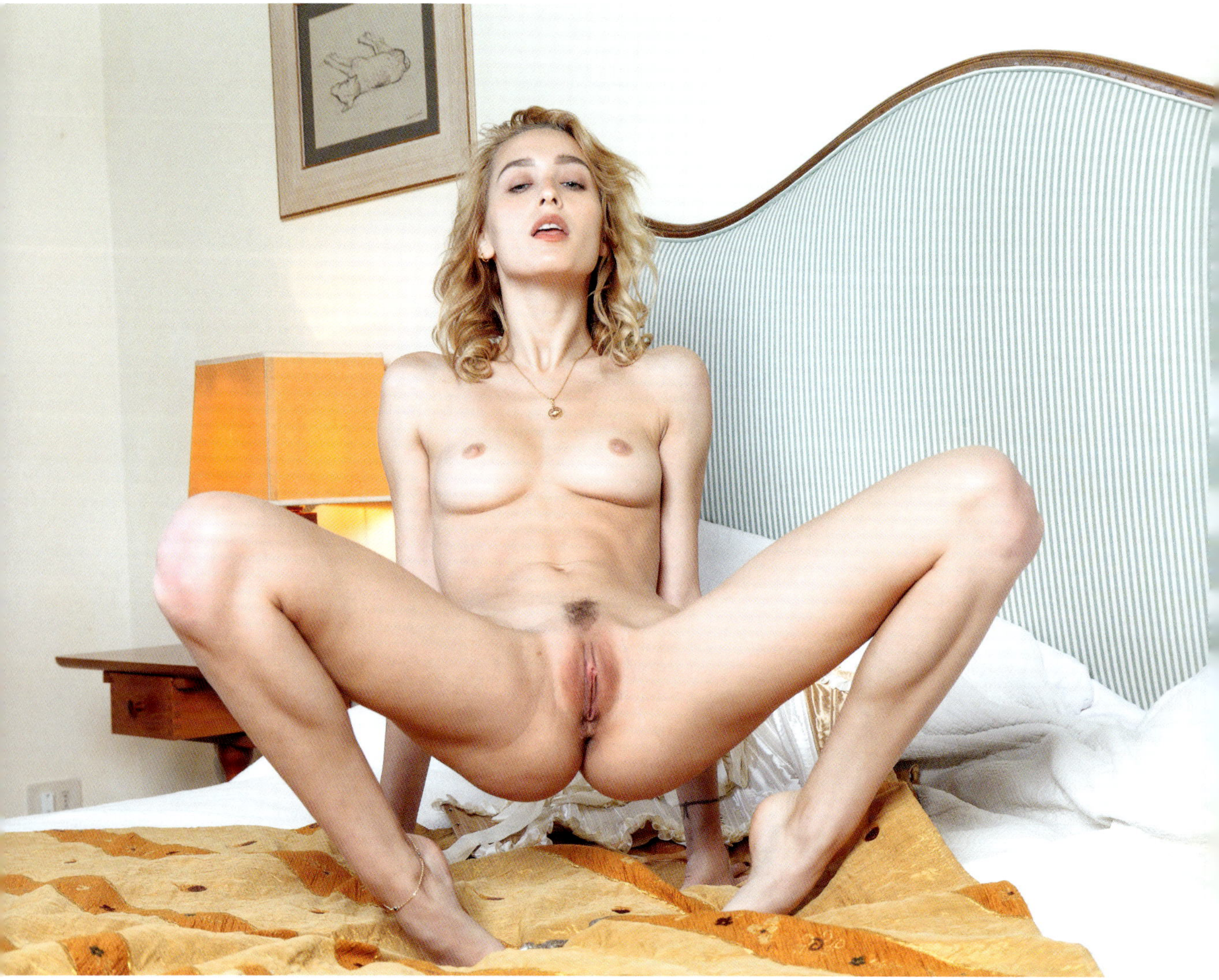

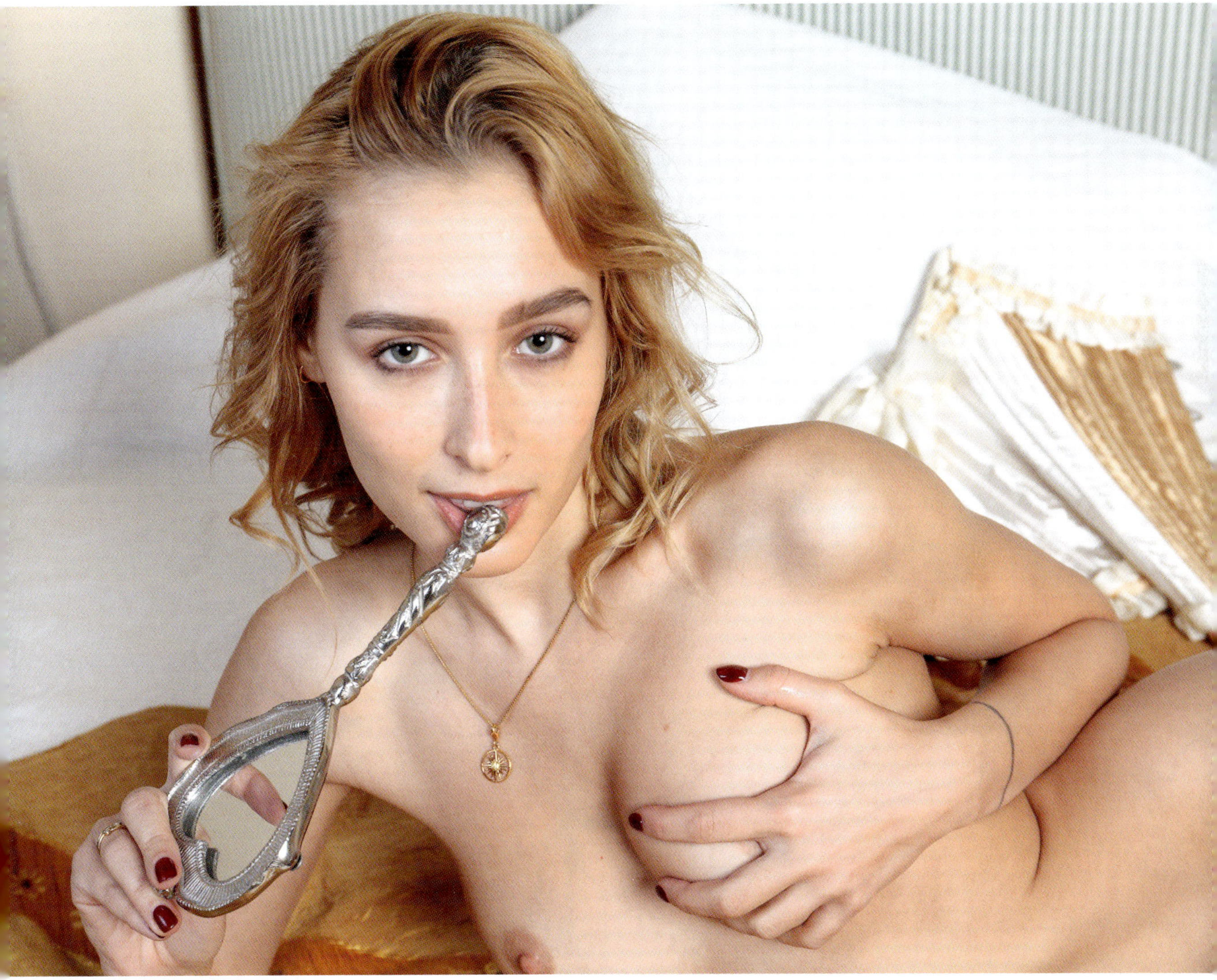

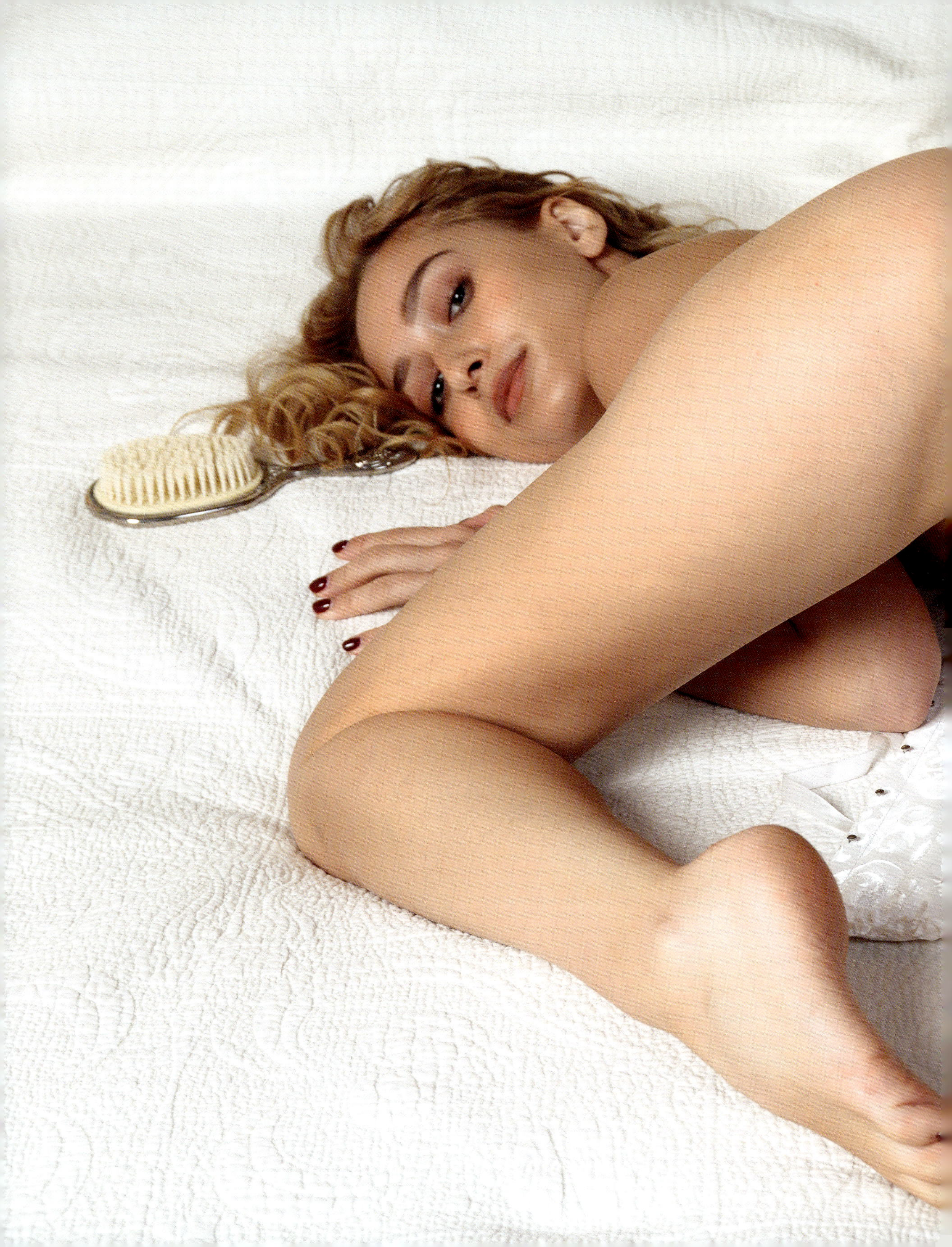

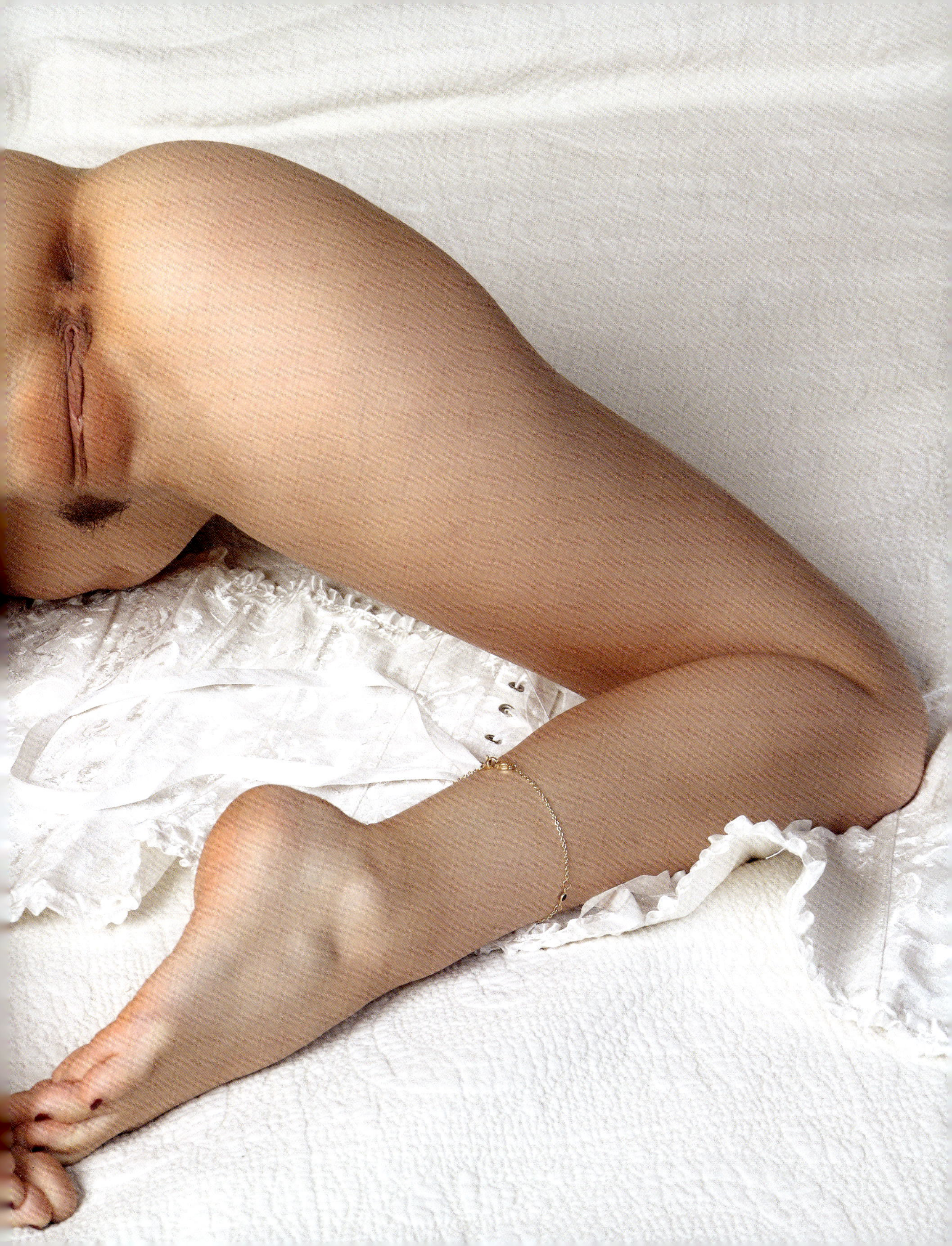

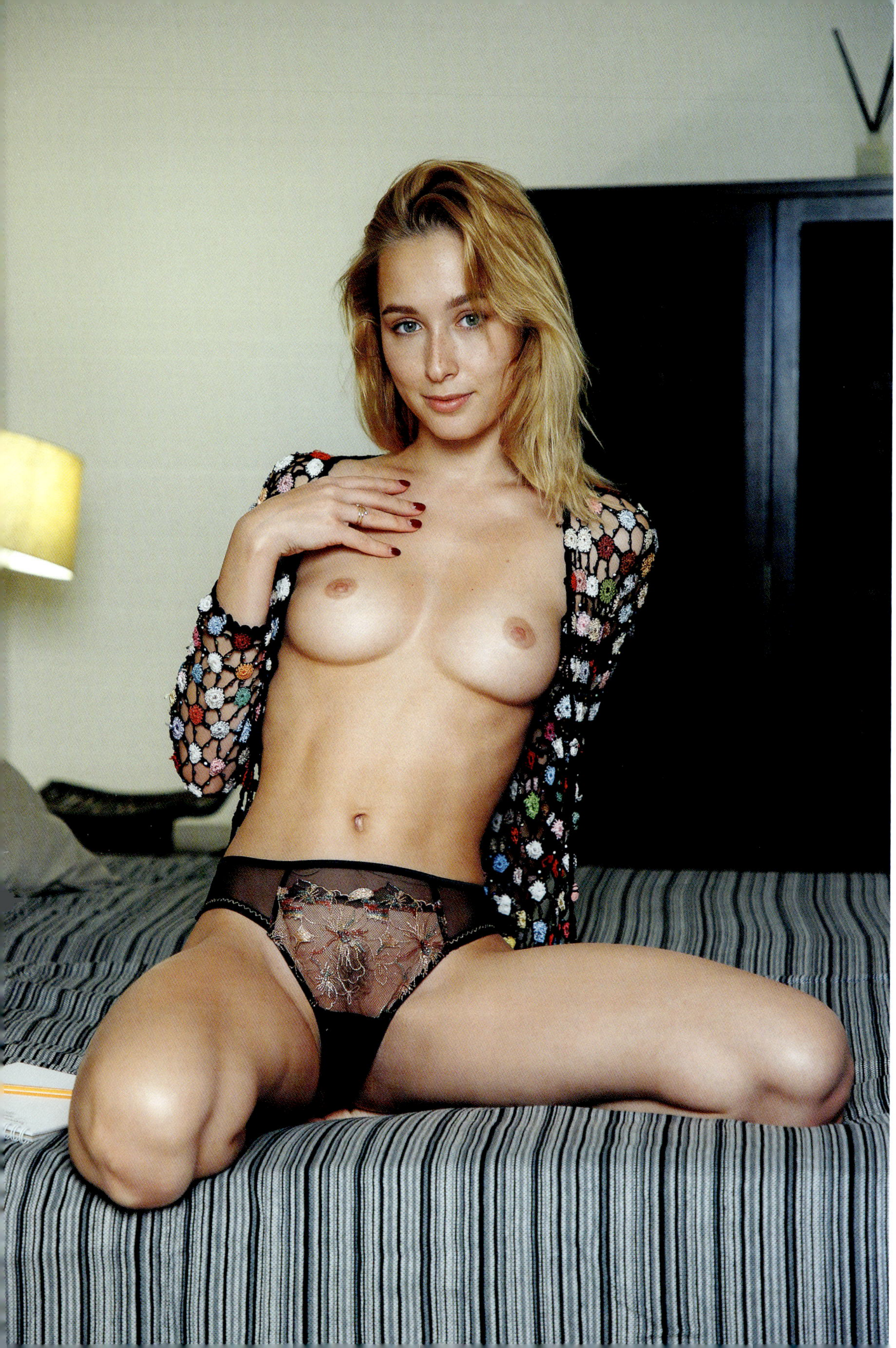

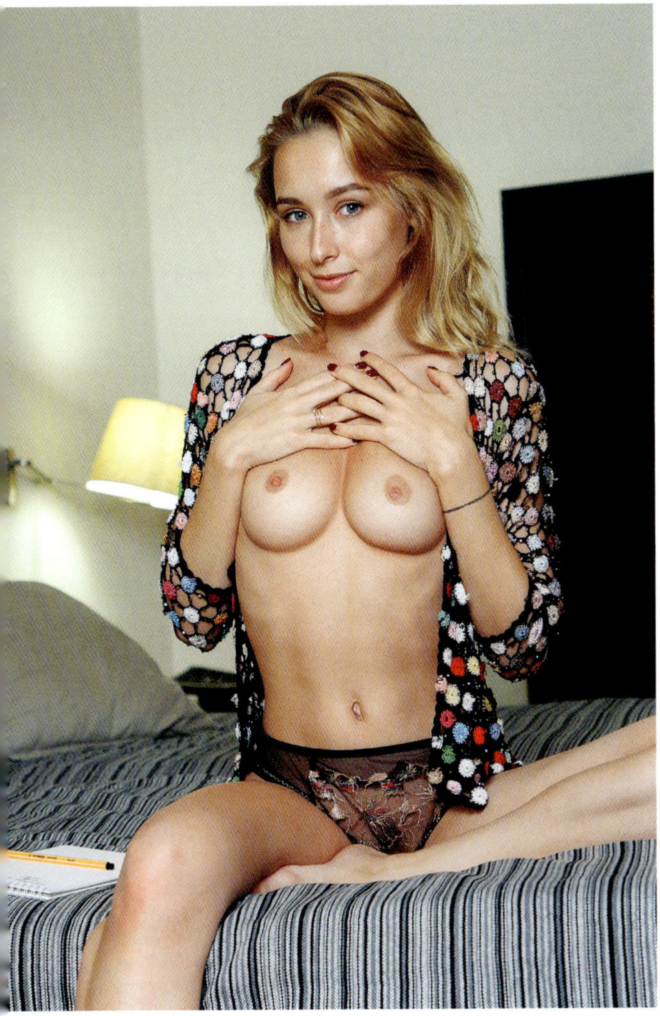

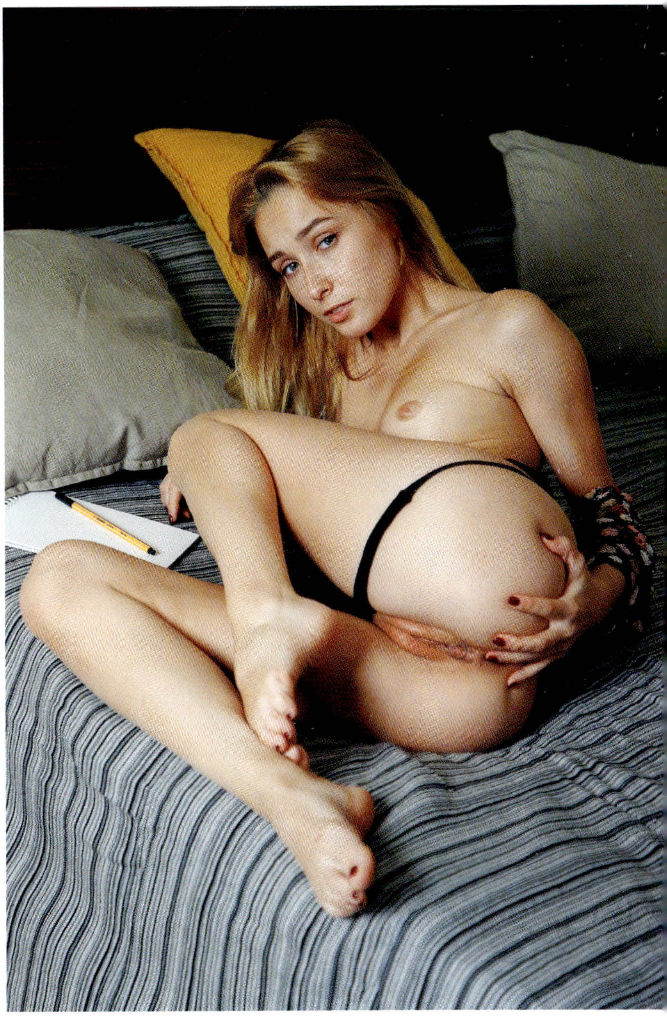

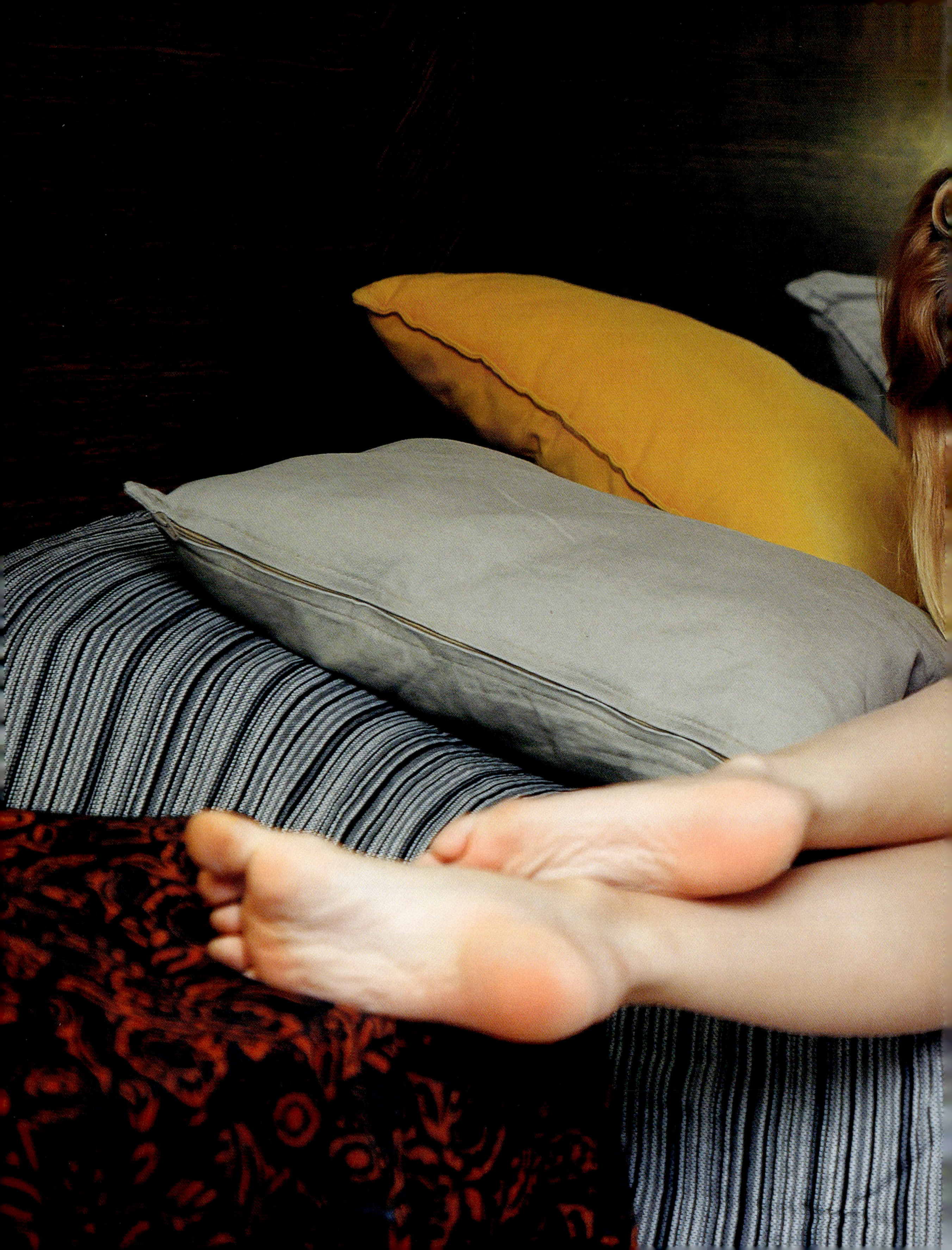

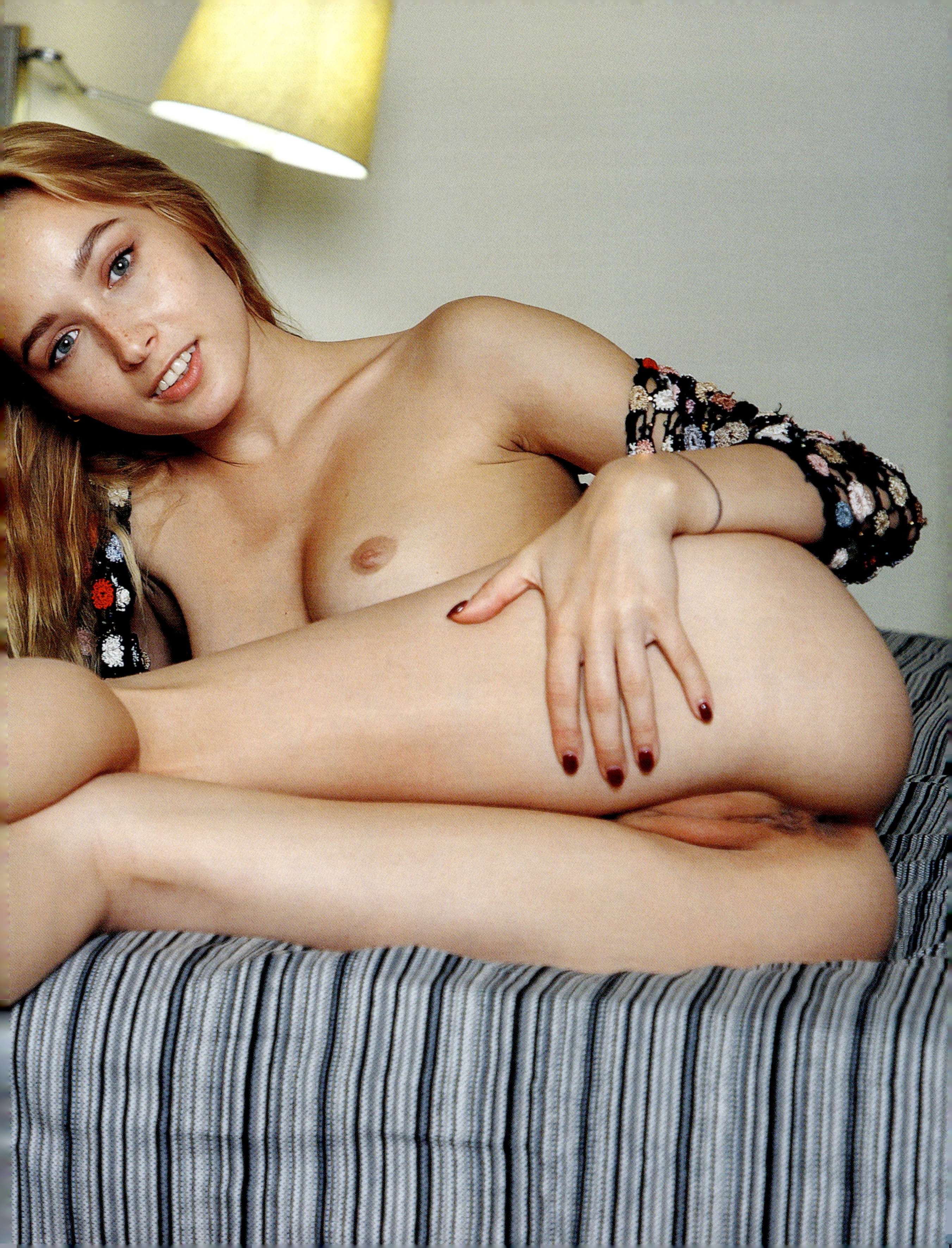

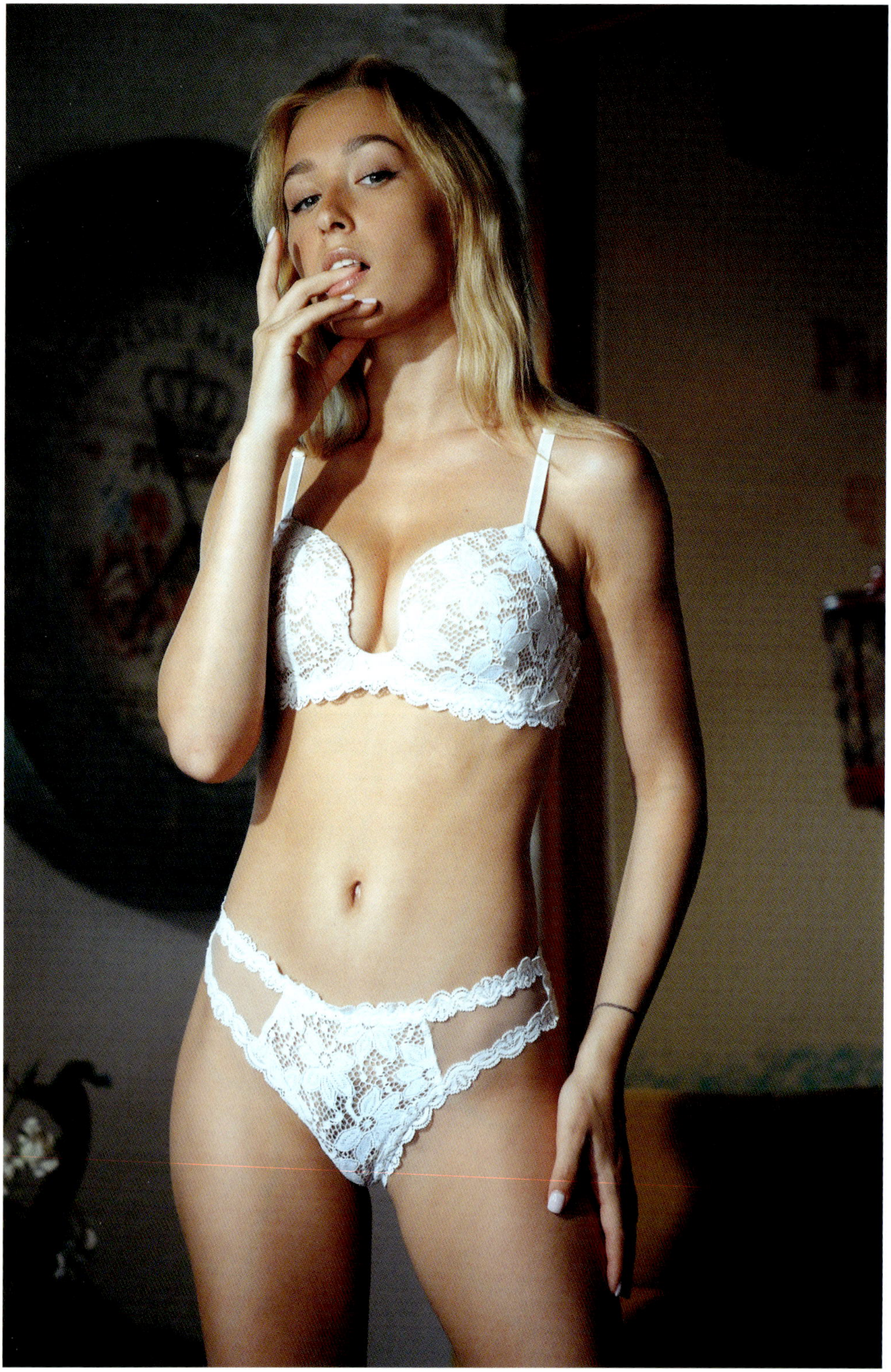

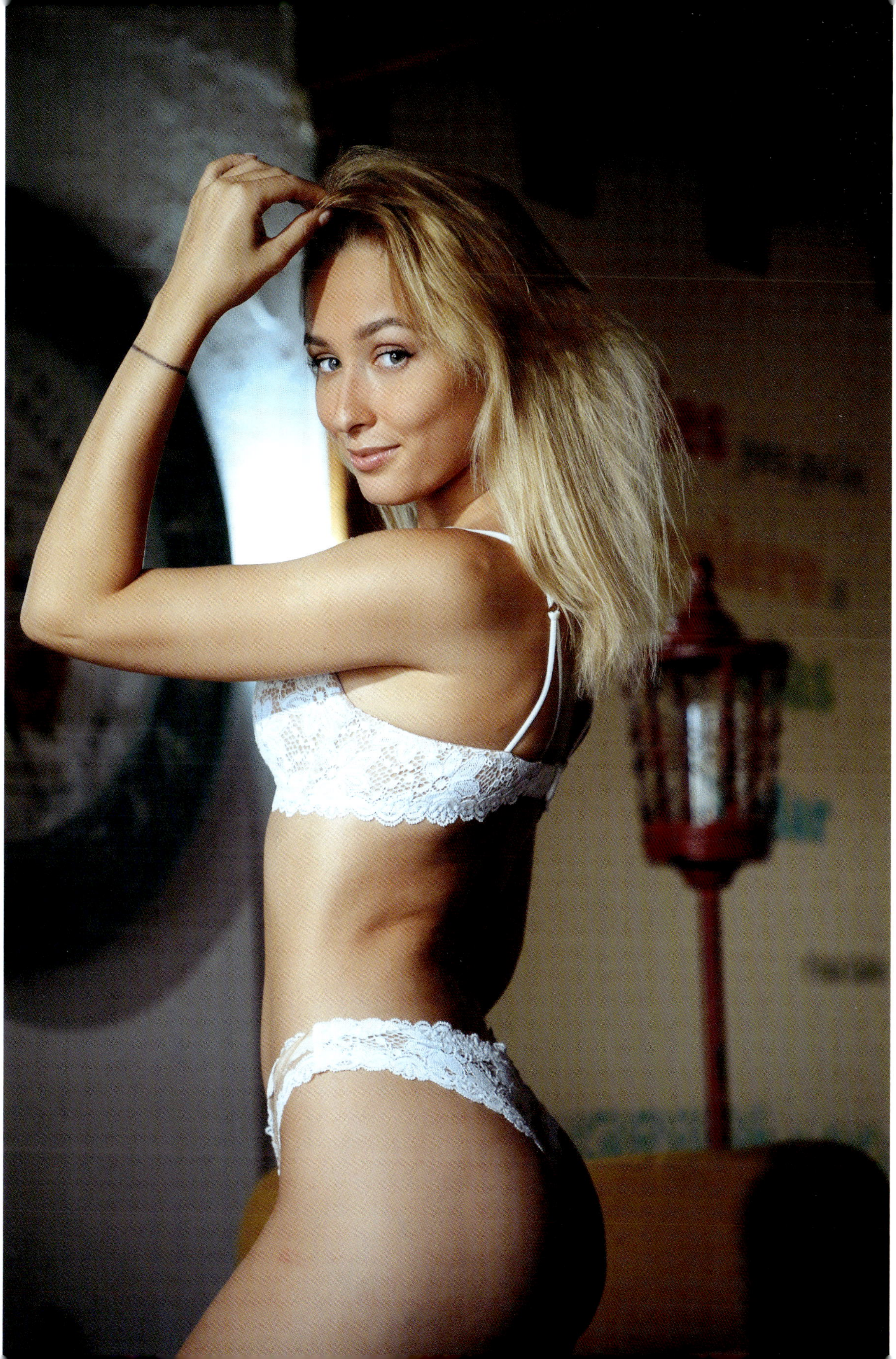

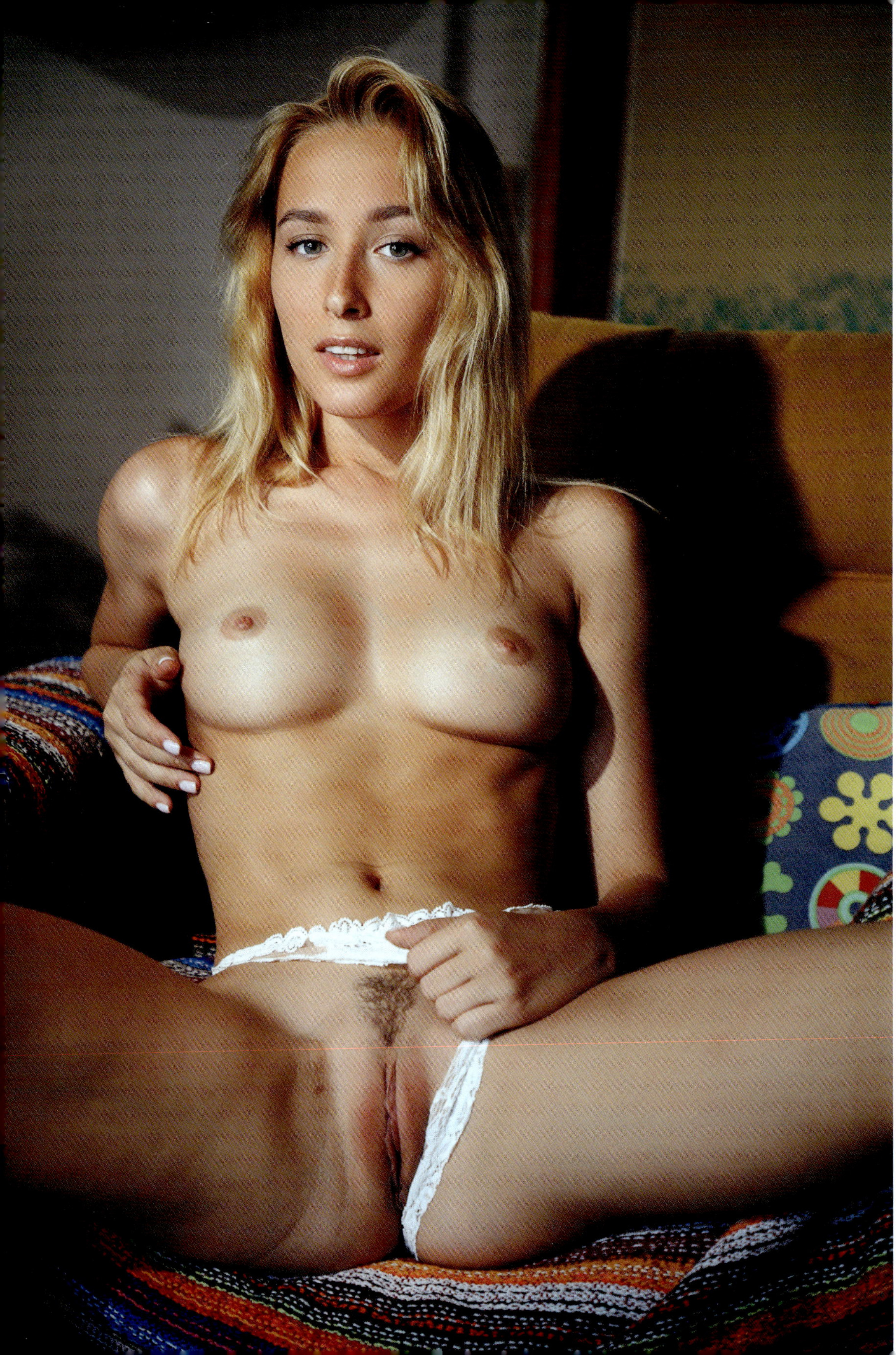

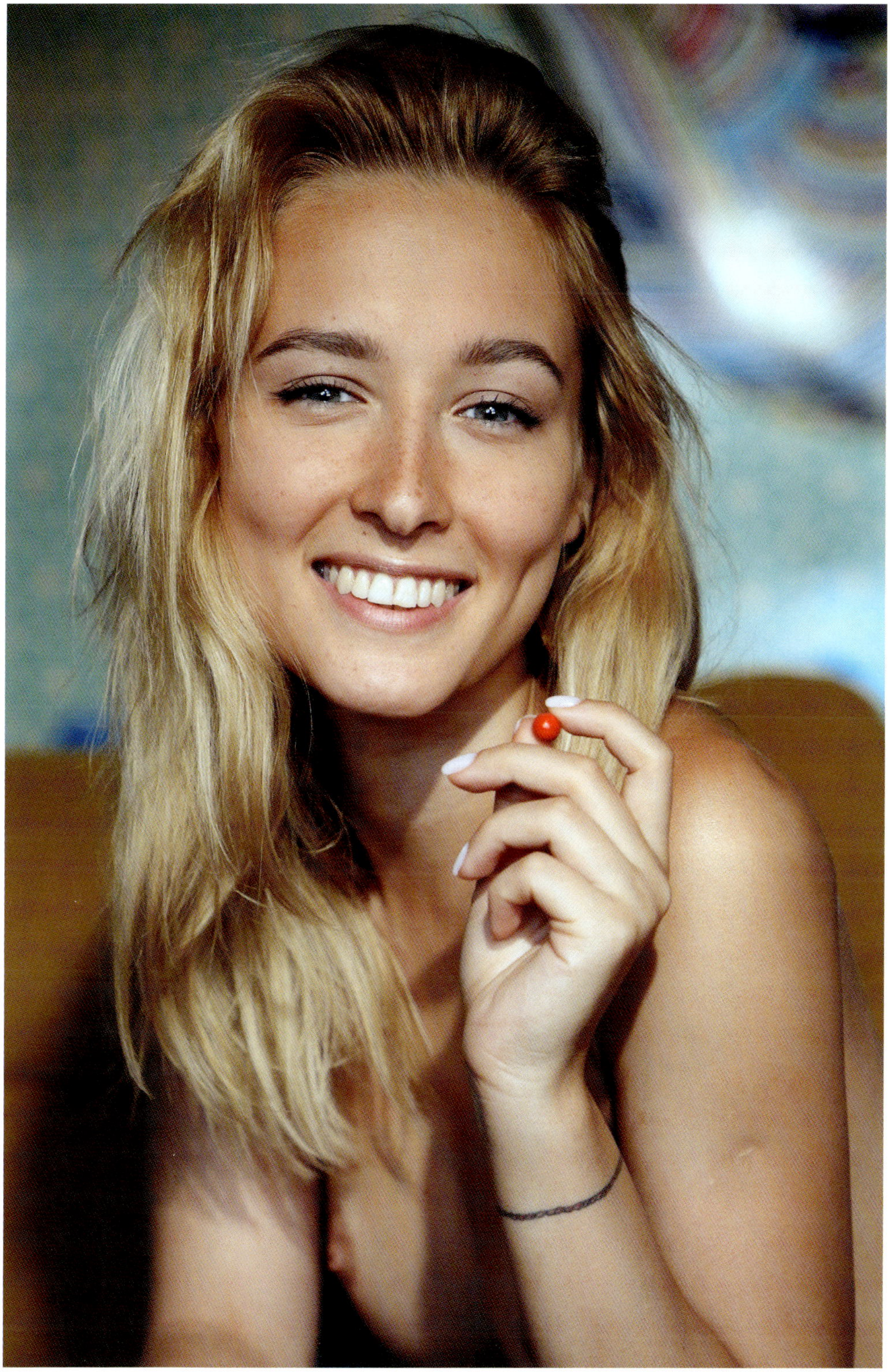

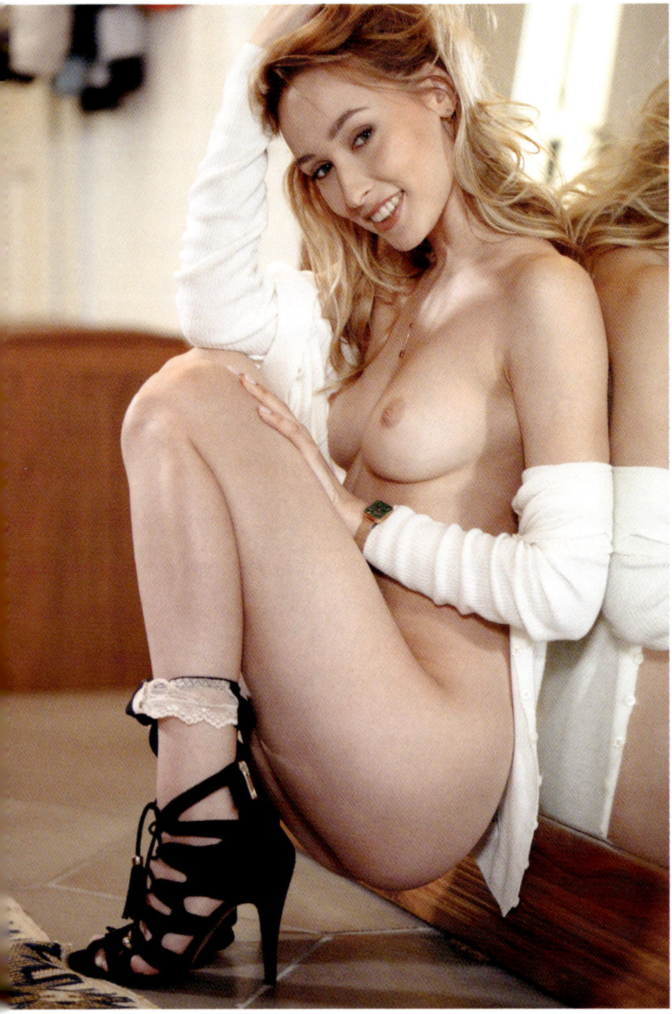

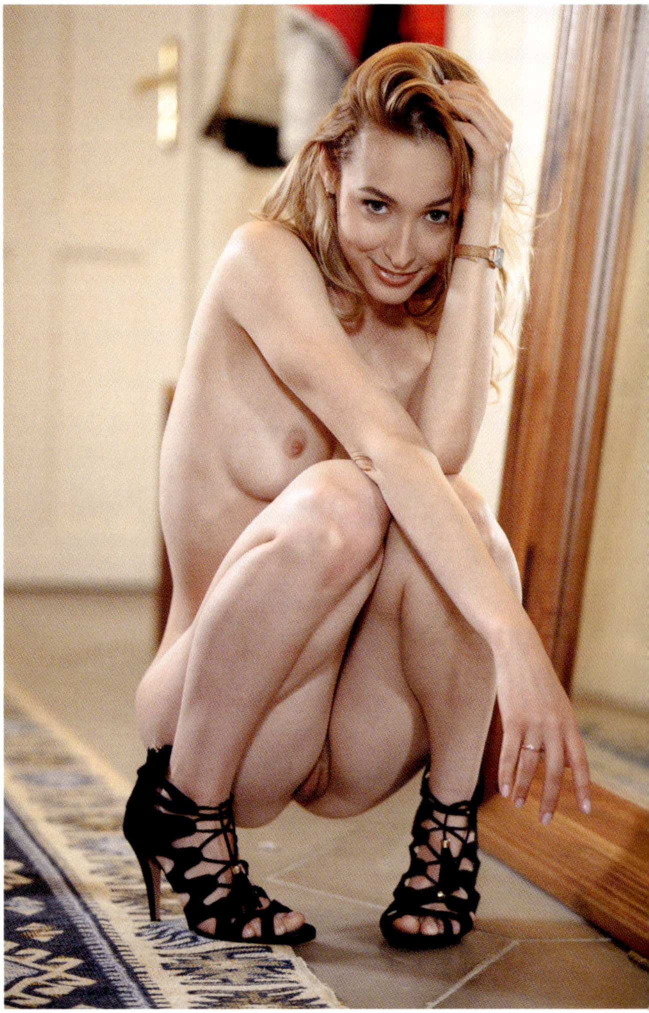

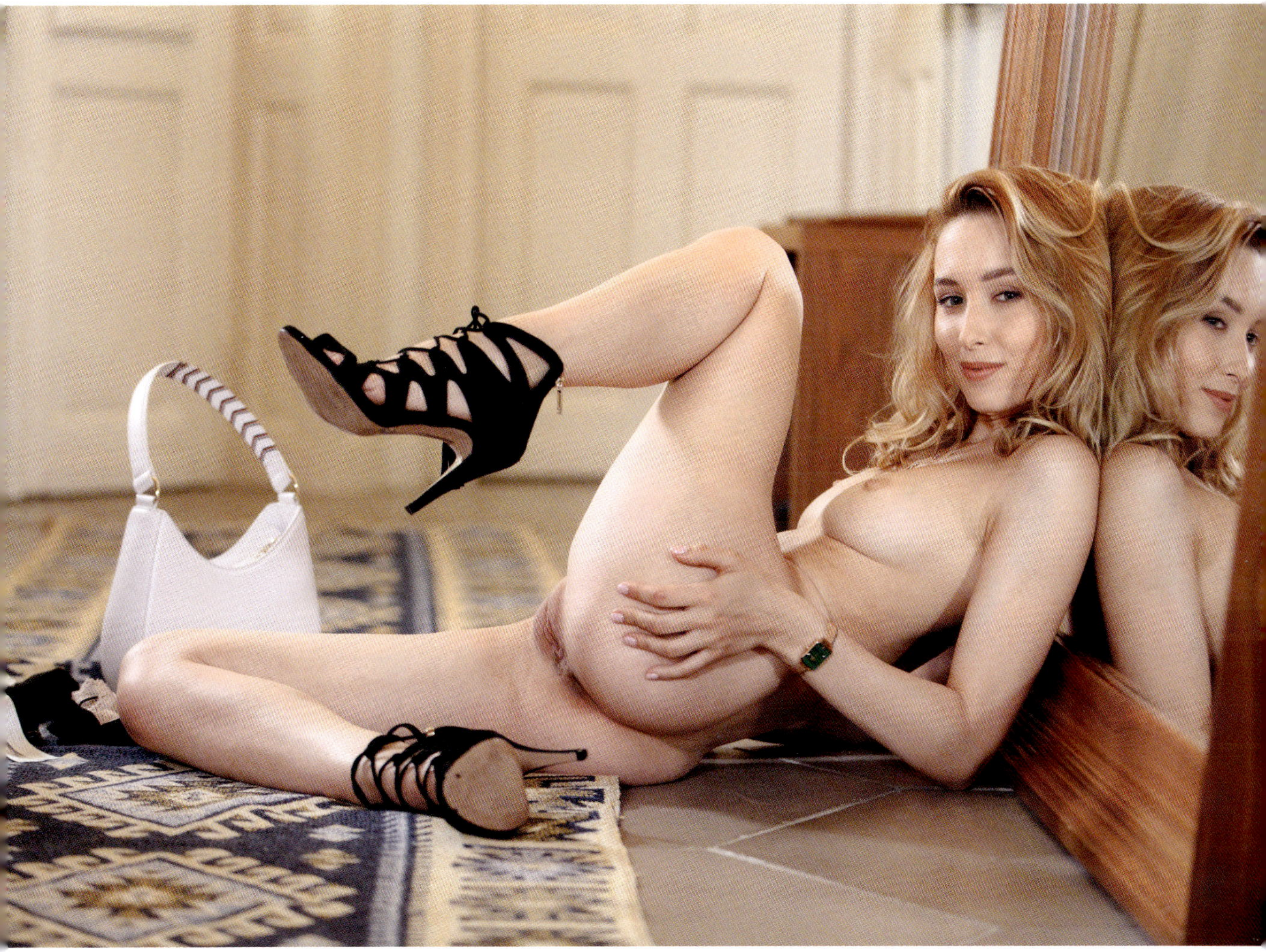

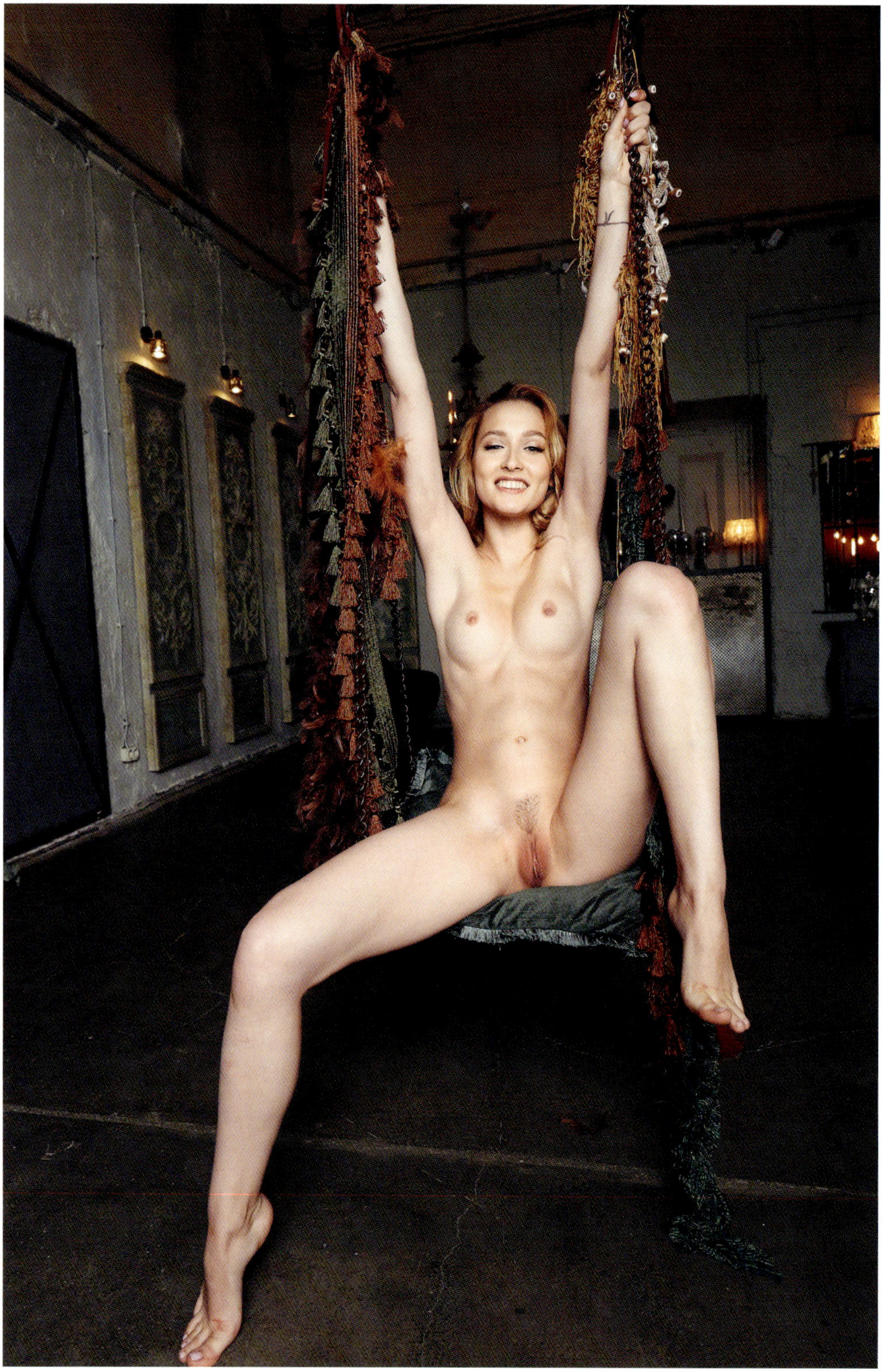

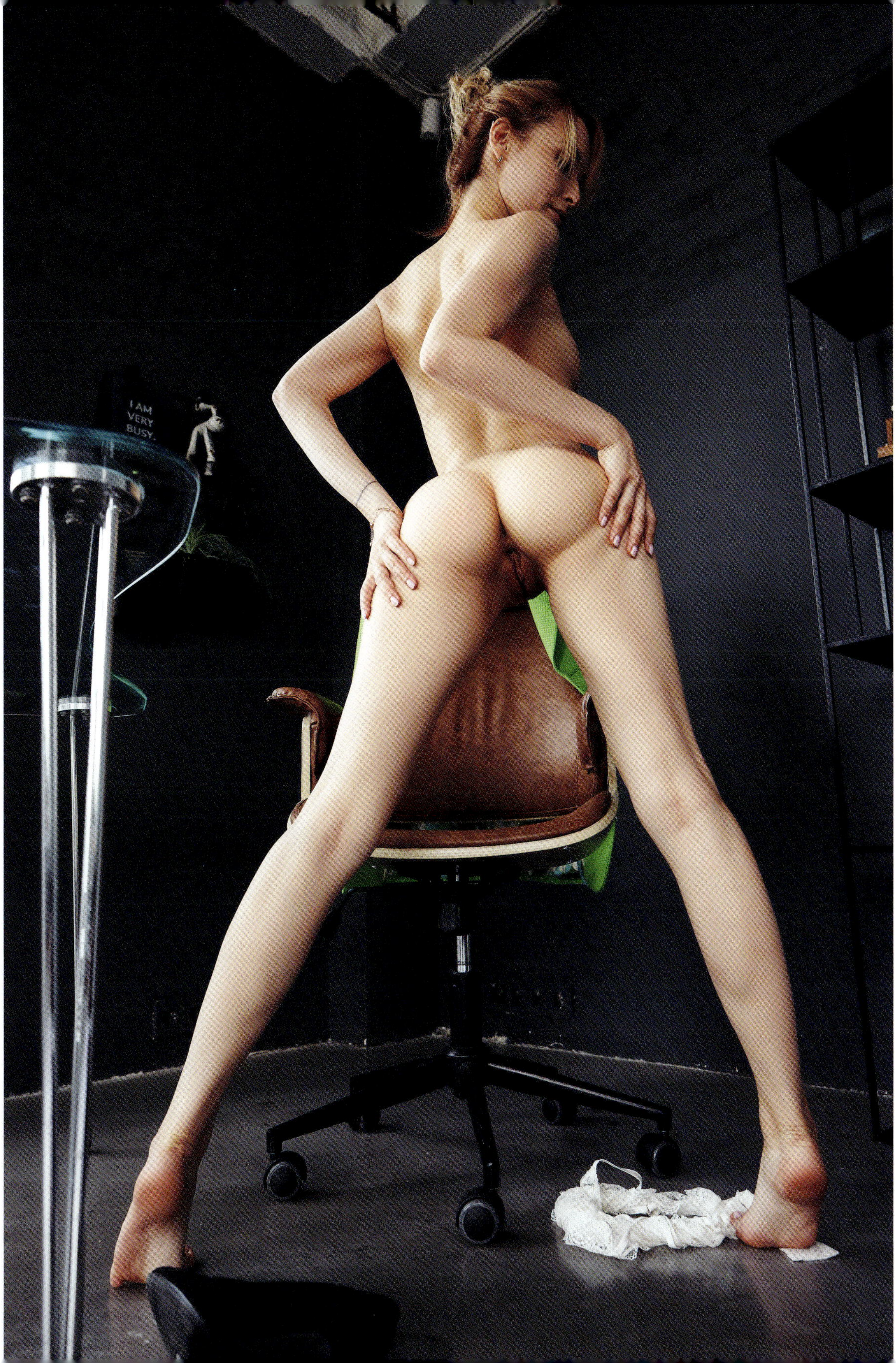
I AM
VERY
BUSY.

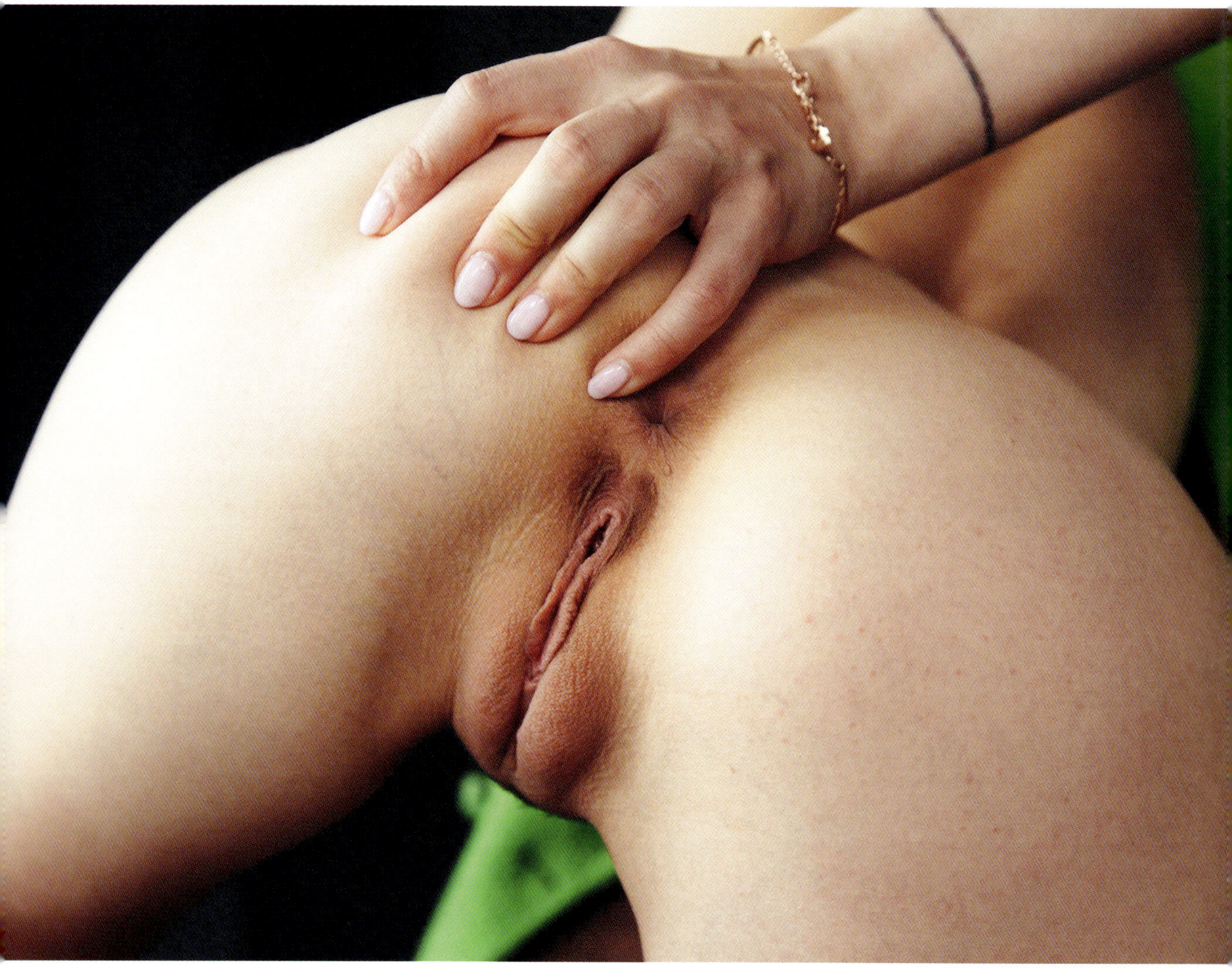

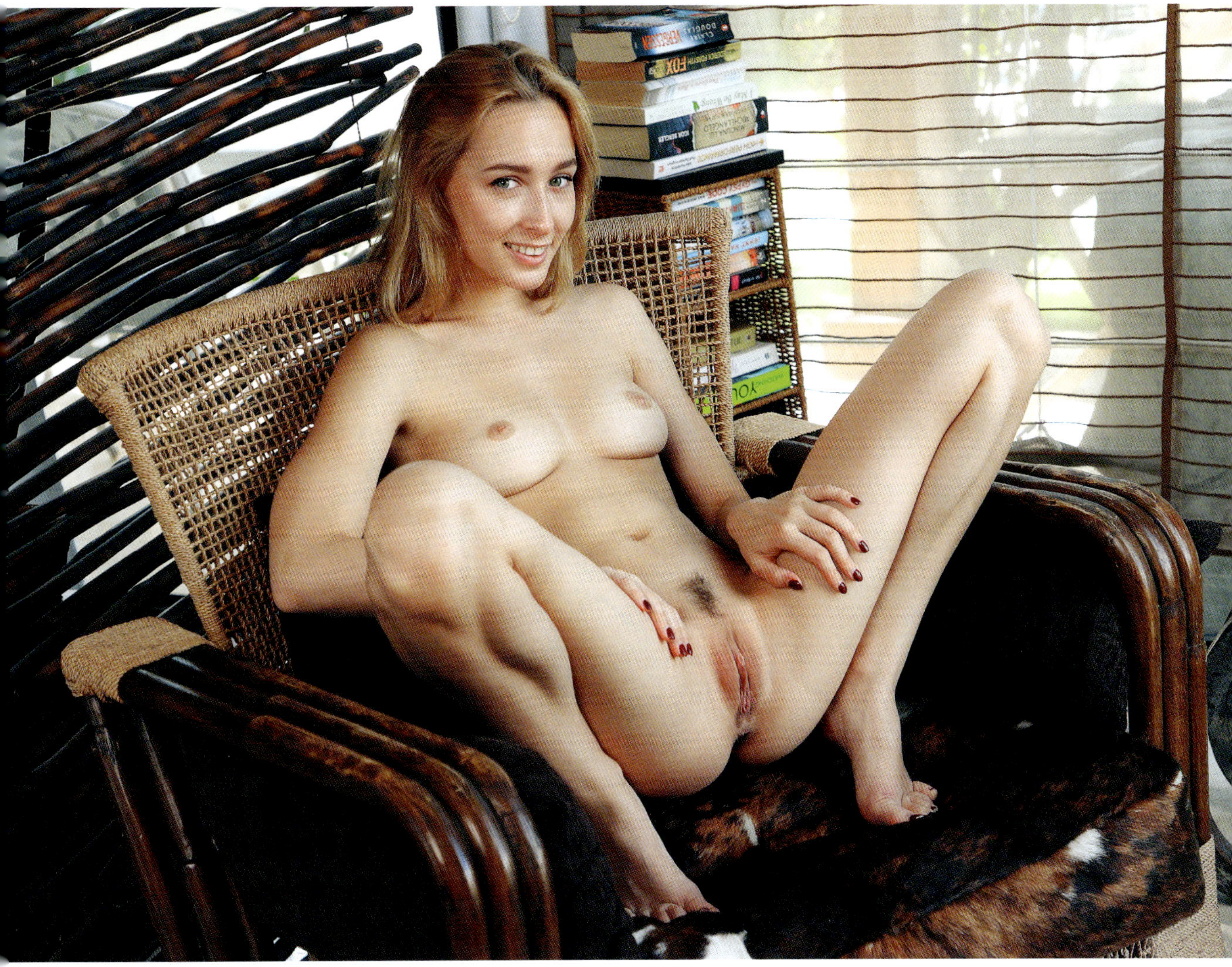

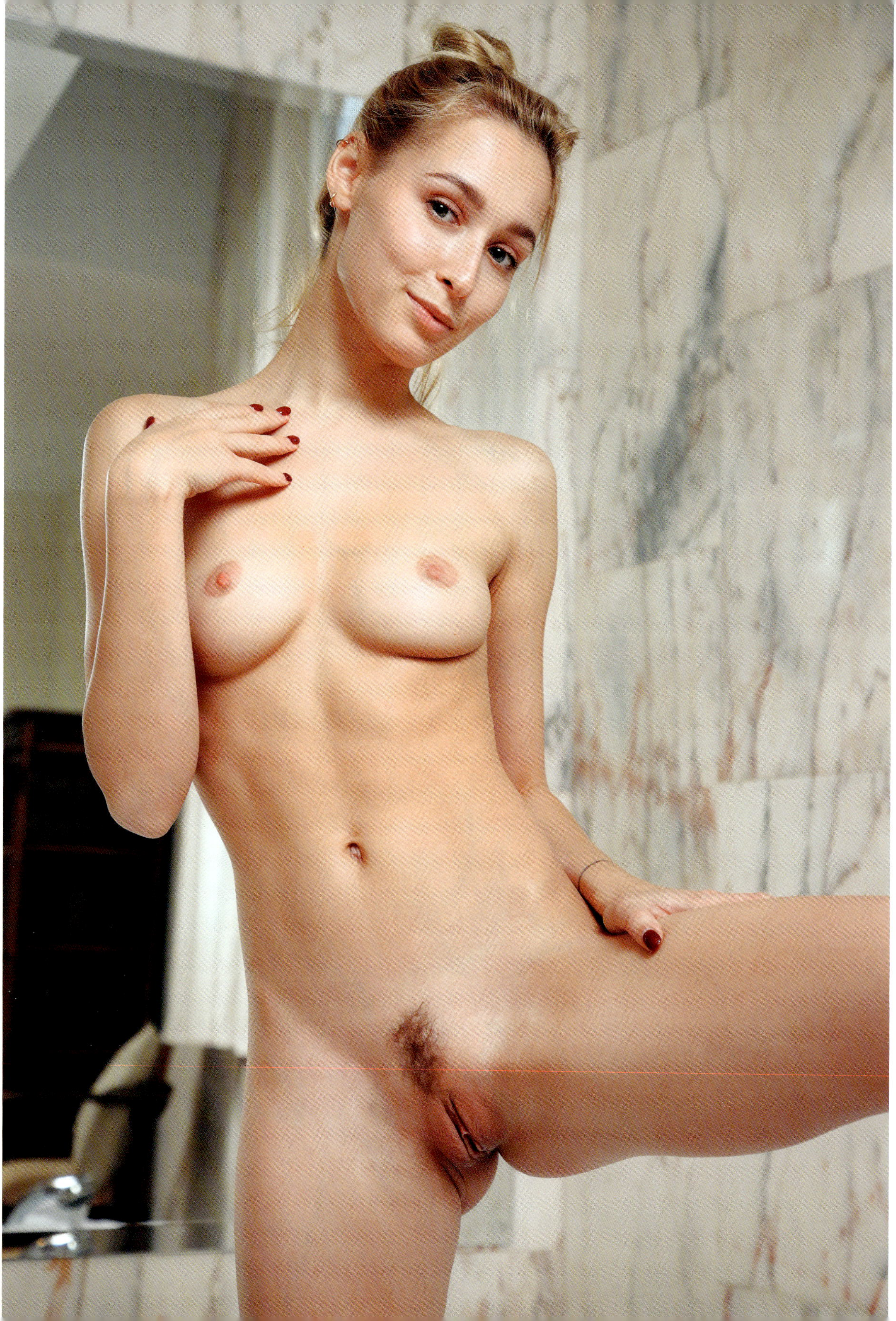

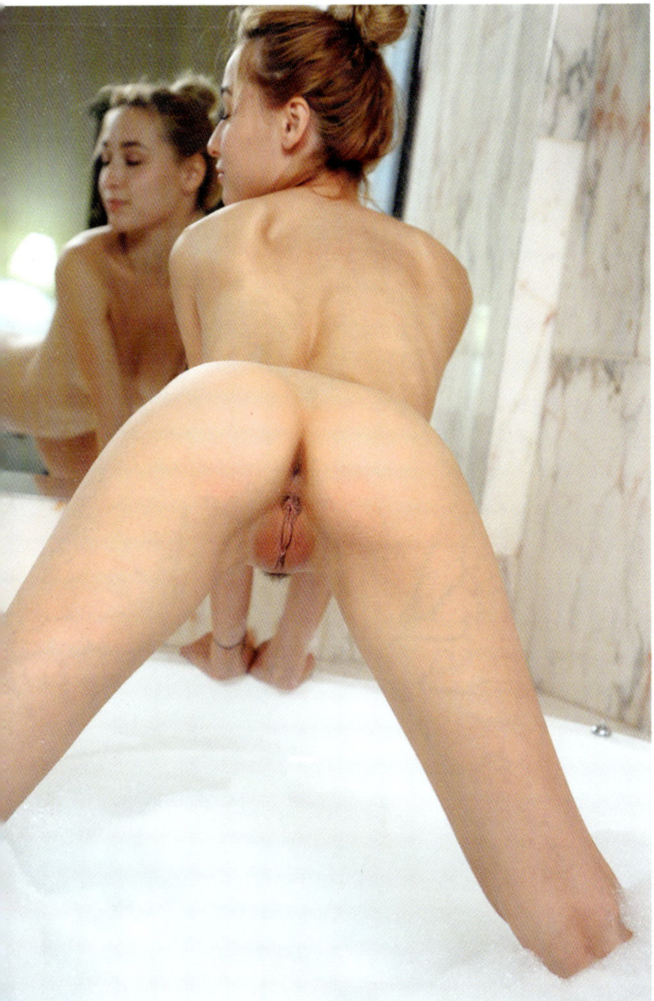
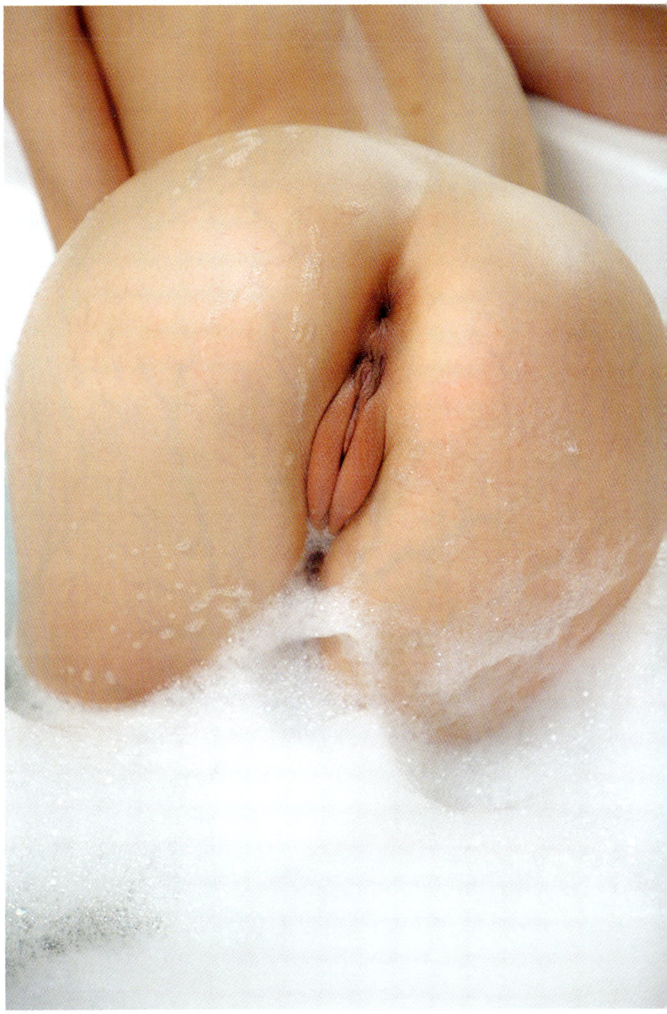

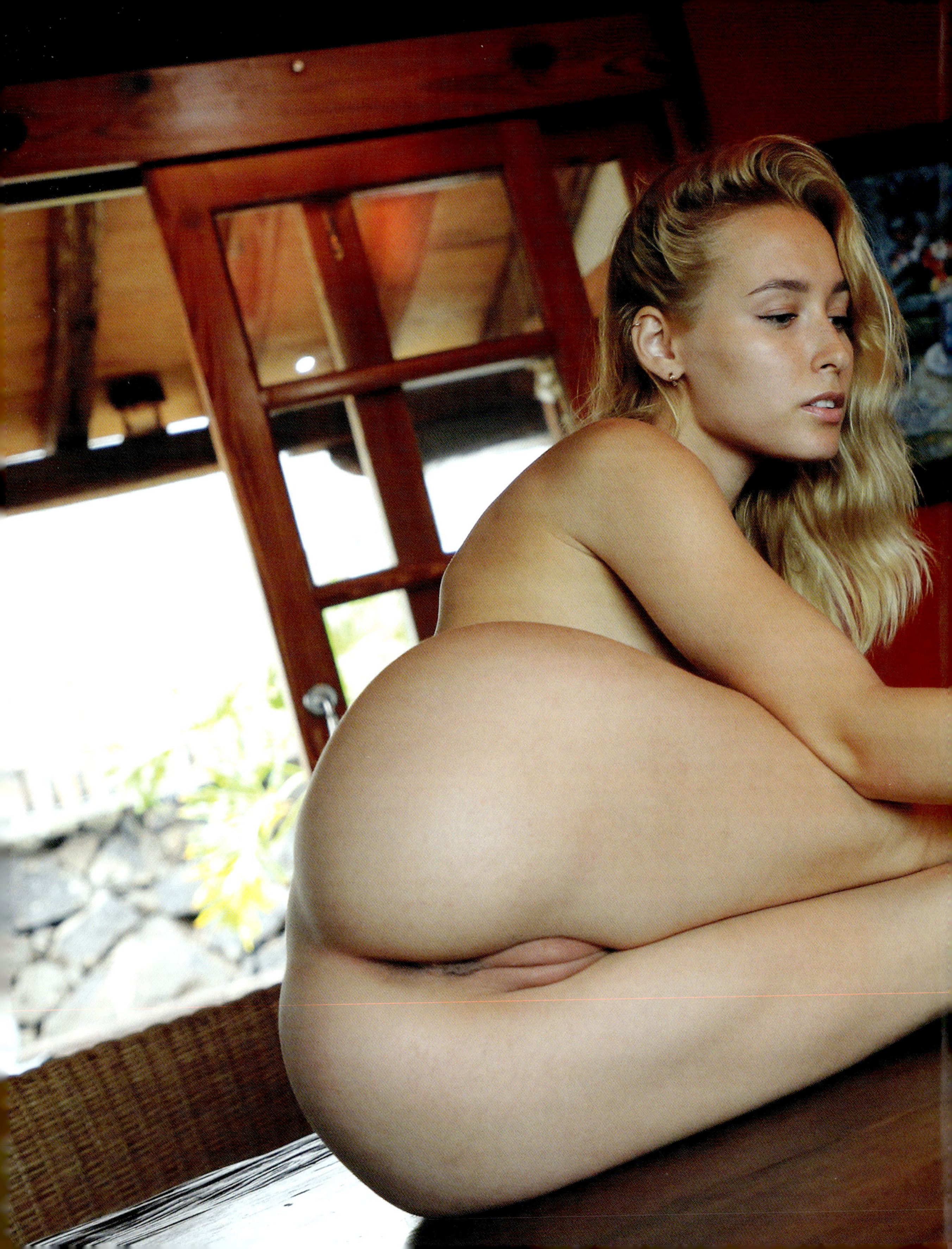

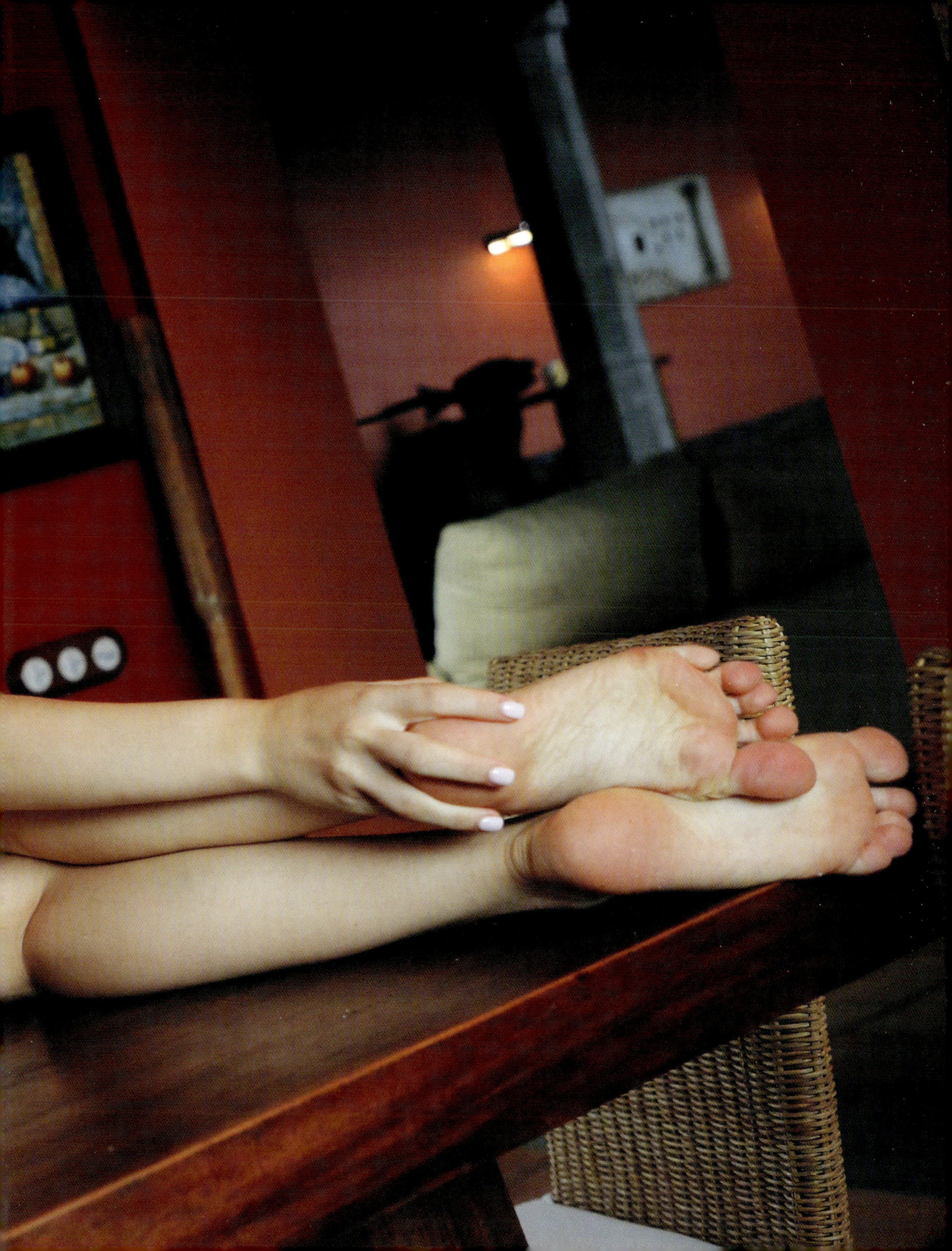

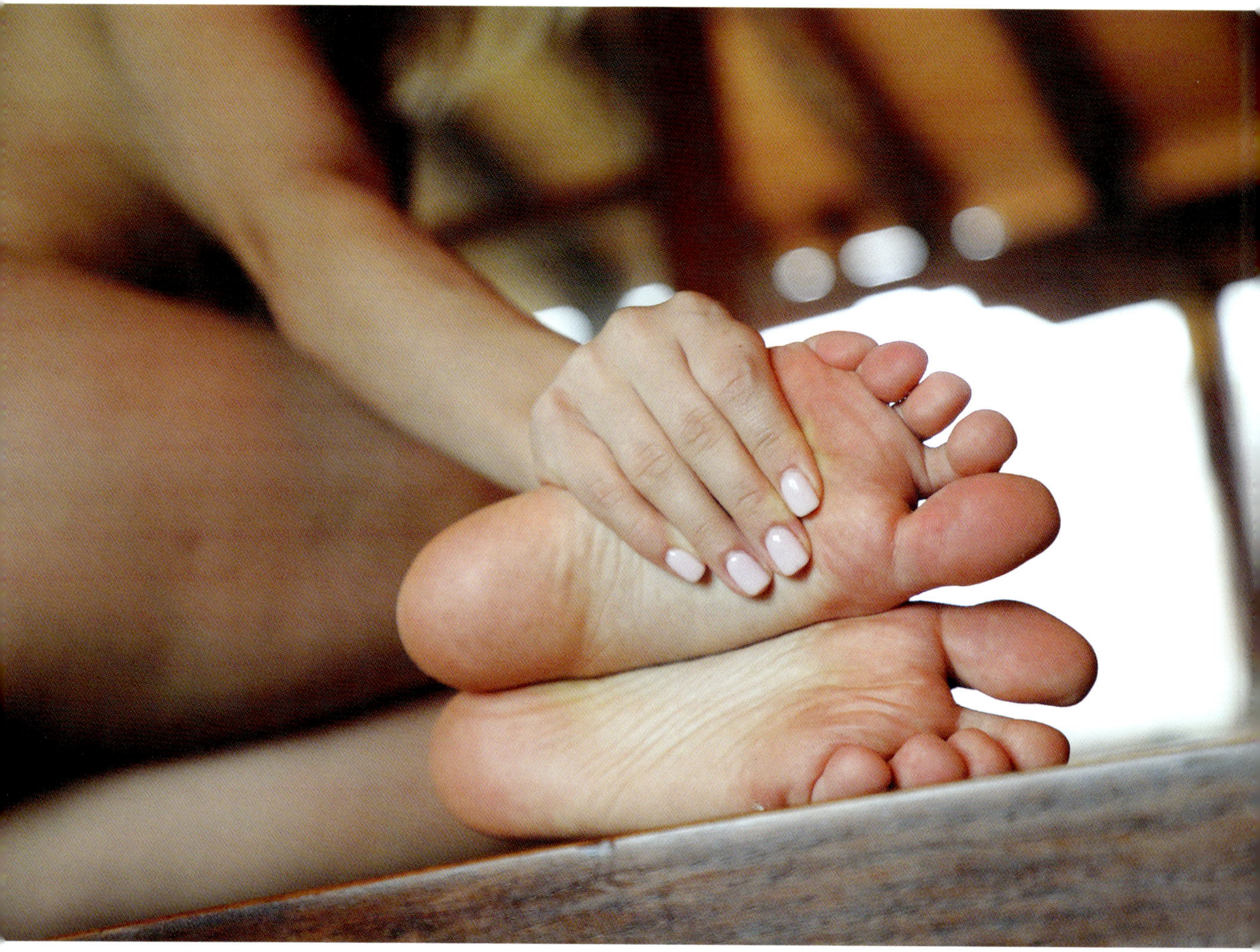

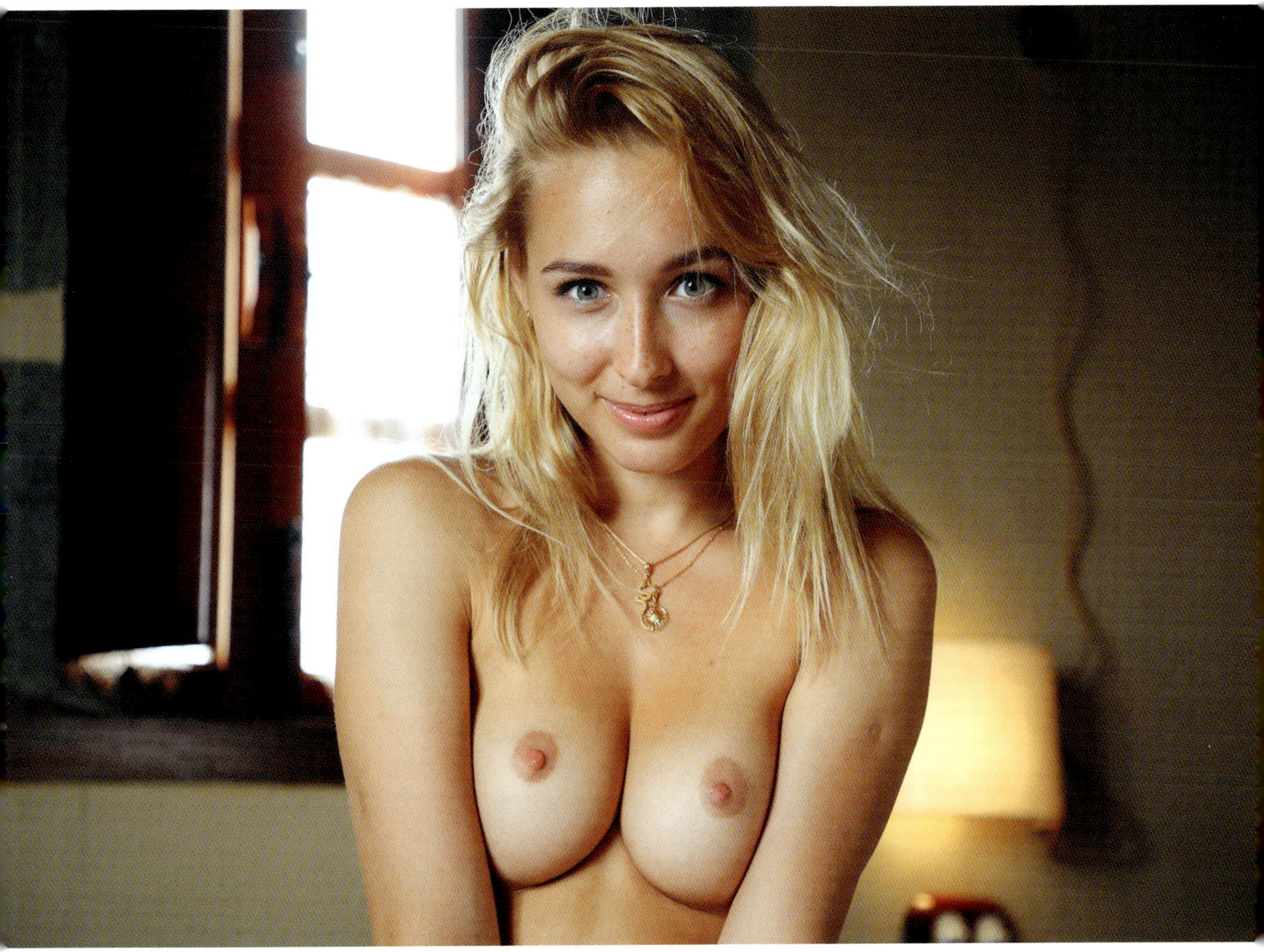

COLLECT THEM ALL: OUR MOST BEAUTIFUL

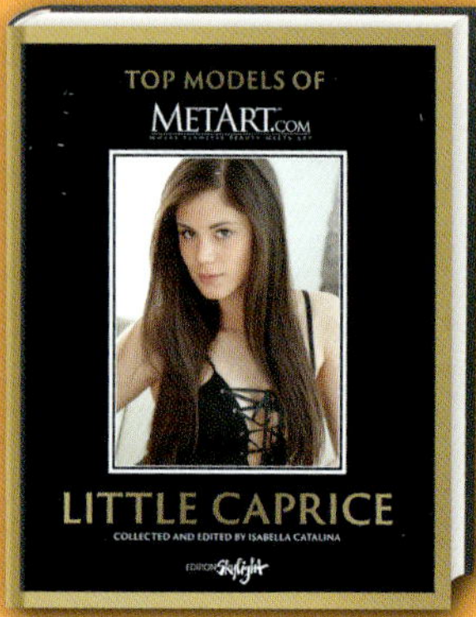

ISBN 978-3-03766-659-3

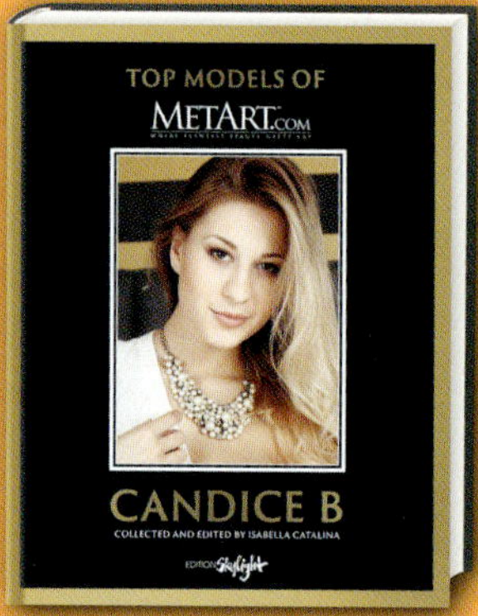

ISBN 978-3-03766-660-9

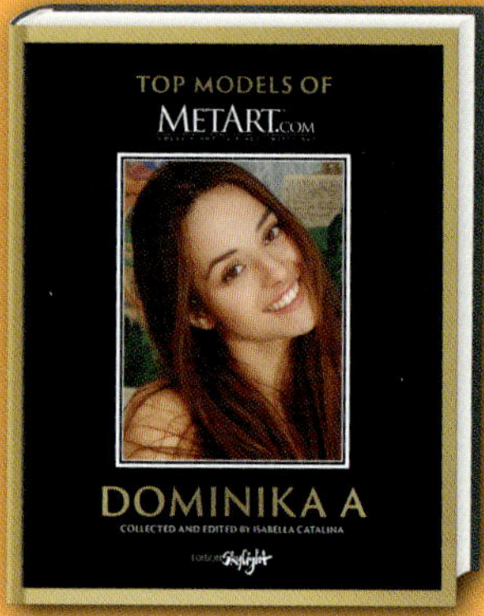

ISBN 978-3-03766-679-1

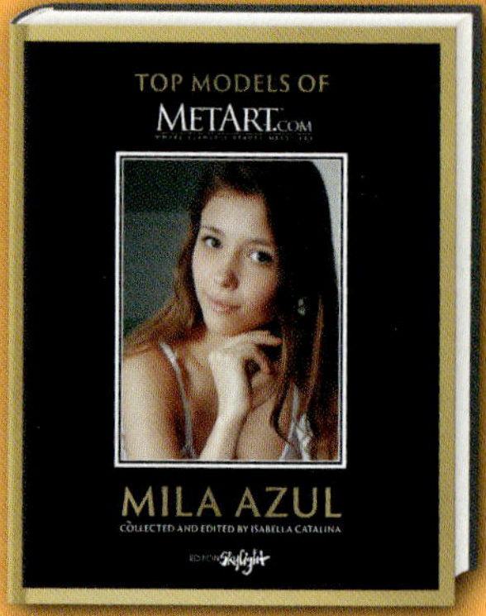

ISBN 978-3-03766-680-7

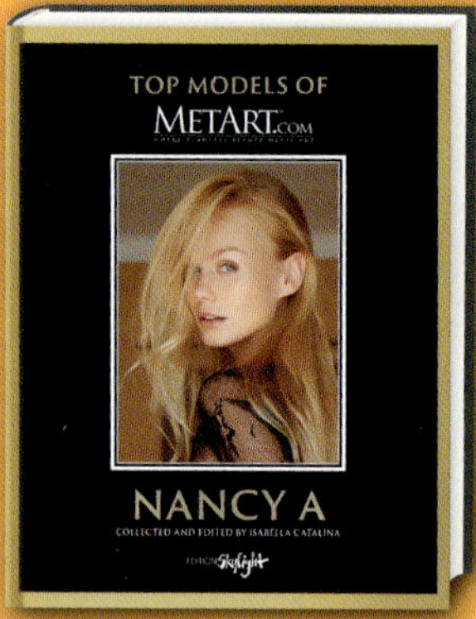

ISBN 978-3-03766-687-6

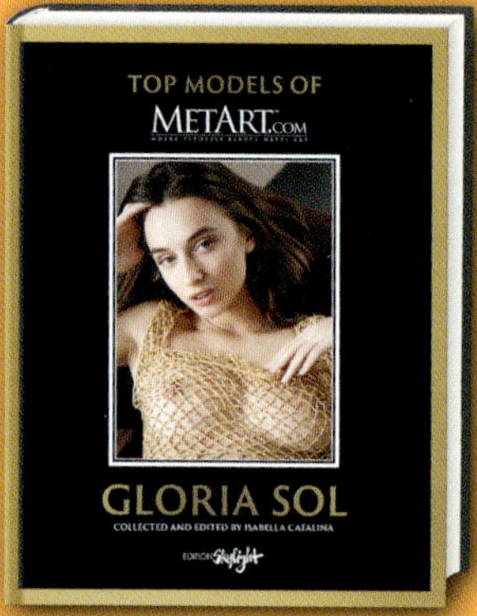

ISBN 978-3-03766-688-3

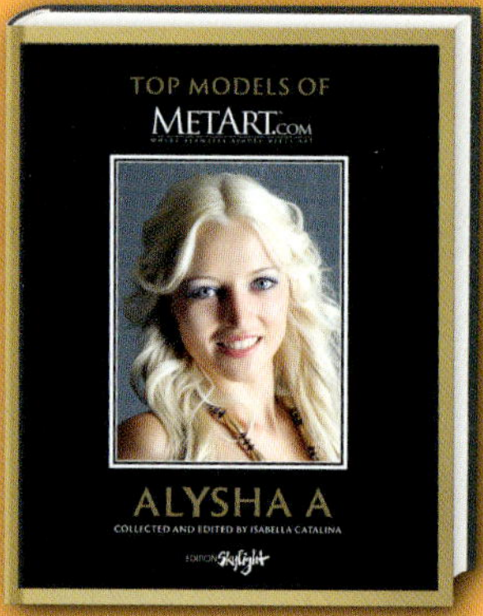

ISBN 978-3-03766-692-0

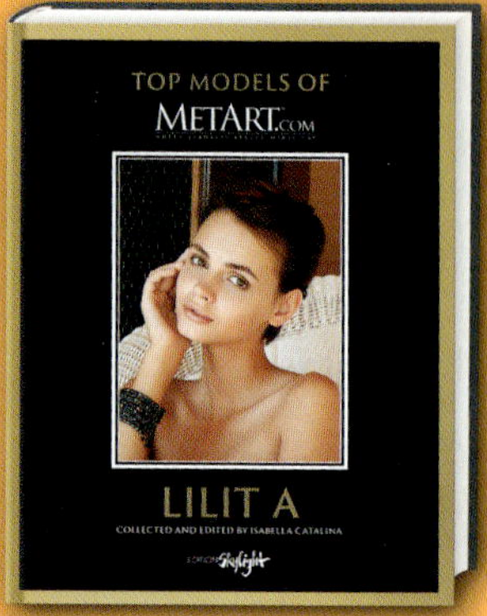

ISBN 978-3-03766-693-7

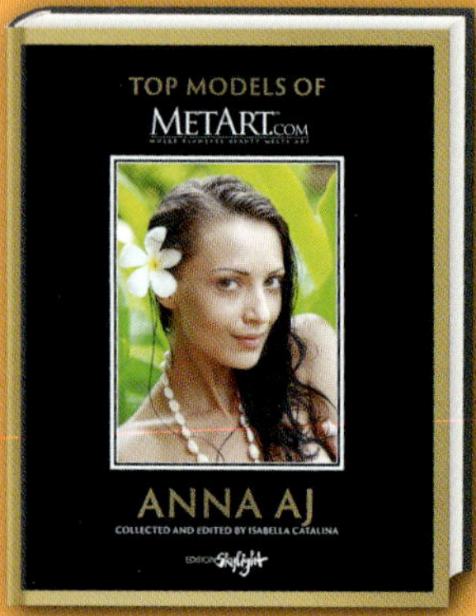

ISBN 978-3-03766-695-1

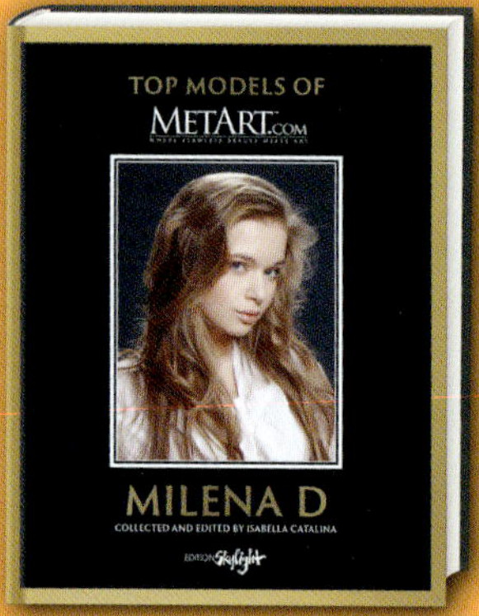

ISBN 978-3-03766-696-8

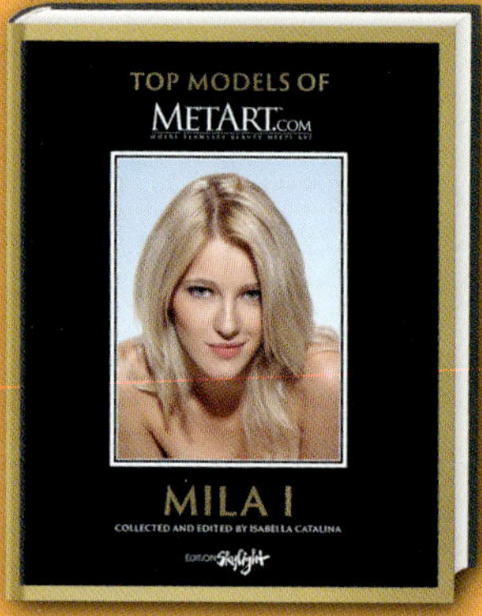

ISBN 978-3-03766-703-3

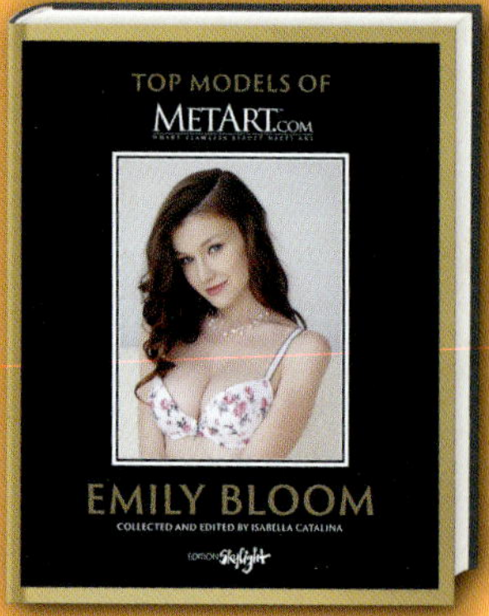

ISBN 978-3-03766-704-0

WWW.EDITION-SKYLIGHT.COM